Department of Economic and Social Affairs

ST/ESA/324

Rethinking Poverty
Report on the World Social Situation 2010

United Nations
New York, 2009

Department of Economic and Social Affairs

The Department of Economic and Social Affairs of the United Nations Secretariat is a vital interface between global policies in the economic, social and environmental spheres and national action. The Department works in three main interlinked areas: (i) it compiles, generates and analyses a wide range of economic, social and environmental data and information on which States Members of the United Nations draw to review common problems and to take stock of policy options; (ii) it facilitates the negotiations of Member States in many intergovernmental bodies on joint courses of action to address ongoing or emerging global challenges; and (iii) it advises interested Governments on the ways and means of translation policy frameworks developed in United Nations conferences and summits into programmes at the country level and, through technical assistance, helps build national capacities.

Note

The designations employed and the presentation of the material in the present publication do not imply the expression of any opinion whatsoever on the part of the Secretariat of the United Nations concerning the legal status of any country or territory or of its authorities, or concerning the delimitations of its frontiers.

The term "country" as used in the text of this report also refers, as appropriate, to territories or areas.

The designations of country groups in the text and the tables are intended solely for statistical or analytical convenience and do not necessarily express a judgement about the stage reached by a particular country or area in the development process.

Mention of the names of firms and commercial products does not imply the endorsement of the United Nations.

Symbols of United Nations documents are composed of capital letters combined with figures.

ST/ESA/324
United Nations publication
Sales No. E.09.IV.10
ISBN 978-92-1-130278-3
Copyright © United Nations, 2009
All rights reserved

Preface

Fifteen years ago, in Copenhagen, global leaders at the World Summit for Social Development described poverty eradication as an ethical, political and economic imperative, and identified it as one of the three pillars of social development. Poverty eradication has since become the overarching objective of development, as reflected in the internationally agreed development goals, including the Millennium Development Goals, which set the target of halving global extreme poverty by 2015.

Yet, global poverty levels have changed very little over the past two decades except in China and East Asia, which have been remarkably successful, and, to some extent, in India. Viewed in terms of the wider definition of poverty adopted by the 1995 Social Summit, which includes deprivation, social exclusion and lack of participation, the situation today may be even more deplorable than a money income poverty line would suggest.

Poverty levels remain stubbornly—and unacceptably—high in sub-Saharan Africa, where there has been little growth except in the half-decade before the current crisis, and in South Asia, despite more rapid and sustained growth. Experience has shown that economic growth alone is necessary, but not sufficient, to greatly reduce poverty in its many dimensions. Indeed, the mixed record of poverty reduction calls into question the efficacy of conventional approaches involving economic liberalization and privatization. Instead, Governments need to play a developmental role, with implementation of integrated economic and social policies designed to support inclusive output and employment growth as well as to reduce inequality and promote justice in society.

Such an approach needs to be complemented by appropriate industrial investment and technology policies as well as by inclusive financial facilities designed to effectively support the desired investments. In addition, new potentially viable production capacities and capabilities need to be fostered through developmental trade and other complementary policies. Structural transformations should promote decent work, while Governments should have enough policy, especially fiscal space, to enable them to play a proactive developmental role and to provide adequate universal social protection.

The world faces crises that pose challenges. The recent food and energy crises made hundreds of millions more vulnerable to hunger and poverty. Moreover, the current global financial and economic crisis threatens to wipe out much of the modest progress in poverty reduction since the 2000 Millennium Summit, while climate change increasingly threatens the lives of the poor. The negative economic and social impacts of these crises highlight vulnerability to poverty, and call into question the sustainability of global poverty reduction. This further underscores the need to rethink poverty reduction strategies and, more broadly, the underlying development paradigm.

This *Report on the World Social Situation* seeks to contribute to rethinking poverty and its eradication. It affirms the urgent need for a strategic shift away from the market fundamentalist thinking, policies and practices of recent decades towards more sustainable development- and equity-oriented policies appropriate to national conditions and circumstances. Such national development strategies, as called for by the 2005 World Summit, should seek to achieve the development goals. Responsible development and counter-cyclical macroeconomic policies to foster productive investments and generate decent employment must be at the core of this effort.

While some modest reforms of global economic governance have been instituted since 2008, too little is being done too slowly to significantly improve conditions, especially for the poor. Much more needs to be done to ensure food security as well as to provide adequate financing and technology support for developing countries to cope with climate change.

In this regard, the General Assembly, in resolution 62/205 of 19 December 2007, proclaimed 2008-2017 as the Second Decade for the Eradication of Poverty. In resolution 63/302 of 9 July 2009, it decided to convene a high-level plenary meeting of the Assembly on the Millennium Development Goals in 2010 to, inter alia, accelerate global progress towards poverty eradication. The *Report on the World Social Situation 2010* makes a compelling case for rethinking poverty and poverty reduction efforts. Ultimately, the primary task going forward is to implement coherent, sustainable approaches that put people at the centre of feasible national development strategies so as to rapidly improve the quality of life of current and future generations.

SHA ZUKANG
Under-Secretary-General for Economic and Social Affairs

Acknowledgements

The *Report on the World Social Situation*, prepared biennially, is the flagship publication on major social development issues of the Department of Economic and Social Affairs of the United Nations Secretariat.

Wenyan Yang led the team from the Division for Social Policy and Development that prepared the present issue of the *Report*. The core team at the Division included Lisa Ainbinder, Renata Kaczmarska, Peggy L. Kelly, Lisa Morrison Puckett, Marta Roig, Amson Sibanda, Sergio P. Vieira and Yiwen Zhu. Nimali S. Ariyawansa, Atsede Mengesha and Sylvie Pailler, also of the Division, provided valuable assistance.

Significant inputs to the *Report* were also received from independent experts Ashwani Saith and Sonali Deraniyagala.

The analysis benefited from a number of background papers prepared especially for the *Report* by prominent experts on social and economic policies, including Jayati Ghosh, Patrick Guillaumont, Aneel Karnani, Mushtaq Khan, Ruth Meinzen-Dick, Sanjay Reddy, Erik Reinert and Lance Taylor.

The *Report on the World Social Situation 2010* was prepared with overall guidance by Jomo Kwame Sundaram. Mr. Jomo Sundaram was ably assisted by Anisuzzaman Chowdhury, who worked hard on some of the most difficult chapters and also contributed a background paper. Most of the background papers will be published in a companion volume.

The *Report* has also benefited from positive feedback from colleagues within and outside the Department of Economic and Social Affairs.

We are grateful to all who have contributed.

Contents

		Page
	Explanatory notes.	xiii
I.	**Rethinking poverty: which way now?**	1
	Eradication of poverty as a moral and ethical imperative	5
	Growth, inequality and eradication of poverty	7
	Multidimensional nature of poverty	8
	Vulnerability	9
	Social exclusion.	10
	Renewal and rethinking	11
II.	**Poverty: the official numbers**	13
	Global poverty trends: 1981-2005	13
	Regional shares and trends	18
	Intraregional poverty trends	20
	Sub-Saharan Africa	20
	East Asia and the Pacific	24
	South Asia.	26
	Latin America and the Caribbean	27
	Middle East and Northern Africa	29
	Eastern Europe and Central Asia.	31
	Least developed countries	33
	Countries of the European Union (EU) and other countries of the Organization for Economic Cooperation and Development (OECD)	36
	Diversity within countries: poverty in China and India	39
	Annex II.1. Poverty: indicators and their relationship	42
III.	**The poverty of poverty measurement**.	45
	The World Bank $1-per-day line	47
	The poverty of poverty lines	49
	Food and the basic needs basket	49
	Non-food basic needs	50
	Ranking households by expenditure	52
	Household size and composition.	53

	Page
Public provisioning	54
Household assets base	54
Intra-household disparities	55
Marginalization and exclusion	55
Self-perception of the poor	55
Inequality	55
Problems of use and interpretation	56
Chronic income poverty or socio-economic vulnerability?	56
Why narrow the target?	57
Is poverty a discrete concept?	58
Towards universalism: life without poverty lines?	60
IV. Deprivation, vulnerability and exclusion	**63**
The need for a new approach	63
Where does this exercise in creative destruction lead: which is the way ahead?	64
Alternative points of entry	65
Social exclusion: a new approach to poverty analysis	65
Social exclusion: ubiquitous presence, multiple forms	67
Regional diversity in its manifestations	67
Social schisms beneath the averages: disparities in life expectancy	69
Identity, exclusion and poverty	71
Ethnicity and poverty: the cases of Native Americans in the United States of America and Roma in Europe	71
Gender and poverty: multiple and multiplied discriminations	74
Migrants and migration: aspirations and exclusions	76
Migration, social exclusion and the impact on poverty and inequality	76
International migrants and the current economic crisis	79
Exclusion's many other forms	81
Conclusion	82
V. Macroeconomic policies and poverty reduction	**83**
Growth performance	85
What role did the macroeconomic policy mix play in a disappointing growth performance?	86
Growth volatility	88

		Page
	Impact on poverty and inequality	89
	The way forward	91
VI.	**Economic liberalization and poverty reduction**	97
	Trade liberalization	98
	Trade and economic growth: the theory	98
	Empirical evidence	100
	Financial liberalization	103
	Privatization	107
	How can privatization reduce poverty?	108
	The way forward	111
VII.	**Labour-market and social policies and poverty reduction**	115
	Labour-market policies: counting the cost for the working poor	115
	Social policies	119
	Social protection	119
	Social pensions and insurance	119
	Social assistance and transfers	120
	Social protection in a time of crisis	120
	Active labour-market policies	122
	Education and poverty reduction	122
	Income-based inequalities	124
	Gender-based inequalities	124
	Health and poverty in developing countries	125
	Pro-poor health policies	126
	Social integration policies	127
	Anti-discrimination policies	128
	Policies designed to reduce inequality in access to opportunities	129
	Policies promoting participation	130
	Effective social integration requires a broad vision	131
	Social policy and poverty reduction: from universalism to targeting and back	131
VIII.	**Poverty reduction programmes**	135
	Microfinance	135
	Conditional cash transfers	138

		Page
	Should cash transfers be conditional?	140
	Conditional cash transfers or job creation?	141
	Unconditional and universal transfers.	141
	Employment guarantee schemes.	143
	Poverty reduction through property rights	144
	Governance reforms and poverty reduction	146
	Concluding remarks.	147
IX.	**Rethinking poverty reduction interventions.**	**151**
	Revisiting recent poverty trends	151
	Critical reflections	152
	Framing policy: some correctives	153
	Policy imperatives.	154
	The crisis: exit strategies	155
	The way forward.	156
Bibliography		**161**

Figures

			Page
I.1	Undernourished people in the developing world, 1990-2008		1
I.2	Gross national income (GNI) per capita and poverty levels in selected developing countries, 2005		9
II.1	World population and number of people living in poverty, 1981-2005		14
II.2	Global and regional trends in extreme poverty, 1981-2005		16
	A.	Number of people living on less than $1.25 a day	16
	B.	Proportion of the population living on less than $1.25 a day	16
II.3	Poverty trends over time, with and without major countries and regions, 1981-2005		17
	A.	Number of people living on less than $1.25 a day	17
	B.	Proportion of the population living on less than $1.25 a day	17
II.4	Poverty in heavily indebted poor countries and least developed countries, 1981-2005		35
II.5	Poverty in landlocked developing countries and small island developing States, 1981-2005		36

		Page
II.6	Relative poverty rates for different income thresholds in OECD countries, mid-2000s	38
IV.1	Inequality in life expectancy has been increasing, 1962-2002	70
VII.1	Ratio of under-five mortality rate for the bottom quintile to that for the top quintile, selected developing countries, late 1980s and mid to late 1990s	127

Tables

		Page
II.1	Regional shares in number of people in the world living on less than $1.25 a day, 1981-2005	19
II.2	Progress made in reducing poverty by half at the regional level, over the period 1990-2005	21
II.3	Proportion of the population living on less than $1.25 a day in countries of sub-Saharan Africa, 1981, 1990 and 2005, and the change needed to reach the 2015 target	22
II.4	Proportion of the population living on less than $1.25 a day in countries of East Asia and the Pacific, 1981, 1990 and 2005, and the change needed to reach the 2015 target	25
II.5	Proportion of the population living on less than $1.25 a day in countries of South Asia, 1981, 1990 and 2005, and the change needed to reach the 2015 target	27
II.6	Proportion of the population living on less than $1.25 a day in countries of Latin America and the Caribbean, 1981, 1990 and 2005, and the change needed to reach the 2015 target	28
II.7	Proportion of the population living on less than $1.25 a day in countries of the Middle East and Northern Africa, 1981, 1990 and 2005, and the change needed to reach the 2015 target	30
II.8	Proportion of the population living on less than $1.25 a day in countries of Eastern Europe and Central Asia, 1981, 1990 and 2005, and the change needed to reach the 2015 target	32
II.9	Proportion of the population living on less than $1.25 a day in least developed countries, landlocked developing countries, heavily indebted poor countries and small island developing States, 1990, 1999 and 2005, and the change needed to reach the 2015 target	37

			Page
V.1	Decadal GDP growth performance of developing regions, 1960-2000		86
VII.1	Average years of education for the poorest and richest quintiles in age group 17-22, selected countries, 1999-2005		124
VII.2	Government expenditure priorities, country groups by income and selected regions, 2005 and 2006		126

Boxes

III.1	Problems in estimating basic non-food needs		51
III.2	Does the choice of approach matter? Soundings from rural China		59
IV.1	The Oglala Sioux people on the Pine Ridge Reservation		72
IV.2	Dalit women: exclusion and violence		75
V.1	Income instability and the people living in poverty		90
V.2	Can aid ease fiscal constraints?		94
VI.1	Trade liberalization and exports in Africa		99
VI.2	Did trade liberalization reduce rural poverty in China?		101
VI.3	Fiscal impact of trade liberalization		103
VI.4	Financial crises and poverty		104
VI.5	Financial liberalization and growth		105
VI.6	Financial deregulation, inequality and poverty		107
VI.7	Privatization in Mongolia		110
VII.1	Urban waste pickers		119
VII.2	Are unemployment compensation programmes feasible in developing and emerging economies?		121
VII.3	User fees: health and poverty effects		128
VII.4	Impact of structural adjustment programmes on health and poverty in Africa		134

Explanatory notes

The following symbols have been used in tables throughout the *Report*:

Two dots (..) indicate that data are not available or are not separately reported.

A dash (—) indicates that the item is nil or negligible.

A hyphen (-) indicates that the item is not applicable.

A minus sign (-) indicates a deficit or decrease, except as indicated.

A full stop (.) is used to indicate decimals.

A slash (/) between years indicates a statistical year, for example, 1990/91.

Use of a hyphen (-) between years, for example, 1990-1991, signifies the full period involved, including the beginning and end years.

Annual rates of growth or change, unless otherwise stated, refer to annual compound rates.

Details and percentages in tables do not necessarily add to totals, because of rounding.

Reference to dollars ($) indicates United States dollars, unless otherwise stated.

When a print edition of a source exists, the print version is the authoritative one. United Nations documents reproduced online are deemed official only as they appear in the United Nations Official Document System. United Nations documentation obtained from other United Nations and non–United Nations sources are for informational purposes only. The Organization does not make any warranties or representations as to the accuracy or completeness of such materials.

The following abbreviations have been used:

AIDS	acquired immunodeficiency syndrome
AP	always poor
CCTs	conditional cash transfers
CPI	consumer price index
DAC	Development Assistance Committee
ECA	Economic Commission for Africa
ECLAC	Economic Commission for Latin America and the Caribbean
EFA	Education for All
ESCAP	Economic and Social Commission for Asia and the Pacific
EU	European Union
EWI	Employing Workers Indicator
FAO	Food and Agriculture Organization of the United Nations
FDI	foreign direct investment
GDP	gross domestic product
GNI	gross national income
GNP	gross national product
HDI	human development index
HIPC	Heavily Indebted Poor Countries

HIV	human immunodeficiency virus
ICP	International Comparison Program
ILO	International Labour Organization
IMF	International Monetary Fund
NAMA	non-agricultural market access
NP	never poor
ODA	official development assistance
OECD	Organization for Economic Cooperation and Development
PETI	Child Labour Eradication Programme
PPP	purchasing power parity
PRSPs	Poverty Reduction Strategy Papers
SAP	structural adjustment programme
SP	sometimes poor
TIM	Trade Integration Mechanism (International Monetary Fund)
UNDP	United Nations Development Programme
UNESCO	United Nations Educational, Scientific and Cultural Organization
UNICEF	United Nations Children's Fund
VAT	value-added tax
WHO	World Health Organization

For analytical purposes, countries are classified as belonging to either of two categories: more developed or less developed. The *less developed regions* (also referred to as *developing countries* in the *Report*) include all countries in Africa, Asia (excluding Japan), and Latin America and the Caribbean, as well as Oceania, excluding Australia and New Zealand. The *more developed regions* (also referred to as *developed countries* in the *Report*) comprise Europe and Northern America, plus Australia, Japan and New Zealand.

The group of *least developed countries* comprises 49 countries (as of 31 July 2009): Afghanistan, Angola, Bangladesh, Benin, Bhutan, Burkina Faso, Burundi, Cambodia, Central African Republic, Chad, Comoros, Democratic Republic of the Congo, Djibouti, Equatorial Guinea, Eritrea, Ethiopia, Gambia, Guinea, Guinea-Bissau, Haiti, Kiribati, Lao People's Democratic Republic, Lesotho, Liberia, Madagascar, Malawi, Maldives, Mali, Mauritania, Mozambique, Myanmar, Nepal, Niger, Rwanda, Samoa, Sao Tome and Principe, Senegal, Sierra Leone, Solomon Islands, Somalia, Sudan, Timor-Leste, Togo, Tuvalu, Uganda, United Republic of Tanzania, Vanuatu, Yemen and Zambia. These countries are also included in the less developed regions.

In addition, the *Report* uses the following country groupings or subgroupings:

Sub-Saharan Africa, which comprises the following countries and areas: Angola, Benin, Botswana, Burkina Faso, Burundi, Cameroon, Cape Verde, Central African Republic, Chad, Comoros, Congo, Côte d'Ivoire, Democratic Republic of the Congo, Djibouti, Equatorial Guinea, Eritrea, Ethiopia, Gabon, Gambia, Ghana, Guinea, Guinea-Bissau, Kenya, Lesotho, Liberia, Madagascar, Malawi, Mali, Mauritania, Mauritius, Mayotte, Mozambique, Namibia, Niger, Nigeria,

Réunion, Rwanda, Saint Helena, Sao Tome and Principe, Senegal, Seychelles, Sierra Leone, Somalia, South Africa, Sudan, Swaziland, Togo, Uganda, United Republic of Tanzania, Zambia and Zimbabwe.

East Asia and the Pacific, which comprises the following countries and areas: American Samoa, Cambodia, China, Fiji, Indonesia, Kiribati, Democratic People's Republic of Korea, Lao People's Democratic Republic, Malaysia, Marshall Islands, Micronesia (Federated States of), Mongolia, Myanmar, Palau, Papua New Guinea, Philippines, Samoa, Solomon Islands, Thailand, Timor-Leste, Tonga, Vanuatu and Viet Nam.

South Asia, which comprises the following countries: Afghanistan, Bangladesh, Bhutan, India, Maldives, Nepal, Pakistan and Sri Lanka.

Middle East and Northern Africa, which includes the following countries and area: Algeria, Djibouti, Egypt, Iran (Islamic Republic of), Iraq, Jordan, Lebanon, Libyan Arab Jamahiriya, Morocco, Syrian Arab Republic, Tunisia, Occupied Palestinian Territory and Yemen.

Eastern Europe and Central Asia, which includes the following countries: Albania, Bosnia and Herzegovina, Bulgaria, Croatia, Czech Republic, Hungary, Montenegro, Poland, Romania, Serbia, Slovakia, the former Yugoslav Republic of Macedonia and the successor countries of the former Union of Soviet Socialist Republics, comprising the Baltic republics and the member countries of the Commonwealth of Independent States. These countries are also referred to as *transition economies* in this *Report*.

Heavily indebted poor countries (as of 30 July 2009): Afghanistan, Benin, Bolivia, Burkina Faso, Burundi, Cameroon, Central African Republic, Chad, Comoros, Congo, Côte d'Ivoire, Democratic Republic of the Congo, Eritrea, Ethiopia, Gambia, Ghana, Guinea, Guinea-Bissau, Guyana, Haiti, Honduras, Kyrgyzstan, Liberia, Madagascar, Malawi, Mali, Mauritania, Mozambique, Nicaragua, Niger, Rwanda, Sao Tome and Principe, Senegal, Sierra Leone, Somalia, Sudan, Togo, Uganda, United Republic of Tanzania and Zambia.

Landlocked developing countries: Afghanistan, Armenia, Azerbaijan, Bhutan, Bolivia, Botswana, Burkina Faso, Burundi, Central African Republic, Chad, Ethiopia, Kazakhstan, Kyrgyzstan, Lao People's Democratic Republic, Lesotho, Malawi, Mali, Mongolia, Nepal, Niger, Paraguay, Republic of Moldova, Rwanda, Swaziland, Tajikistan, the former Yugoslav Republic of Macedonia, Turkmenistan, Uganda, Uzbekistan, Zambia and Zimbabwe.

Small island developing States and areas: American Samoa, Anguilla, Antigua and Barbuda, Aruba, Bahamas, Bahrain, Barbados, Belize, British Virgin Islands, Cape Verde, Commonwealth of the Northern Mariana Islands, Comoros, Cook Islands, Cuba, Dominica, Dominican Republic, Fiji, French Polynesia, Grenada, Guam, Guinea-Bissau, Guyana, Haiti, Jamaica, Kiribati, Maldives, Marshall Islands, Mauritius, Micronesia (Federated States of), Montserrat, Nauru, Netherlands Antilles, New Caledonia, Niue, Palau, Papua New Guinea, Puerto Rico, Saint Kitts and Nevis, Saint Lucia, Saint Vincent and the Grenadines, Samoa, Sao Tome and Principe, Seychelles, Singapore, Solomon Islands, Suriname, Timor-Leste, Tonga, Trinidad and Tobago, Tuvalu, United States Virgin Islands and Vanuatu.

Chapter I
Rethinking poverty: which way now?

Despite remarkable progress achieved since the Second World War, especially in parts of Asia, abject poverty remains widespread in many parts of the world. According to the World Bank's much cited "dollar-a-day" international poverty line, which was revised in 2008 to $1.25 a day in 2005 prices, there are still 1.4 billion people living in poverty, although this represents a decline from the 1.9 billion in 1981. This figure is higher than the 2004 estimate of 984 million made with the old measure of $1-a-day.

Poverty is the principal cause of hunger and undernourishment. According to most recent estimates of the Food and Agriculture Organization of the United Nations (FAO, 2009), the number of hungry people worldwide is 963 million (figure I.1), or about 14.6 per cent of the estimated world population of 6.6 billion, representing an increase of 142 million over the figure for 1990-1992. Most of the undernourished are in developing countries. Insofar as the poverty line is supposed to be determined principally in terms of the money income needed to avoid going hungry, the large discrepancy between the numbers for poverty and hunger and especially between their apparent trends becomes a source of rather fundamental concerns about the significance of the measures being used and cited.

Poverty claims the lives of 25,000 children each day. They "die quietly in some of the poorest villages on earth, far removed from the scrutiny and the

Figure I.1
Undernourished people in the developing world, 1990-2008

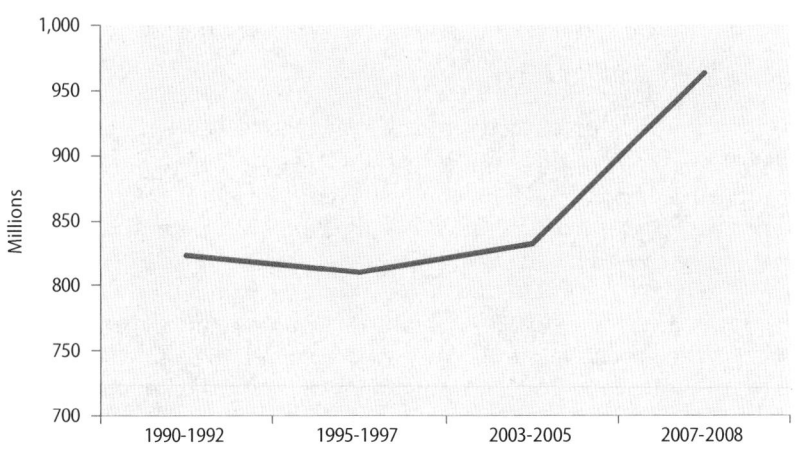

Source: Food and Agriculture Organization of the United Nations (2008; 2009).

conscience of the world. Being meek and weak in life makes these dying multitudes even more invisible in death" (United Nations Children's Fund, 2000). About 27-28 per cent of all children in developing countries are estimated to be underweight or stunted. According to 2005 school enrolment data, about 72 million children of primary school age in the developing world were not in school, and more than half of them—57 per cent—were girls (United Nations, 2007b). Nearly 1 billion people entered the twenty-first century unable to read or even sign their name (United Nations Children's Fund, 1999). About 1.1 billion people in developing countries do not have adequate access to water, while 2.6 billion lack basic sanitation (United Nations Development Programme, 2006).

Poverty and inequality are closely related, and inequality appears to have been on the rise worldwide in recent decades at both national and international levels. More than 80 per cent of the world's population live in countries where income differentials are widening. The poorest 40 per cent of the world's population account for only 5 per cent of global income. On the other hand, the richest 20 per cent account for 75 per cent of world income (United Nations Development Programme, 2007).

Extreme poverty does not entail just having unsatisfied material needs or being undernourished. It is often accompanied by a degrading state of powerlessness. Even in democratic and relatively well-governed countries, poor people have to accept daily humiliations without protest. Often, they cannot provide for their children and have a strong sense of shame and failure. When they are trapped in poverty, the poor lose hope of ever escaping from their hard work for which they often have nothing to show beyond bare survival (Singer, 2009).

In recognition of the gravity of the problem, world leaders participating in the 2000 Millennium Summit adopted the United Nations Millennium Declaration,[1] which became the basis for the formulation of the Millennium Development Goals. The overarching goal is to halve world poverty by 2015. The Millennium Development Goals have been elaborated as global time-bound and quantified targets for addressing several key dimensions of extreme poverty, including income poverty, hunger, disease, lack of shelter, and exclusion. Since the importance of poverty reduction was reaffirmed by the General Assembly in 2001, that goal has received the most attention.

Progress in meeting this poverty target is now seriously threatened by the worst financial and economic crisis since the Great Depression of the 1930s, which hit the world before it could fully recover from the sudden surges in energy and food prices. FAO (2009) estimated that soaring food prices had pushed another 115 million people into conditions of chronic hunger in 2007 and 2008 and noted (p. 6) that "The impact is most severe in Africa, where many countries are highly dependent on imported cereals (in some cases for

---

[1] See General Assembly resolution 55/2 of 8 September 2000.

up to 80 per cent of their dietary energy supplies) and undernourishment is already rife". FAO uses national income and income distribution to estimate how many people have received a level of income that would lead to undernourishment. What applies to these figures also holds for the World Bank's estimates, namely, that figures based on actual surveys of living conditions and on actual nutrition levels can be expected to be higher (Svedberg, 2000).

According to estimates contained in a press release of the World Bank (2009b), the food and energy price hikes in 2007-2008 increased the global poverty headcount by as many as 155 million people in 2008. The World Bank has not revised these estimates following the price declines. While oil prices have fallen precipitously since August 2008, food prices have declined since their early 2008 highs, but remain significantly higher than before the spikes.

The World Bank predicted a contraction of the world economy in 2009 by between 0.5 and 1.0 per cent, which was supposed to add another 60 million people to the ranks of the poor in developing countries. This prediction was based on the World Bank's new international poverty line—$1.25 purchasing power parity dollars a day in 2005—and on the parametric assumption that a decline of growth by 1 per cent adds 20 million people to the ranks of the poor (World Bank, 2008b; 2009c). As noted in the aforementioned World Bank press release:

> New estimates for 2009 suggest that lower economic growth rates will trap 46 million more people on less than USD 1.25 a day than was expected prior to the crisis. An extra 53 million people will be trapped on less than USD 2 a day. This is on top of the 130 million–155 million people pushed into poverty in 2008 because of soaring food and fuel prices.[2]

The subsequent downwardly revised economic growth/recession forecasts will certainly portray an exacerbation of the situation.

The Department of Economic and Social Affairs of the United Nations Secretariat (United Nations, 2009b) estimates that the drop in per capita income growth in 2009 will slow poverty reduction significantly. Between 73 million and 100 million more people will remain poor or fall into poverty than would have if the pre-crisis growth rate had continued. Most of the impact of this setback will be felt in East and South Asia where between 56 million and 80 million people, about half of whom are in India, are likely to be affected. The crisis is expected to keep from 12 million to 16 million more people in poverty in Africa and another 4 million in Latin America and

---

2 There is, however, some confusion regarding the projected increase in poverty. In an Op-Ed piece written for *The New York Times*, Robert Zoellick, President of the World Bank, stated that the economic crisis has already pushed an estimated 100 million people back into poverty (Zoellick 2009). If this is correct, then nearly 29 per cent of the gains in global poverty reduction have been wiped out. This estimate is based on claims that since 1997, 350 million people have graduated out of poverty as measured by the poverty line of $1.25 a day (see Lin, 2008).

the Caribbean. These projections most likely underestimate the true poverty impact of the crisis, as its distributional consequences have not been fully accounted for.

According to estimates by the International Labour Organization (2009a), the global unemployment rate increased to 6.0 per cent in 2008 from 5.7 per cent in 2007, while the total number of unemployed increased by 10.7 million, reaching about 190 million in 2008. Workers at the lower end of the job ladder, including youth and female workers, are more likely to lose their jobs or to suffer income losses. Also, workers are already shifting out of dynamic export-oriented sectors and are either becoming unemployed or moving to lower-productivity activities (which includes moving back from urban to rural areas). In China alone, 20 million workers had been so affected by the end of 2008. These trends are likely to jeopardize poverty reduction in more structural terms as it may take some time before economies readjust and workers can shift back to activities yielding higher remuneration.

Children, especially girls, are expected to suffer major health and education setbacks as a result of the crises. Shrinking household budgets force families to pull children out of school, with girls more likely than boys to be affected. Preliminary forecasts for 2009-2015 indicate that a total of from 1.4 million to 2.8 million infants—700,000 in Africa alone—may die if the crisis persists (World Bank, 2009b; 2009e).

It is clear, therefore, that the global food, energy, and financial and economic crises are reversing the modest progress achieved thus far towards achieving the internationally agreed development goals. In addition, climate change is posing a serious risk to poverty reduction and threatening to undo decades of development efforts. As stated in the Johannesburg Declaration on Sustainable Development (United Nations, 2002b; chap. I, resolution 1, annex), "the adverse effects of climate change are already evident, natural disasters are more frequent and more devastating and developing countries more vulnerable" (para. 13). Although climate change is a global phenomenon, its negative impacts are more severely felt by poor people and poor countries, according to the Synthesis Report of the Third Assessment Report of the International Panel on Climate Change (2001), owing to the economic importance of climate-sensitive sectors (for example, agriculture and fisheries) in those countries, and their limited human, institutional and financial capacity to anticipate and respond to the adverse effects of climate change. Many sectors providing basic livelihood services to the poor in developing countries are not even able to cope with today's climate variability and stresses.

The fact that prospects for future advancement in terms of poverty reduction are thus in jeopardy will need to be considered at the high-level plenary meeting of the General Assembly on the Millennium Development Goals to be held in 2010. The high-level meeting will review progress and chart the course towards achieving the Goals to which world leaders committed at the 2000 Millennium Summit.

The decision taken by the General Assembly in its resolution 63/302 of 9 July 2009 to hold the high-level plenary meeting reflects its recognition of the need to consolidate achievements and ensure future progress towards poverty eradication. In the same spirit, the Assembly proclaimed the Second United Nations Decade for the Eradication of Poverty (2008-2017) in its resolution 62/205 of 19 December 2007. Thus, the time is right for re-examining the complex issue of poverty in order to learn from past experiences and inform future efforts to eradicate poverty and to ensure the attainment of the Millennium Development Goals—hence, the choice of poverty as the theme for the *Report on the World Social Situation 2010*.

The theme of poverty is in fact intimately linked to the themes of the *Report on the World Social Situation 2005* (United Nations, 2005a) and the *Report on the World Social Situation 2007* (United Nations, 2007a). The *Report on the World Social Situation 2005* focused on growing inequalities around the world, which present a major hurdle for poverty eradication and achievement of the Millennium Development Goals. The *Report on the World Social Situation 2007* focused on the issue of employment. The promotion of decent and productive employment for **all** has been identified as the key instrument for addressing the problem of poverty and inequality. The 2005, 2007 and 2010 issues of the *Report on the World Social Situation* thus all serve as reminders of the commitments made by world leaders at the World Summit for Social Development held in Copenhagen in 1995 and the great efforts that still need to be made to achieve a world free of poverty, hunger and injustice.

Eradication of poverty as a moral and ethical imperative

The eradication of poverty is a moral and ethical imperative, rooted in the principles governing the United Nations. To live a life free from poverty and hunger is one of the human rights and fundamental freedoms enshrined in the Universal Declaration of Human Rights.[3] Article 25 (1) of the Declaration states that "Everyone has the right to a standard of living adequate for the health and well-being of himself and of his family, including food, clothing, housing and medical care and necessary social services". This right is further reaffirmed in the International Covenant on Economic, Social and Cultural Rights and the International Covenant on Civil and Political Rights.[4] These human rights instruments acknowledge that human rights derive from the inherent dignity of the human person. Extreme poverty has also been recognized by the General Assembly as a violation of human rights, even of the right to life itself.[5] Moreover, in the Charter of the United Nations it was determined that

---

[3] General Assembly resolution 217 A (III) of 10 December 1948.
[4] General Assembly resolution 2200 A (XXI), annex.
[5] See General Assembly resolution 59/186 of 20 December 2004 entitled "Human rights and extreme poverty".

one mission of the United Nations would be to promote "higher standards of living, full employment, and conditions of economic and social progress and development" through international cooperation (Articles 55 and 56).

The persistence of poverty, especially in its extreme form, flouts the purposes and principles of the Charter of the United Nations. It is particularly worrisome that during periods of high economic growth and global plenty, so many people remain consigned to a life of material deprivation which may end in early death. Of particular concern is the fact that poverty is often associated with unalterable characteristics (such as race and ethnicity) and shocks (such as health pandemics and environmental catastrophes) that are beyond the control of those affected.

Poverty is also a violation of elementary absolute standards of social justice. Social justice emphasizes core principles of non-discrimination and equality, including equal entitlement to fulfilment through exercise of civil, political, economic, social and cultural rights. These principles necessarily give rise to a set of socio-economic priorities that direct the focus of policy to issues of vulnerability, discrimination and segregated development. Social justice requires that everyone should have a minimal standard of living, and that people living in poverty should receive assistance when they lack the means to live lives that affirm their human worth and dignity.

At the World Summit for Social Development, world leaders committed to eradicating poverty through decisive national actions and international cooperation (United Nations, 1996). The Summit emphasized that people are at the centre of development; thus, the ultimate goal of development is both to improve living conditions and to empower people to participate fully in the economic, social and political spheres. It firmly placed the goal of eradicating poverty at the centre of national and international policy agendas, a goal enshrined in resolution 50/107 of 20 December 1995, by which the General Assembly proclaimed the First United Nations Decade for the Eradication of Poverty (1997-2006).

Five years after the Copenhagen Summit, the General Assembly held its twenty-fourth special session in Geneva, which resulted in the adoption of proposals for further initiatives for social development.[6] Representatives of Governments reiterated their "determination and duty to eradicate poverty, promote full and productive employment, foster social integration and create an enabling environment for social development" (sect. I, para. 5) while reaffirming their "resolve to reinforce solidarity with people living in poverty" (sect. I, para. 10).

At the Millennium Summit, held in New York in 2000, world leaders restated that "men and women have the right to live their lives and raise their children in dignity, free from hunger and from the fear of violence, oppression and injustice" (General Assembly resolution 55/2, para. 6) and that "no

---

6 General Assembly resolution S-24/2 of 1 July 2000, annex.

individual and no nation must be denied the opportunity to benefit from development" (ibid.). They vowed (para. 11) that they would "spare no effort to free our fellow men, women and children from the abject and dehumanizing condition of extreme poverty, to which more than 1 billion of them are currently subjected" and were "committed to making the right to development a reality for everyone and to freeing the entire human race from want". To this end, world leaders further resolved to achieve the Millennium Development Goals set out in the Millennium Declaration, the first of which was to halve, by 2015, the proportion of the world's people living on less than one dollar a day and the proportion of people who suffered from hunger.

The commitment and dedication to eradicating poverty as a moral and ethical imperative, as expressed in the Millennium Declaration, were reaffirmed in the 2005 World Summit outcome.[7] To ensure follow-up of the implementation of major United Nations conferences and summits, including the World Summit for Social Development, the General Assembly decided that the Economic and Social Council should hold annual ministerial reviews to monitor progress towards achieving the internationally agreed development goals, including the Millennium Development Goals.[8]

The commitments and mandates emanating from the major United Nations conferences and summits strongly affirmed the intimate relationship between poverty eradication and the realization of human rights and social justice. They are inseparable goals; not only is eradicating poverty a means to improve the living conditions of people living in poverty, but it is an end in itself.

Growth, inequality and eradication of poverty

A basic lesson to be drawn from successful development experiences is that sustained poverty reduction depends on a fast pace of economic growth. However, the connection between growth and poverty is not a direct one, and the variation associated with the stylized trends that it reflects is a reminder that the impact both of the way in which additional income is distributed and of the features of the employment component matters to poverty outcomes.

The East Asian experience, perhaps the most successful example of rapid poverty reduction in the modern era, confirms that countries with a more equal distribution of assets and income can grow faster than countries with a higher degree of inequality. Higher productivity among smallholders, significant human capital investments, scale economies linked to larger domestic markets and greater political stability are just some of the factors suggested to account for the fact that greater equality coincided with faster growth. Rapid

---

7 See General Assembly resolution 60/1.
8 See General Assembly resolution 61/16 of 20 November 2006, entitled, "Strengthening of the Economic and Social Council", para. 8.

expansion of industrial investment and jobs enabling the absorption of surplus labour leaving the rural economy was also a characteristic feature of this experience (Khan, 2007).

The long-term success of poverty reduction in East Asian countries was not the automatic outcome of the unleashing of market forces. Rather, it rested on the State's forging a social contract in which a nascent entrepreneurial class accepted, in return for State support for socializing investment risk and bolstering profits, some degree of direction with respect to its investment decisions. This contract was designed both to ensure expansion of jobs in labour-intensive manufacturing as a means of absorbing unskilled labour and reducing poverty, and to effect a shift to more technologically demanding activities which were more likely to guarantee continued competitive advantage in the international markets and rising living standards in the future.

By contrast, the Latin American region has been described as being caught in a "vicious circle" of persistent poverty, insecurity and unstable growth, which has been perpetuated by a persistent and widespread tendency to underinvest in productive assets and social capital (Perry and others, 2006). Similar poverty traps have been identified in other developing regions by a growing body of research (Jomo and Baudot, 2007).

Perception of the links among growth, employment and distribution can be obscured where there is an undue focus on levels of extreme poverty. In this respect, the dollar-a-day benchmark may not serve as the best guide to policymakers in respect of their identifying the structural obstacles that hinder growth acceleration and ensuring that faster growth translates into poverty reduction.

Multidimensional nature of poverty

Poverty is not simply a lack of adequate income. It is a multidimensional phenomenon that extends beyond the economic arena to encompass factors such as the inability to participate in social and political life (Sen, 1979; 1985; 1987). In short, poverty is the deprivation of one's ability to live as a free and dignified human being with the full potential to achieve one's desired goals in life. The Programme of Action of the World Summit for Social Development (United Nations, 2006, resolution 1, annex II) characterized poverty as follows:

> Poverty has various manifestations, including lack of income and productive resources sufficient to ensure sustainable livelihoods; hunger and malnutrition; ill health; limited or lack of access to education and other basic services; increased morbidity and mortality from illness; homelessness and inadequate housing; unsafe environments; and social discrimination and exclusion. It is also characterized by a lack of participation in decision-making and in civil, social and cultural life (para. 19).

While this characterization is very broad and seeks to capture various dimensions of poverty, it manages to encompass in a balanced manner such aspects as restrictions in opportunities, vulnerability to shocks and social exclusion.[9] These three aspects combined contribute to a truly multidimensional perspective on poverty.

They are not, however, dissociated from issues of growth and income. Indeed, the scatter plot involving several developing countries contained in figure I.2 demonstrates that lower levels of poverty are associated with high per capita incomes.

From the multidimensional perspective, what matters is a focus on the opportunities—such as a set of endowments, access to markets, etc.—that are available to people. If an individual does not possess sufficient endowments or capabilities, such as a basic education, or does not have the opportunity to acquire them, he or she will have a limited ability to escape poverty.

Vulnerability

The concept of vulnerability captures the likelihood that people will fall into poverty owing to shocks to the economic system or personal mishaps. Vulnerability is thus a reflection of economic insecurity. Although poor people

Figure I.2
Gross national income (GNI) per capita and poverty levels in selected developing countries, 2005

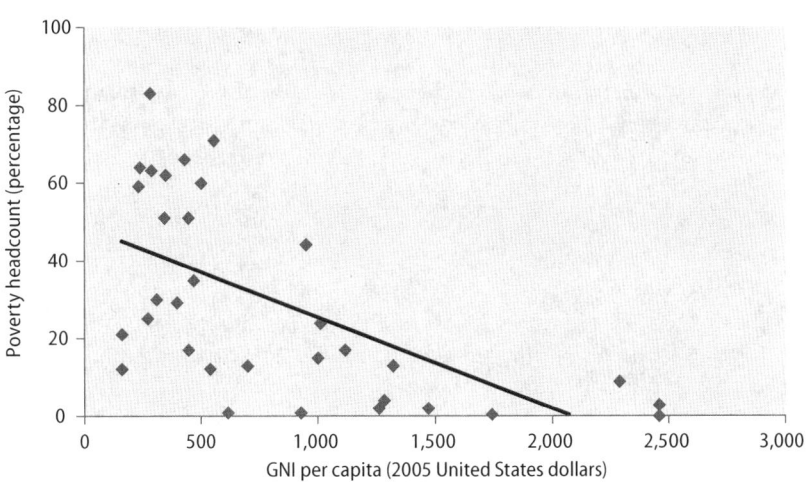

Source: World Bank, Development Research Group (2009).

---

9 The majority of these aspects are reflected in the Millennium Development Goals and their benchmarks and indicators, except for inclusion/exclusion and participation.

are usually among the most vulnerable, not all vulnerable people are poor, a distinction which facilitates differentiation among lower-income populations. Many people not currently living in poverty face a high risk of becoming poor if faced with a change in situation such as job loss or the major illness of a family member. Such individuals, while not poor per se, are highly vulnerable to falling into poverty. In addition, people already living in poverty are vulnerable to being pushed into deeper poverty when faced with mishaps.

Estimates show that a large number of people on the edge of poverty, especially those just above the official poverty line, are economically insecure. If the World Bank's poverty line of $2 per day is used, instead of its line of $1 per day, poverty rates rise dramatically in many developing countries, reflecting the extent of vulnerability of their population to small shifts in their opportunity set.

Because commonly used poverty measures are generally fixed in time, they tend to miss this dynamic aspect of poverty. Unlike poverty, which is assessed after the fact, vulnerability "focuses on assessing the extent of the threat of poverty or low well-being, measured ex ante, before the veil of uncertainty has been lifted" (Dercon, 2005, p. 486).

Social exclusion

The approach based on social exclusion focuses on the lack of participation of individuals or groups in society. Certain groups such as women or specific socio-ethnic communities may be excluded from the labour market and education, while others may be excluded from the political process. Hence, analyses of different social groups based on gender, age, religion, ethnicity, geographical location, occupation and health status are particularly important. While this perspective originated in developed countries in the wake of the crisis in the welfare State, it has become prominent in the literature on poverty in both developed and developing countries as a consequence of rising inequalities and concerns about race and ethnicity and the need to promote more harmonious societies (Figueiredo and de Haan, 1998; Buvinic, Mazza and Deutsch, 2004; de Haan, 2007).

Perhaps the real significance of a multidimensional approach to poverty lies in the fact that it allows for an expanded public policy agenda. In many cases where social performance indicators, such as health and education, far exceeded expectations based on levels of gross national product (GNP) per capita, these results were achieved through transformative social policies, for example, in China, Costa Rica, Cuba, Kerala State of India, Sri Lanka and many formerly socialist countries. Those policies, which were holistic, inclusive and universalistic, can provide lessons to developing countries struggling to overcome poverty in its various dimensions. Many of the major social transformations were achieved despite low average income levels. Conversely, many countries that raised average income levels significantly but failed to adopt a more transformative social agenda remained underperformers in terms of health, education and social inclusion. This highlights the limitations of approaches that are excessively focused on income. The role of poverty lines and narrow Government targeting mechanisms was small in cases where poverty reduction was successful and significant as well as in cases where such reduction did not occur despite significant increases in average per capita incomes.

Renewal and rethinking

Since the adoption of the United Nations Millennium Declaration in 2000, many countries in Africa and Latin America have seen rapid economic growth, often benefiting from higher commodity prices. Most developing countries achieved macroeconomic stability, and their public finances achieved some degree of balance, after two decades of austere adjustment programmes. Global financial markets were awash in liquidity, with investors ready to invest in developing-country debt and equity. Foreign direct investment (FDI) was also rising strongly, especially in resource-rich countries, as mining companies raced to take advantage of higher mineral commodity prices. Strong growth in China and India helped further to bring down global poverty rates, not only in their own economies but also in the economies of their main trading partners. As noted by Addison (2009, p. 174): "For those convinced that economic growth offers the main route to poverty reduction, that the market mechanism works wonders, and that the poor always benefit from globalization, the world looked good."

However, the optimism started to crumble with the crises in food and energy prices and the current global financial and economic crisis. The dominant growth-based paradigm which underpinned poverty reduction strategies in the past two to three decades has come under serious scrutiny. Further, the World Bank has revised its "dollar-a-day" methodology and its own poverty estimates, but criticisms continue to highlight their methodological problems and the implications of such problems. Thus, controversies about actual trends in global poverty continue, while raising, in the process, serious doubts about the effectiveness of poverty reduction strategies.

The present publication represents a contribution to this debate. Following the review of global poverty trends contained in chapter II, chapters III and IV reflect on broader issues of measurement, with a view to widening the understanding of poverty in its various dimensions. They underscore the fact that the issue of poverty reduction is a great deal more nuanced and complex than the narrow technocratic vision underlying the conventional wisdom. Chapters V to VIII critically examine the conventional policy framework and popular poverty reduction programmes in the context of the persistence of poverty, rising inequality and lacklustre growth performance in many developing countries until very recently. Chapter IX argues that a commitment to eradicating poverty and to enhancing equity and social integration requires persistent actions directed towards sustainable economic growth, productive employment creation and social development, entailing an integrated approach to economic and social policies for the benefit of **all** citizens. Moreover, it calls for more developmentally oriented and progressive State activism and universalism—as opposed to selectivity—in the approach to social policy.

It is hoped that, through the highlighting of the moral obligation to address poverty as a human right, the temptation to cut social spending will be resisted during the current period of economic hardship. While ultimate responsibility for tackling poverty and climate change lies with national Governments, the developed world must support the efforts of developing countries to achieve the internationally agreed development goals so as to ensure the creation of a peaceful, inclusive and prosperous world free of hunger, indignity and deprivation.

Chapter II
Poverty: the official numbers

Monitoring and reporting on the levels, patterns and trends of poverty have become a standard part of anti-poverty programme design and assessment. With the steady internationalization of the poverty agenda, development organizations, both multilateral and bilateral, have demanded a template for regular reporting, and new concepts, definitions, data sets and instruments have been generated to meet this demand. Every major development organization produces its own report card, often ranking countries in terms of their performance. Special interest usually attaches to the annual *Human Development Reports* of the United Nations Development Programme (UNDP) and, of late, the Millennium Development Goals progress reports; however, it is perhaps the reports of the World Bank on the incidence of poverty based on the dollar-a-day criterion that generate the greatest interest and commentary in the development community. Statistics have an awesome power, and these global accounting exercises present statistical data to journalists, researchers, practitioners and activists as irrefutable facts. What, then, are those ostensible facts? The present chapter provides a summary of the currently most influential versions, largely associated with the World Bank's dollar-a-day poverty estimates.

Global poverty trends: 1981-2005[1]

Poverty is most often measured in monetary terms, captured by levels of income or consumption per capita or per household. The commitment made in the Millennium Development Goals to eradicate absolute poverty by halving the number of people living on less than US$ 1.25 dollar a day represents the most publicized example of an income-focused approach to poverty.

Based on this measure, the last 20 years have seen significant reductions in the depth and severity of extreme poverty in the developing world.[2] In absolute terms, extreme income poverty has fallen substantially, with the number of

---

[1] The present chapter uses the revised series of country-level poverty data issued by the World Bank in August 2008 following the findings of the 2005 International Comparison Program. These data are available on PovcalNet, a web-based interactive research tool which can be used to replicate Bank poverty estimates and test alternative assumptions regarding, inter alia, the poverty line or country groupings. Despite many criticisms, the Bank's approach remains highly influential, and provides the prevailing benchmark for discussions of the extent and trends of poverty globally, including in the United Nations system. Hence, what we think we know continues to rely heavily on the accuracy of the poverty estimates generated by the Bank.

[2] For definitions of terms, see annex II.1.

people living on less than $1.25 a day having declined from a high of 1.9 billion in 1981 to a low of 1.4 billion in 2005. In relative terms, the proportion of people living in extreme poverty dropped from 52.0 to 25.7 per cent during this period (Chen and Ravallion, 2008).[3]

Notwithstanding the continued growth in the world's population, the absolute number of people living in extreme poverty has fallen, regardless of whether the poverty-line income threshold is set at $1.25 or raised to $2 or $2.50 per day (figure II.1). This has occurred in the midst of an expanding global economy, which has resulted, on average, in higher per capita incomes in both developed and developing countries (Sachs, 2008; United Nations, 2005a). Since the 1960s, gross domestic product (GDP) in low-income countries has grown at an average of 4.1 per cent per annum, while GDP in middle-

Figure II.1
World population and number of people living in poverty, 1981-2005

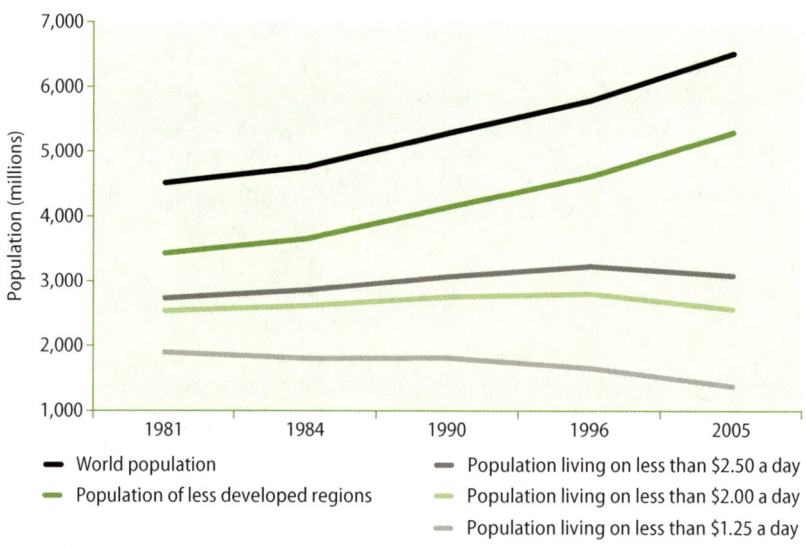

Sources: United Nations, Department of Economic and Social Affairs, Population Division; and World Bank, Development Research Group (2009).

---

3 For many developing countries, the estimation of current and past poverty levels is a complex task given the general lack of reliable data. In these countries, information on the depth, severity and duration of poverty may be limited, and available information may be unreliable. To address some of these data gaps, the research programme of the World Bank Poverty and Inequality Group has been engaged in improving current data as well as methods and tools for poverty and inequality analysis through, inter alia, producing new household-level data (notably through the Group's Living Standards Measurement Study), monitoring poverty and inequality using household-level data, developing more reliable "poverty maps", and rolling out computational tools such as ADePT and PovCalNet (see http://go.worldbank.org/NT2A1XUWP0).

and high-income countries has grown at an average of 4.2 and 3.2 per cent per annum, respectively (Soubbotina, 2004).

By 2050, the world's population is projected to surpass 9 billion, with developing countries accounting for most of the 2.3 billion increase. The population of the developing world is expected to rise from 5.6 billion in 2009 to 7.9 billion in 2050. In contrast, the population of the developed regions is expected to increase slightly, from 1.23 billion to 1.28 billion (United Nations, Department of Economics and Social Affairs, Population Division, 2009). The continued rapid increase in the population of developing countries highlights the importance of having appropriate policies designed to promote the sustained economic growth and structural transformation of their economies so as to ensure durable poverty reduction. Although the income-based (per capita) conventional poverty measure is sensitive to population growth, careful analysis does not provide any support for the Malthusian claim that poverty can be attributed to population growth in excess of output growth, especially food production. Instead, the demographic transitions experienced by a wide variety of societies suggest that family sizes tend to decline with higher incomes and greater economic security. Conversely, poor families tend to have more children in the hope of increasing contributions to household income as well as of ensuring continued economic security as parents age (Leibenstein, 1957; Mamdani, 1972; Robbins, 1999).

As can be seen from figure II.2.A, faster rates of decline in the number of people living on less than $1.25 a day occurred between 1999 and 2005. A significant proportion of this decline can be largely attributed to the rise in living standards in East Asia and the Pacific which accompanied explosive economic growth, particularly in China. Other regions of the world also experienced a decline in the incidence of poverty, with the exception of Eastern Europe and Central Asia, where the proportion of people living on less than $1.25 a day increased from 1.7 to 3.7 per cent between 1981 and 2005 (figure II.2.B). While this declining trend in poverty levels is welcome, it is also important to point out that poverty rates remain unacceptably high in sub-Saharan Africa and South Asia.

Figure II.3 presents global poverty trends with and without some major countries and regions, thereby illustrating the role that these countries and regions play in shaping the global trends. The absolute global poverty level in 2005 was about 1.4 billion; however when China is excluded from the analysis, poverty increased from 1.1 billion in 1981 to about 1.3 billion in 1999, before declining to about 1.2 billion in 2005 (figure II.3.A). However, if sub-Saharan Africa is left out, the number of people living on less than $1.25 a day falls precipitously, from 1.7 billion in 1981 to 986 million in 2005. Without the rapidly growing developing economies of Brazil, the Russian Federation, India and China, the absolute number of people living in extreme poverty actually went up, from 619 million in 1981 to about 699 million in 2005. However, in terms of incidence, poverty levels declined across all regions (figure II.3.B).

Figure II.2
Global and regional trends in extreme poverty, 1981-2005

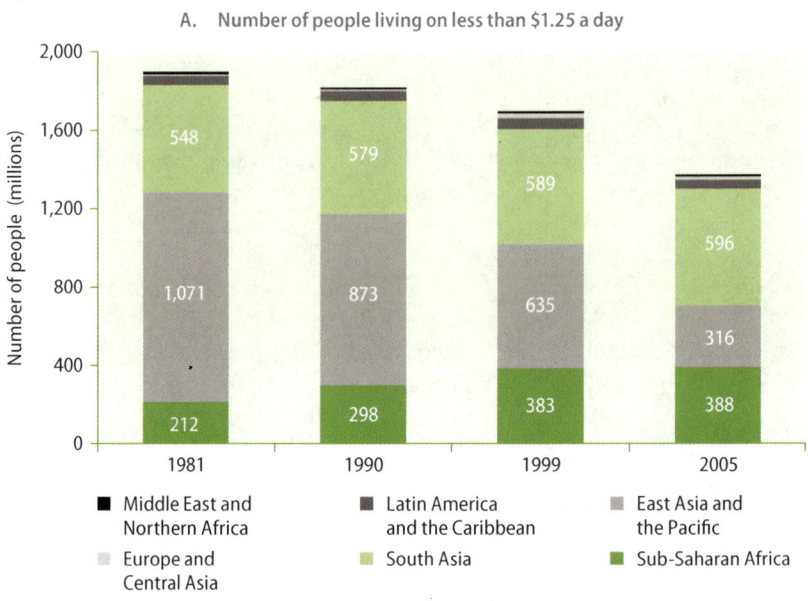

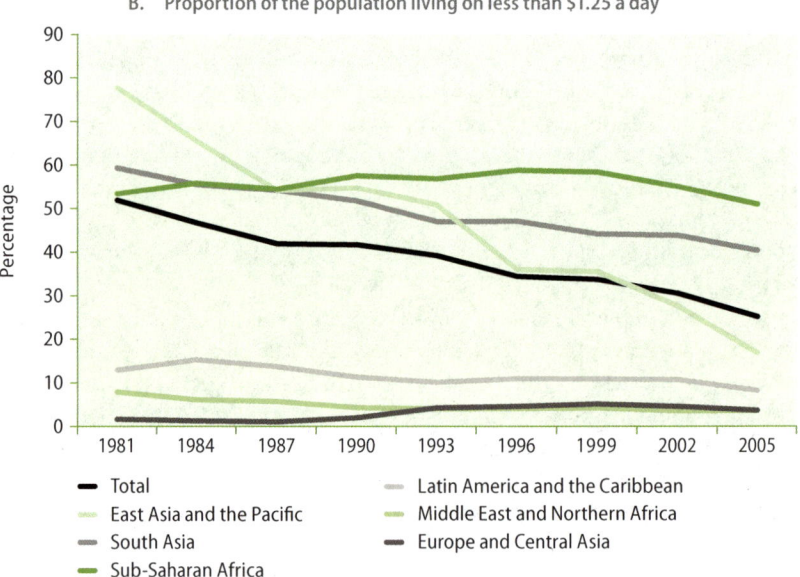

Source: World Bank, Development Research Group (2009).

Figure II.3
Poverty trends over time, with and without major countries and regions, 1981-2005

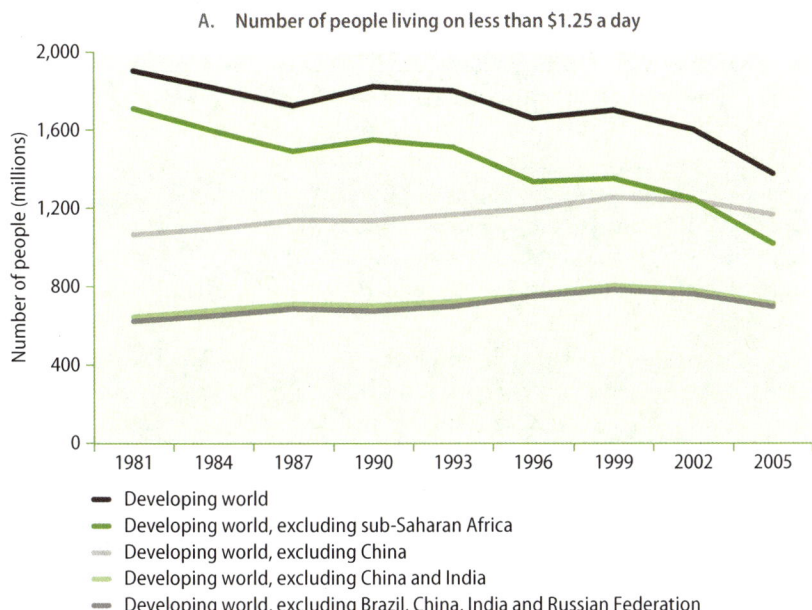

A. Number of people living on less than $1.25 a day

- Developing world
- Developing world, excluding sub-Saharan Africa
- Developing world, excluding China
- Developing world, excluding China and India
- Developing world, excluding Brazil, China, India and Russian Federation

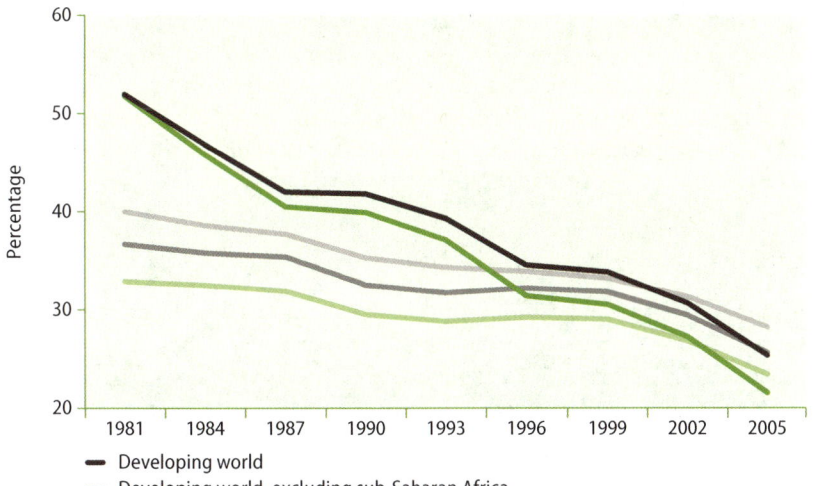

B. Proportion of the population living on less than $1.25 a day

- Developing world
- Developing world, excluding sub-Saharan Africa
- Developing world, excluding China
- Developing world, excluding China and India
- Developing world, excluding Brazil, China, India and Russian Federation

Source: World Bank, Development Research Group (2009).

With sub-Saharan Africa excluded, the incidence of poverty in the developing world declined by 31 percentage points between 1981 and 2005, while a developing world without China saw the incidence of poverty drop from about 40 to 28 per cent during this period.

The dramatic drop in poverty levels has been attributed to, inter alia, improved rates of economic performance and higher wages, as well as the provision of social protection systems. Unfortunately, in the context of the current global economic and financial crisis, which is slowing down rates of economic growth, faster rates of population growth in developing countries without commensurate increases in productive employment and with a lack of comprehensive social protection have exacerbated the declines in real per capita incomes and have thus contributed to a rise in the number of poor persons.

The contraction in the global economy has already resulted in massive job losses, with the global unemployment rate having increased from 5.7 to 6 per cent between 2007 and 2008 (International Labour Organization, 2009a). Data on recent global employment trends released by the International Labour Organization (ILO) also show that based on growth projections, the number of unemployed persons globally could rise by 20 million in 2009 as a result of the economic crisis (International Labour Organization, 2009a). It is also estimated that the number of the unemployed could rise by 50 million if the global economic outlook worsens to the point where increases in unemployment match the magnitudes witnessed in the 1990s. This will bring the global unemployment rate to above 7 per cent. The number of the working poor is also likely to rise, particularly in emerging and developing countries where growth was primarily export-led. Besides posing serious challenges with respect to Government social spending and social stability, given the long lag in employment recovery, this increase will in all likelihood erase progress made over the last decade in reducing extreme poverty through the generation of decent work opportunities for all.[4]

Regional shares and trends

Although global trends are informative, they tend to conceal significant diversity in poverty levels across regions. The transformative power of sustained economic growth combined with urbanization trends has propelled some countries to middle-income status (particularly those in East Asia) while a few others are poised to join the high-income status group. For other regions, the lack of strong and sustained economic growth and persisting income in-

---

4 Employment recovery generally lags from four to five years behind output recovery. Historical evidence culled by Reinhart and Rogoff (2009), based on 14 cases, suggests that it takes 4.8 years for the unemployment rate to revert to its pre-crisis level, even though GDP returns to its pre-crisis level in 1.9 years.

equalities have meant that the number of poor people continues to grow. Consequently, the spatial distribution of poor people within and across regions is changing. Before examining what is happening to levels of poverty across regions, it is important to determine where poor people live. One way to do this is to compare the share of poor people living in each region.

As shown in table II.1, the distribution of extremely poor people (defined as those living on less than $1.25 a day) across developing regions has changed significantly since 1981 when East Asia and the Pacific had the highest share of the number of poor people. It is now South Asia and sub-Saharan Africa that have the highest shares. In 1981, China and other East Asian countries accounted for 57 per cent of extremely poor people in the world. However, over a span of less than 25 years, the East Asian and Pacific region managed to reduce its global share of extremely poor people to about 23 per cent by 2005. In contrast, the share of the world's extremely poor people increased in South Asia, from 29 per cent in 1981 to 43 per cent in 2005. The share of poor people in sub-Saharan Africa more than doubled over the same period, having gone from 11 per cent in 1981 to 28 per cent in 2005. These changes are partly accounted for by high rates of population growth in the absence of strong economic and productive employment growth, as well as by the failure in both regions to achieve significant structural change.

In other words, the changing picture of the distribution of poverty across the regions reflects the broad nature of their economic performances. In the case of East Asia and the Pacific, there is little doubt that strong economic

Table II.1
Regional shares in number of people in the world living on less than $1.25 a day, 1981-2005 (*percentage*)

Region	1981	1984	1987	1990	1993	1996	1999	2002	2005
East Asia and the Pacific	56.50	52.39	47.81	48.16	47.09	37.57	37.44	31.61	22.97
Eastern Europe and Central Asia	0.37	0.32	0.28	0.50	1.12	1.32	1.43	1.35	1.26
Latin America and the Caribbean	2.21	2.89	3.04	2.37	2.33	3.15	3.23	3.64	3.35
Middle East and Northern Africa	0.72	0.64	0.69	0.53	0.55	0.64	0.68	0.64	0.80
South Asia	28.91	30.28	33.09	31.94	31.17	35.89	34.72	38.42	43.26
Sub-Saharan Africa	11.27	13.48	15.09	16.49	17.74	21.43	22.50	24.33	28.37
Total (per cent)	100	100	100	100	100	100	100	100	100
Total number of poor (millions)	1 896.2	1 808.2	1 720	1 813.4	1 794.9	1 656.2	1 696.2	1 603.1	1 376.7

Source: World Bank, Development Research Group (2009).

growth and structural change, particularly in China, have been important contributors to the phenomenal decrease in the region's share of people living below the $1.25-a-day poverty line. Africa's recent growth surge, particularly since 2002 (Economic Commission for Africa, 2008), had offered some hope of reducing levels of extreme poverty. However, the recent global financial and economic crisis, which came on the heels of food and energy price hikes, is set to reverse recent gains (United Nations, 2009b). Moreover, Africa's recent growth surge had been driven by commodity exports which did not induce much structural change. Instead, it reinforced Africa's narrow export base; hence, its growth could not be sustained.

Table II.2 reveals that East Asia and the Pacific is the only region that has already attained the Millennium Development Goal of halving poverty by 2015. Other regions on track to meet this goal are Eastern Europe and Central Asia, Latin America and the Caribbean, and the Middle East and Northern Africa. In contrast, halving poverty remains a major challenge in South Asia and sub-Saharan Africa. These two subregions actually saw a significant increase in the shares of people living on less than $1.25 a day over the period 1990-2005.

Intraregional poverty trends

It is important to remember that all poverty is local. Hence, efforts to reduce poverty tend to be vigorously waged first and foremost at the country level. Analysis of intraregional poverty can therefore reveal considerable diversity in respect of the patterns and trends in poverty rates across countries that help to spur countries and their development partners to action. The present section will therefore provide a detailed description of poverty trends by income at intraregional levels. Such a focus will help illuminate the discussion and understanding of poverty patterns and trends that followed the publication of a World Bank report (Chen and Ravallion, 2008) whose purpose was to show that "the developing world is poorer than we thought, but no less successful in the fight against poverty".

Sub-Saharan Africa

Although the absolute number of people living in extreme poverty has been on the rise in sub-Saharan Africa, the incidence of poverty fell marginally, from 54 to 51 per cent between 1981 and 2005 (table II.3), after having risen briefly to 59 per cent in 1996. However, this regional trend disguises large country differences. For instance, in 1981, the proportion of people living on less than $1.25 a day had varied from a low of 3.6 per cent in Gabon to a high of 89.9 per cent in Swaziland. This pattern persisted into 2005, with the proportion in extreme poverty ranging from a low of 4.8 per cent in Gabon to a high of 86.1 per cent in Liberia. These differences are strongly correlated with differences in respect of both economic growth and the severity of income inequal-

Table II.2
Progress made in reducing poverty by half at the regional level, over the period 1990-2005

	East Asia and the Pacific	Eastern Europe and Central Asia	Latin America and the Caribbean	Middle East and Northern Africa	South Asia	Sub-Saharan Africa
	Percentage living on less than $1.25 a day					
2005	16.8	3.7	8.2	3.6	40.3	50.9
1999	35.5	5.1	10.9	4.2	44.1	58.4
1990	54.7	2.0	11.3	4.3	51.7	57.6
2015 target	27.4	1.0	5.7	2.2	25.9	28.8
Change needed to achieve the target	a	-2.7	-2.6	-1.4	-14.5	-22.1
	Annual rate of change (percentage)					
1990-2005	-7.6	4.2	-2.1	-1.2	-1.6	-0.8
1990-1999	-4.7	11.0	-0.4	-0.2	-1.7	0.2
1999-2005	-11.7	-5.2	-4.6	-2.6	-1.5	-2.3
Rate needed to achieve target from 2005 level	a	-12.3	-3.7	-5.0	-4.4	-5.5
	Percentage point change					
1990-1999	-19.2	3.1	-0.4	-0.1	-7.6	0.8
1999-2005	-18.7	-1.4	-2.7	-0.6	-3.8	-7.5

Source: World Bank, Development Research Group (2009).
a By 2005, the region had achieved the 2015 target of halving poverty, using 1990 as the baseline.

ity, especially in countries of Southern Africa. For example, the Gini coefficient was above 50 per cent in all five Southern African countries in 2005, with Namibia registering the world's highest level of income inequality. Table II.3 also shows that only seven sub-Saharan African countries had poverty rates below 25 per cent in 2005,[5] up from two (Côte d'Ivoire and Gabon) in 1981. In general, countries with extremely high poverty levels also trail behind in respect of a number of demographic and social indicators such as life expectancy at birth, infant mortality, and children's school enrolment and completion rates.

Further insights into country-level poverty trends can be gained by examining progress made in meeting the Millennium Development Goal target of halving extreme poverty rates by 2015. Among the 19 African countries with extremely high poverty levels (that is, those where more than half of the

[5] Botswana, Cape Verde, Côte d'Ivoire, Gabon, Kenya, Mauritania and South Africa.

Table II.3
Proportion of the population living on less than $1.25 a day in countries of sub-Saharan Africa, 1981, 1990 and 2005, and the change needed to reach the 2015 target (*percentage*)

Country	Proportion living on less than $1.25 a day			2015 target	Annual rate of change (1990-2005)	Change needed to achieve the target (2005-2015)	Annual rate of change needed to achieve the target (2005-2015)
	1981	1990	2005				
	Countries with the proportion of the poor above 50 per cent in 2005						
Liberia	74.5	83.2	86.1	41.6	0.2	−44.5	−7.3
United Republic of Tanzania	65.4	70.3	82.4	35.2	1.1	−47.2	−8.5
Burundi	85.2	84.5	81.3	42.3	−0.3	−39.0	−6.5
Rwanda	66.5	70.5	74.4	35.2	0.4	−39.2	−7.5
Malawi	85.3	90.5	73.9	45.2	−1.4	−28.7	−4.9
Guinea	86.6	92.6	69.8	46.3	−1.9	−23.5	−4.1
Mozambique	60.8	84.0	68.2	42.0	−1.4	−26.2	−4.8
Madagascar	85.9	68.4	67.8	34.2	−0.1	−33.6	−6.8
Niger	57.4	65.0	65.9	32.5	0.1	−33.4	−7.1
Central African Republic	79.5	80.8	64.4	40.4	−1.5	−24.0	−4.7
Zambia	53.6	62.8	64.3	31.4	0.2	−32.9	−7.2
Swaziland	89.9	83.7	62.4	41.8	−2.0	−20.6	−4.0
Nigeria	47.2	49.1	62.4	24.5	1.6	−37.9	−9.3
Democratic Republic of Congo	31.9	80.2	59.2	40.1	−2.0	−19.1	−3.9
Chad	61.1	55.9	58.7	27.9	0.3	−30.8	−7.4
Burkina Faso	73.0	61.9	55.0	30.9	−0.8	−24.1	−5.8
Congo, Republic of	61.9	66.3	54.1	33.2	−1.4	−20.9	−4.9
Uganda	66.2	68.7	51.5	34.3	−1.9	−17.2	−4.1
Mali	81.5	85.2	51.4	42.6	−3.4	−8.8	−1.9
	Countries with the proportion of the poor at or below 50 per cent in 2005						
Benin	53.5	66.0	50.0	32.9	−1.9	−17.1	−4.2
Sierra Leone	59.4	63.1	49.9	31.6	−1.6	−18.3	−4.6
Comoros	53.3	51.4	46.1	25.7	−0.7	−20.4	−5.8
Namibia	45.4	43.3	43.8	21.6	0.1	−22.2	−7.1
Guinea-Bissau	31.2	41.3	42.5	20.7	0.2	−21.8	−7.2
Angola	63.6	47.3	42.5	23.7	−0.7	−18.8	−5.8

Country	Proportion living on less than $1.25 a day			2015 target	Annual rate of change (1990-2005)	Change needed to achieve the target (2005-2015)	Annual rate of change needed to achieve the target (2005-2015)
	1981	1990	2005				
Ethiopia	66.2	65.9	39.0	32.9	−3.5	−6.1	−1.7
Togo	35.2	33.8	38.7	16.9	0.9	−21.8	−8.3
Lesotho	44.1	57.7	38.7	28.8	−2.7	−9.9	−3.0
Senegal	68.3	65.8	33.5	32.9	−4.5	−0.6	−0.2
Gambia	64.3	67.9	31.3	33.9	−5.2	a	a
Ghana	48.9	50.7	30.0	25.3	−3.5	−4.7	−1.7
Cameroon	43.0	45.7	27.5	22.8	−3.4	−4.7	−1.9
Botswana	35.6	25.6	23.1	12.8	−0.7	−10.3	−5.9
South Africa	34.7	22.1	20.6	11.0	−0.5	−9.6	−6.3
Côte d'Ivoire	6.7	17.3	20.4	8.7	1.1	−11.7	−8.5
Kenya	38.4	35.4	19.7	17.7	−3.9	−2.0	−1.1
Cape Verde	52.3	36.0	18.4	17.9	−4.5	−0.5	−0.3
Mauritania	38.9	45.9	13.4	22.9	−8.2	a	a
Gabon	3.6	1.9	4.8	1.0	6.2	−3.8	−14.9
Total	**53.7**	**57.9**	**51.2**	**28.8**	**−0.8**	**−22.4**	**−5.5**

Source: World Bank, Development Research Group (2009).
a By 2005, the country had achieved the 2015 target of halving poverty, using 1990 as the baseline.

national population live on less than $1.25 a day), 12 countries managed to reduce poverty levels between 1990 and 2005. Although these declines are encouraging, they still leave a large proportion of the total population living in extreme poverty, and all 19 countries face major challenges in meeting the 2015 Millennium Development Goal target. For instance, in Liberia, poverty levels increased between 1990 and 2005; moreover, the estimated extreme poverty headcount (86 per cent) would need to be cut by half in order for the 2015 target (41.6) to be reached; that is, Liberia will have to reduce poverty at an annual rate of 7 per cent from now to 2015 to achieve the target. Huge challenges face all the sub-Saharan African countries that have extremely high levels of poverty, including Africa's most populous country, Nigeria, which saw its level of poverty increase by 20 per cent between 1990 and 1999 before recording a modest 7 per cent decrease between 1999 and 2005. Furthermore, income inequality has grown in the largest countries of sub-Saharan Africa, including South Africa, the Democratic Republic of the Congo, the United Republic of Tanzania and Kenya.

Among countries with lower levels of poverty (at or below 50 per cent), only the Gambia and Mauritania succeeded in halving the 1990 levels of poverty by 2005. On the other hand, a few other countries, Cape Verde, Senegal and Kenya, seem to be on track to meet the Millennium Development Goal target by 2015: they need to reduce the poverty levels that prevailed in 2005 by less than 2 per cent in order to meet the 2015 target. Overall, however, the goal of eradicating extreme poverty will continue to be a major challenge in a large number of African countries and huge efforts will continue to be required to halve extreme poverty by 2015.

East Asia and the Pacific

The East Asian and Pacific region has recorded some of the fastest declines in levels of extreme poverty in the world. The proportion of people with income levels below the $1.25 poverty line declined from 67 per cent in 1981 to about 9 per cent in 2005 (table II.4), translating as the movement of more than 755 million people out of extreme poverty in about 25 years. A decline of this magnitude in less than a quarter-century is a historic first. However, although this regional picture is outstanding, it is also equally important to acknowledge huge intraregional differences in levels of absolute poverty. As table II.4 shows, all East Asian and Pacific countries recorded significant declines in poverty with the exception of Papua New Guinea, where poverty remained largely unchanged between 1981 and 2005.

As already mentioned, the most impressive reductions occurred in China. Since 1979, China's economy has experienced high and sustained growth following successful land and economic reforms. Over the last 25 years, China successfully moved from agriculture to manufacturing activities and saw an annual trend of real gross domestic product (GDP) growth of just under 10 per cent (Ghosh, 2008a). China's manufacturing sector doubled its share of the workforce and tripled its share of output. The rate of extreme poverty at the national level declined from a high of 84 per cent in 1981 to a low of 16 per cent in 2005. The decline occurred in both rural and urban areas: the rural poverty rate fell from 94 to 26 per cent and the urban poverty rate fell from 45 to less than 2 per cent during this period.

Although China's poverty eradication efforts overshadow in their scale the progress made by other countries in the region, a number of other countries with large populations have also successfully moved millions of people out of poverty—namely, Indonesia, the Philippines, Thailand, Malaysia and Viet Nam. They have been able to capitalize effectively on the opportunities offered by strong growth to significantly reduce extreme poverty. Indeed, the big three success stories—China, Indonesia and Viet Nam—together account for an absolute drop in the numbers of the extreme poor of 718 million. Without the progress of these countries, the global poverty record would have appeared far less successful.

Despite this tremendous effort, the region is still home to about 316 million people living on less than $1.25 day. Compared with those of neighbouring countries, poverty rates remain very high in Cambodia (40 per cent), Timor-Leste (44 per cent) and the Lao People's Democratic Republic (36 per cent). Poverty has remained high in these countries partly because economic growth rates have been comparatively low (Economic and Social Commission for Asia and the Pacific, 2007).

Yet, although progress has been uneven across the region, almost all countries are on track to meet the 2015 target. The prospects for halving poverty remain a major challenge, however, for Papua New Guinea, the Philippines and Timor-Leste. In the Philippines, for instance, even if the incidence of poverty declined from 30 per cent in 1990 to 23 per cent in 2005, at an annual rate of about 2 per cent, the country will need to reduce the number of people living in extreme poverty at an annual rate of 4 per cent in order to reach its 2015 target.

Table II.4
Proportion of the population living on less than $1.25 a day in countries of East Asia and the Pacific, 1981, 1990 and 2005, and the change needed to reach the 2015 target (*percentage*)

Country	Proportion living on less than $1.25 a day			2015 target	Annual rate of change (1990-2005)	Change needed to achieve the target (2005-2015)	Annual rate of change needed to achieve the target (2005-2015)
	1981	1990	2005				
Timor-Leste	82.1	71.3	43.6	35.7	-3.3	-7.9	-2.0
Cambodia	86.1	77.3	40.2	38.7	-4.4	-1.5	-0.4
Lao People's Democratic Republic	88.0	65.9	35.7	32.9	-4.1	-2.8	-0.8
Papua New Guinea	29.5	43.0	29.7	21.5	-2.5	-8.2	-3.2
Indonesia (rural)	73.8	57.1	24.0	28.6	-5.8	a	a
Indonesia (urban)	63.8	47.8	18.7	23.9	-6.3	a	a
Viet Nam	90.4	34.2	22.8	17.1	-2.7	-5.7	-2.9
Philippines	31.4	29.7	22.6	14.8	-1.8	-7.8	-4.2
Mongolia	62.4	34.9	22.4	17.5	-3.0	-4.9	-2.5
China	84.0	60.2	15.9	30.1	-8.9	a	a
China (rural)	94.1	74.1	26.1	37.0	-6.7	a	a
China (urban)	44.5	23.4	1.7	11.7	-16.0	a	a
Malaysia	3.8	1.9	0.5	1.0	-8.9	a	a
Thailand	21.9	9.4	0.4	4.7	-21.0	a	a
Total	**66.8**	**39.1**	**9.3**	**24.4**	**-7.6**		

Source: World Bank, Development Research Group (2009).
a By 2005, the country had achieved the 2015 target of halving poverty, using 1990 as the baseline.

South Asia

South Asia is the developing subregion with the largest number of poor people: 43 per cent of the developing world's 1.4 billion poor people live in South Asian countries. The absolute number of people living in extreme poverty increased from 548.3 million to 595.6 million between 1981 and 2005. Rates of population growth in these countries have remained high and have led to an enlargement of both the total population as well as the numbers living in extreme poverty. In recent years, economic growth has been relatively high in the three largest countries in the region, India, Bangladesh and Pakistan, which recorded annual rates of growth of GDP per capita above 5 per cent in 2000-2006.[6] As a result, the subregion saw the proportion of those living in extreme poverty decline in relative terms, from a high of 59 per cent in 1981 to 40 per cent in 2005 (table II.5). However, such growth has not been sufficiently inclusive and pro-poor to reduce the absolute number of persons living in poverty. Income inequalities have grown steadily in India since the early 1980s, in both urban and rural areas. The same pattern can be observed in Bangladesh. South Asian countries have been unable to generate sufficient decent work opportunities to lift working poor people out of poverty. The structural change of the subcontinental economies has also been slow; for example, manufacturing accounts for about 17 per cent of GDP in Bangladesh and for about 28 per cent in India and Pakistan, as opposed to close to 35 per cent in China (World Bank, 2008c).

The headcount index declined in almost all countries with data on income poverty, with the exception of Bangladesh, where the estimated proportion of people living below the $1.25 a day poverty line increased from 44 per cent in 1981 to 51 per cent in 2005. In India alone, the poverty headcount fell by 18 percentage points, from 60 per cent in 1981 to 42 per cent in 2005. Pakistan also experienced a decline in the headcount index from 73 to 23 per cent during the same period.[7] Yet, table II.5 shows that, in terms of progress in meeting the Millennium Development Goal target of halving extreme poverty by 2015,

---

6 Growth rates calculated based on World Bank data of GDP per capita in purchasing power parities (PPPs), as shown in the United Nations Key Global Indicators database (http://data.un.org) (accessed 8 June 2009).

7 The sharp decline in the poverty headcount in Pakistan potentially highlights the problems with data on and measurement of poverty. The ups and downs reflected in the poverty data collected during the 1990s are questionable. It is possible that the data from this period are not comparable. The variation could also be a result of sensitivity in respect of the poverty lines. Alternative sources of information report different poverty trends; for instance, the latest Human Development Report for Pakistan reports an increase in poverty during the 1990s, while a report by the Asian Development Bank cites several studies that showed a trend for the 1990s that was the reverse of the one reported by the World Bank (see http://hdr.undp.org/en/reports/nationalreports/asiathepacific/pakistan/ and http://www.adb.org/documents/reports/poverty_pak/chapter_2.pdf). Data problems may also be responsible for a reported rise in poverty in Bangladesh, which appears counter-intuitive, given the rise in GDP per capita.

Table II.5
Proportion of the population living on less than $1.25 a day in countries of South Asia, 1981, 1990 and 2005, and the change needed to reach the 2015 target (*percentage*)

Country	Proportion living on less than $1.25 a day			2015 target	Annual rate of change (1990-2005)	Change needed to achieve the target (2005-2015)	Annual rate of change needed to achieve the target (2005-2015)
	1981	1990	2005				
Nepal	—	77	54.7	38.5	-2.3	-16.2	-3.5
Bangladesh	44.2	49.9	50.5	24.9	0.1	-25.6	-7.1
India	59.8	51.3	41.6	25.7	-1.4	-15.9	-4.8
India (rural)	62.5	53.9	43.8	27.0	-1.4	-16.9	-4.7
India (urban)	51	43.5	36.2	21.8	-1.2	-14.4	-5.0
Bhutan	47.4	51	26.8	25.5	-4.3	-1.3	-0.5
Pakistan	72.9	58.5	22.6	29.3	-6.3	a	a
Sri Lanka	31	15	10.3	7.5	-2.5	-2.8	-3.2
Total	**59.4**	**51.7**	**40.3**	**25.9**	**-1.6**	**-14.5**	**-4.4**

Source: World Bank, Development Research Group (2009).
a By 2005, the country had achieved the 2015 target of halving poverty, using 1990 as the baseline.

several countries in the region, including Bangladesh, India, Nepal and Sri Lanka, will need higher rates of poverty reduction than recorded since 1990 if they are to meet the 2015 target.

Latin America and the Caribbean

Over the last 25 years, Latin America and the Caribbean has had mixed results in eradicating poverty. While poverty declined in most countries, levels of poverty went up in the Plurinational State of Bolivia, Guyana, Haiti, Panama, Paraguay, Peru and the Bolivarian Republic of Venezuela and in urban areas of Argentina[8] (table II.6). These disparities are to a large extent a reflection of the huge inequalities in the distribution of income across the region and within countries. For example, 12 out of 23 countries in the world with Gini coefficients above 50 per cent in 2005 were in Latin America. It is estimated that, in Latin American and Caribbean countries, the per capita income of households in the tenth decile is about 17 times greater than that of the poorest 40 per cent of households (Economic Commission for Latin America and the Caribbean, 2008). Nonetheless, poverty levels have declined at the regional level owing to strong per capita GDP growth, averaging over 3 per cent per annum between

---

8 Poverty data are not available for rural areas of Argentina.

Table II.6
Proportion of the population living on less than $1.25 a day in countries of Latin America and the Caribbean, 1981, 1990 and 2005, and the change needed to reach the 2015 target (*percentage*)

Country	Proportion living on less than $1.25 a day			2015 target	Annual rate of change (1990-2005)	Change needed to achieve the target (2005-2015)	Annual rate of change needed to achieve the target (2005-2015)
	1981	1990	2005				
Haiti	54.6	56.8	58.0	28.4	0.1	−29.6	−7.1
Honduras	—	43.5	22.2	21.8	−4.5	−0.4	−0.2
Bolivia (Plurinational State of)	2.0	4.0	19.6	2.0	10.6	−17.6	−22.8
Saint Lucia	24.0	26.8	17.8	13.4	−2.7	−4.4	−2.8
Nicaragua	21.0	39.5	15.8	19.8	−6.1	a	a
Suriname	17.2	18.6	14.2	9.3	−1.8	−4.9	−4.2
El Salvador	14.8	15.9	13.5	8.0	−1.1	−5.6	−5.3
Guatemala	46.7	37.2	12.1	18.6	−7.5	a	a
Venezuela (Bolivarian Republic of)	6.2	3.1	10.0	1.6	7.8	−8.5	−18.6
Ecuador	11.1	14.2	9.8	7.1	−2.5	−2.7	−3.2
Paraguay	4.8	5.9	9.3	3.0	3.0	−6.4	−11.5
Panama	6.0	15.8	9.2	7.9	−3.6	−1.3	−1.5
Peru	1.0	1.3	8.2	0.7	12.3	−7.6	−25.3
Brazil	17.1	15.5	7.8	7.8	−4.6	0.0	0.0
Guyana	3.1	8.4	7.3	4.2	−0.9	−3.1	−5.5
Dominican Republic	16.6	14.9	5.0	7.5	−7.3	a	a
Argentina (urban)	0.0	0.4	4.5	0.2	16.1	a	a
Costa Rica	21.4	9.2	2.4	4.6	−9.0	a	a
Mexico	9.8	5.4	1.7	2.7	−7.7	a	a
Chile	6.3	4.4	0.7	2.2	−12.3	a	a
Trinidad and Tobago	0.0	4.4	0.5	2.2	−14.5	a	a
Jamaica	5.6	0.2	0.2	0.1	0.0	−0.1	−6.9
Total	**11.5**	**9.8**	**8.4**	**5.7**	**−2.1**	**−2.6**	**−3.7**

Source: World Bank, Development Research Group (2009).
a By 2005, the country had achieved the 2015 target of halving poverty, using 1990 as the baseline.

2003 and 2007. Such growth, the highest the region has experienced since the 1970s, resulted in an increase in the average labour income of the poorest (Economic Commission for Latin America and the Caribbean, 2009).

This trend in poverty is consistent with the findings of the Economic Commission for Latin American and the Caribbean (ECLAC), based on a series of household surveys in 18 countries.[9] The most recent figures from these surveys show that poverty has continued on a downward trend. According to ECLAC, about 34 per cent of the population of Latin America and the Caribbean were living in poverty in 2007, among whom 13 per cent were living in extreme poverty. In absolute numbers, 184 million were considered poor, among whom 68 million were living in extreme poverty (Economic Commission for Latin America and the Caribbean, 2008).

According to World Bank estimates, in 2005, most countries in the region were on track to halve poverty rates by 2015. This was accounted for largely by the fact that poverty levels had been very low in 1990, which is the base year for measuring progress made by countries towards the achievement of the Millennium Development Goals. However, for a number of countries, the target remains a major challenge. For Haiti to halve its poverty rate by 2015, it will have to reduce poverty levels at an annual rate of 7.1 per cent from 2005 onward. The country's poverty levels have practically remained unchanged since 1981. For the Plurinational State of Bolivia and the Bolivarian Republic of Venezuela, two countries that saw sharp increases in the incidence of poverty between 1990 and 2005 and increases in income disparities during the same period that were among the world's highest, much higher annual rates of poverty reduction are required even though their poverty levels are much lower than that of Haiti.

Middle East and Northern Africa

The Middle East and Northern Africa region has managed to reduce both the incidence of poverty and the absolute number of people living in extreme poverty despite poor economic performance in the last two decades. The incidence of poverty in the region is the lowest in the developing world. It dropped from 7.9 per cent in 1981 to 3.6 per cent in 2005 (table II.7). In absolute terms, the number of poor people has declined from 13.7 million to 11 million. Unlike other middle-income countries, the countries of the Middle East and Northern Africa have been very successful in reducing extreme poverty owing in part to improvements in the health and education levels of the general population, as well as to the availability of extensive food and energy subsidies in several countries. For example, between 1980 and 2000, the regional child mortality rate plunged from 138 per thousand live births to 47 per thousand, the average years of schooling per person over age 15 rose from 2.6 to 5.5 years, and life expectancy at birth increased by 10 years, from 58 to 68 years (Iqbal, 2006). Gains of this magnitude within the social dimensions of development which

---

9 The findings of these surveys are reported on a regular basis in the issues of the *Social Panorama of Latin America*, published by the Economic Commission for Latin America and the Caribbean.

enhance human capabilities are known to contribute to reductions in poverty at the household level even when per capita incomes stagnate.

While poverty rates are low at the regional level, poverty levels and trends differ across countries. For example, table II.7 shows that, while 12 per cent of Egypt's population had lived below the $1.25 poverty line in 1981, the incidence of poverty dropped to 2 per cent in 2005. In contrast, poverty rates increased sharply in Djibouti (from 6.1 to 18.6 per cent) and Yemen (from 9.1 to 17.5 per cent) over the same period, giving them the highest poverty rates in the region. Poverty levels are lower in oil-rich Gulf countries which are able to use the vast wealth derived from oil and gas to subsidize consumption goods and social services for their citizens (Iqbal, 2006). Net oil importers in the Middle East and Northern Africa region were impacted negatively by the recent increases in the prices of energy and food. This created fiscal burdens for Governments, increased production costs for small businesses, and reduced the food intake of poor families.

Despite the decline in poverty at the regional level, fighting poverty is still a major concern for many countries in the region. Although per capita income is high as a result of high prices of oil and gas, not all segments of society have benefited. Egypt, the Islamic Republic of Iran, Jordan and Tunisia have al-

Table II.7
Proportion of the population living on less than $1.25 a day in countries of the Middle East and Northern Africa, 1981, 1990 and 2005, and the change needed to reach the 2015 target (*percentage*)

Country	Proportion living on less than $1.25 a day			2015 target	Annual rate of change (1990-2005)	Change needed to achieve the target (2005-2015)	Annual rate of change needed to achieve the target (2005-2015)
	1981	1990	2005				
Djibouti	6.1	1.8	18.6	0.9	15.6	−17.7	−30.3
Yemen	9.1	4.9	17.5	2.5	8.5	−15.1	−19.7
Algeria	3.8	6.2	4.3	3.1	−2.4	−1.2	−3.3
Morocco	10.4	2.5	3.0	1.3	1.2	−1.8	−8.8
Egypt	12.0	4.5	2.0	2.3	−5.4	a	a
Islamic Republic of Iran	4.0	3.9	1.5	2.0	−6.4	a	a
Tunisia	9.7	5.9	1.0	3.0	−11.8	a	a
Jordan	0.0	2.8	0.4	1.4	−13.0	a	a
Total	7.9	4.3	3.6	2.2	−1.2	−1.4	−5.0

Source: World Bank, Development Research Group (2009).
a By 2005, the country had achieved the 2015 target of halving poverty, using 1990 as the baseline.

ready cut by more than half the poverty rates that prevailed in 1990, although some increases did occur in Egypt and the Islamic Republic of Iran between 1999 and 2005. According to the World Bank (2004), Egypt and the Islamic Republic of Iran managed to lower levels of poverty by considerably reducing poverty in urban areas and, in the case of the latter, sharp declines in urban poverty managed to offset an increase in rural poverty.

Eastern Europe and Central Asia

Given the very low levels of absolute poverty in Eastern Europe, it is more illuminating to use an absolute poverty line of $2 a day, considering the cost of the heating and warm clothing that are required in this region (Alam and others, 2005). According to this measure, there had been 21.7 million poor people in Eastern Europe in 1981. This figure dropped to 5 million in 2005, attesting to a significant decline in poverty in the region. On the other hand, in Central Asia, the number of poor according to the $2-a-day measure increased from 13.2 million in 1981 to 36.1 million in 2005. However, unlike Eastern Europe, Central Asia shares many of the characteristics of other developing regions and hence $1.25 a day perhaps represents a more appropriate poverty line for Central Asia. Application of this measure shows that the number in absolute poverty in Central Asia increased more than 4 times, from 3.7 million in 1981 to 16.1 million in 2005. The difference between the poverty levels in Central Asia according to the two poverty lines ($2 a day and $1.25 a day)—20 million people in 2005—can be taken as a rough measure of vulnerability.

Another feature of the region is the widening of intercountry disparities in extreme poverty (table II.8). The highest levels of absolute poverty are found in Central Asian countries such as Georgia, Kyrgyzstan, Tajikistan, Turkmenistan and Uzbekistan, countries whose economies were centrally planned during the Soviet period and hence which shared many structural similarities. Differences in levels of absolute poverty in these countries were considerably lower in the early 1980s largely because of the significant resource transfers, including guaranteed employment, subsidies and social safety nets, that these countries received from the central budget. In contrast, the Eastern European countries, although also under the Soviet influence, were primarily responsible for meeting their own budgetary needs. The fact that, in a large majority of those countries, extreme absolute poverty was very low during the period 1981-2005 has been attributed to the growth in wages and employment opportunities as well as adequate social transfers (Alam and others, 2005). In contrast, levels of absolute poverty actually increased in a number of Central Asian countries. Consequently, these countries face a substantially bigger challenge in respect of halving poverty by 2015.

In large measure, this sharp increase in absolute poverty is associated with the collapse of the Soviet Union and the transition to market economies in the early 1990s, which witnessed large declines in real output and high

Table II.8
Proportion of the population living on less than $1.25 a day in countries of Eastern Europe and Central Asia, 1981, 1990 and 2005, and the change needed to reach the 2015 target (*percentage*)

Country	Proportion living on less than $1.25 a day			2015 target	Annual rate of change (1990-2005)	Change needed to achieve the target (2005-2015)	Annual rate of change needed to achieve the target (2005-2015)
	1981	1990	2005				
Uzbekistan	0.0	4.9	38.8	2.5	13.8	−36.4	−27.6
Kyrgyzstan	0.0	4.8	21.8	2.4	10.1	−19.4	−22.1
Tajikistan	1.4	1.5	21.5	0.8	17.8	−20.8	−33.6
Georgia	2.5	2.9	13.4	1.5	10.2	−12.0	−22.2
Turkmenistan	21.9	34.2	11.7	17.1	−7.2	a	a
Republic of Moldova	20.2	15.2	8.1	7.6	−4.2	−0.5	−0.6
Armenia	0.9	6.3	4.7	3.2	−2.0	−1.6	−4.0
Turkey	4.5	1.5	2.7	0.8	3.9	−2.0	−12.8
Kazakhstan	0.0	0.5	1.2	0.3	5.8	−1.0	−15.7
Albania	0.2	0.9	0.9	0.5	0.0	−0.5	−6.9
Romania	0.0	0.0	0.8	0.0		−0.8	−0.1
Lithuania	0.0	0.0	0.4	0.0		−0.4	−0.1
The former Yugoslav Republic of Macedonia	0.0	0.0	0.3	0.0		−0.3	0.0
Bosnia and Herzegovina	0.0	0.0	0.2	0.0		−0.2	0.0
Russian Federation	0.7	1.4	0.2	0.7	−13.0	a	a
Poland	0.0	1.3	0.1	0.7	−17.1	a	a
Ukraine	3.0	1.2	0.1	0.6	−16.6	a	a
Azerbaijan	13.4	16.1	0.0	8.1		a	a
Belarus	0.0	0.0	0.0	0.0		a	a
Bulgaria	0.0	0.0	0.0	0.0		a	a
Croatia	0.0	0.0	0.0	0.0		a	a
Czech Republic	0.0	0.0	0.0	0.0		a	a
Estonia	0.0	0.0	0.0	0.0		a	a
Hungary	0.0	0.0	0.0	0.0		a	a
Latvia	0.0	0.0	0.0	0.0		a	a
Slovakia	0.0	0.0	0.0	0.0		a	a

Country	Proportion living on less than $1.25 a day			2015 target	Annual rate of change (1990-2005)	Change needed to achieve the target (2005-2015)	Annual rate of change needed to achieve the target (2005-2015)
	1981	1990	2005				
Slovenia	0.0	0.0	0.0	0.0		a	a
Total	1.7	2.0	3.7	1.0	4.2	−2.7	−12.3

Source: World Bank, Development Research Group (2009).
a By 2005, the country had achieved the 2015 target of halving poverty, using 1990 as the baseline.

inflation. During the transition, the political, economic and social institutions in these formerly centrally planned economies underwent major changes which affected the distribution of public and private resources, both across and within countries. In particular, public social services crumbled in most of these countries (Bandara, Malik and Gherman, 2004), which contributed to the rise in poverty and inequalities as well as greater regional disparities, especially between rural and urban areas (Cukrowski, 2006; Anderson and Pomfret, 2004). On average, within-country income inequalities rose faster in this region than in any other between the early 1980s and the late 1990s. In particular, successor republics of the former Soviet Union such as Turkmenistan, the Russian Federation and Uzbekistan, as well as the three Baltic States, saw their Gini coefficient increase by more than 10 points between 1981 and 1999.

Least developed countries

Further insight and nuance into poverty patterns and trends around the world can be gleaned from an examination of the situation in the least developed countries. This group of countries[10] is home to 750 million people, or 12 per cent of the world's population. It is claimed that the economic growth prospects of these countries have been undermined by their geography, with 28 of them being landlocked or small island States (Gallup, Sachs and Mellinger, 1998; Collier, 2007). Controlling for economic policies and institutions, some researchers contend that the location and climate of the continent of Africa have had a negative impact on its income levels and growth. In particular, they note that these geographical factors affect growth through their impact on agricultural productivity, transport costs and a debilitating disease burden. In addition, landlocked countries also tend to be held hostages by their neighbours if the latter have poor transport links to the coast; consequently, landlocked countries find it more difficult to reap the benefits of globalization inasmuch as they are hamstrung in their ability to export commodities or any manufac-

---

10 The current list of the least developed countries comprises 49 countries: 33 in Africa, 15 in Asia and the Pacific, and 1 in Latin America.

tured products (Collier, 2007). Countries with access to the sea therefore tend to have higher incomes than their landlocked counterparts because they have better and cheaper access to global markets.

Although 38 per cent of the people in "bottom billion societies"[11] live in countries that have no sea access, serious research has questioned the findings of studies that give prominence to geography and climate. For example, Nordhous and Chen (2009) found that a substantial part of the "latitude effect" (distance from the equator) does not reflect geophysical variables such as climate, elevation, distance from coastlines and rivers, and similar factors: variables other than purely geographical ones are responsible for much of the poor economic performance of low-latitude regions. In this regard, an International Monetary Fund (IMF) study (Hernández-Catá, 2000) has raised questions about the methodological soundness of the influential study by Bloom and Sachs (1998) which relied only on cross-country data and hence may have picked up fixed effects specific to Africa other than those related to geography or climate. According to Hernández-Catá, if landlockedness had been a growth-inhibiting factor, then the economies of Switzerland and the Czech Republic would have been given a very low probability of success starting from the seventeenth century. Even in Africa, landlocked Bostwana grew impressively in the 1990s, and a tropical climate has not hampered growth in Thailand, Malaysia and Indonesia and several southern states of the United States of America. While recognizing the disadvantages of geography faced by many African countries, then World Bank economist Benno Ndulu (2006, pp. 215-216) has made the following point:

> The most important message I am trying to convey in this paper is that offsetting natural or geographical disadvantages is a choice for which public action is important. Malaria can be eradicated, and it was in many areas where it was once preponderant. Fragmentation can be overcome through integration and deliberate effort to offset its negative effects. For example, Tanzania was able to overcome the potential of high ethnolinguistic fractionalization through a deliberate effort to create national unity and a single language among 132 tribes. Remoteness, likewise, can be overcome and distance can be bridged through improvements in infrastructure. Botswana's experience perhaps best embodies all aspects of this message.

In other words, what matters for sustained economic growth and poverty reduction is the nature of public policy and action.

Figure II.4 shows the absolute number of poor people and the incidence of poverty in heavily indebted poor countries and the least developed countries. In absolute terms, the number of people living on less than $1.25 a day in both

---

11 These are the people living in failing States (a group of about 50) who are dropping further and further behind the majority of the world's people, often falling into an absolute decline in living standards (Collier, 2007).

Figure II.4
Poverty in heavily indebted poor countries and least developed countries, 1981-2005

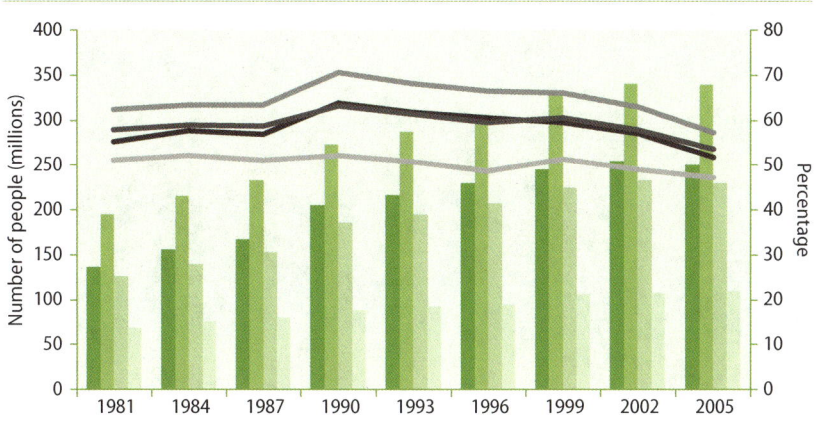

Left axis data:
- Heavily indebted poor countries
- Least developed countries
- Least developed countries (Africa)
- Least developed countries (Asia and the Pacific)

Right axis data:
- Heavily indebted poor countries (percentage)
- Least developed countries (percentage)
- Least developed countries (Africa) (percentage)
- Least developed countries (Asia and the Pacific) (percentage)

Source: World Bank, Development Research Group (2009).

groups of countries increased between 1981 and 2002, and declined, slowly, only between 2002 and 2005, the number being larger in the least developed countries of Africa than in the least developed countries of Asia and the Pacific. However, in relative terms, the proportion of people living in extreme poverty has been declining since 1990 in both the heavily indebted poor countries (HIPC) and in the least developed countries.

Figure II.5 shows that, among all landlocked developing countries and small island developing States, African landlocked developing countries have the highest proportion of people living in extreme poverty, followed by Asian landlocked developing countries. However, the numbers of people living in extreme poverty have been on the decline since the early 1990s.

In terms of overall poverty reduction efforts, all least developed countries face a major hurdle (table II.9). In order for all least developed countries to reduce the 1990 poverty headcount of 67.9 per cent to the 2015 target of 33.9 per cent, they will have to significantly accelerate the pace of poverty reduction efforts. Starting from 2005, least developed countries will have had to

Figure II.5
Poverty in landlocked developing countries and small island developing States, 1981-2005

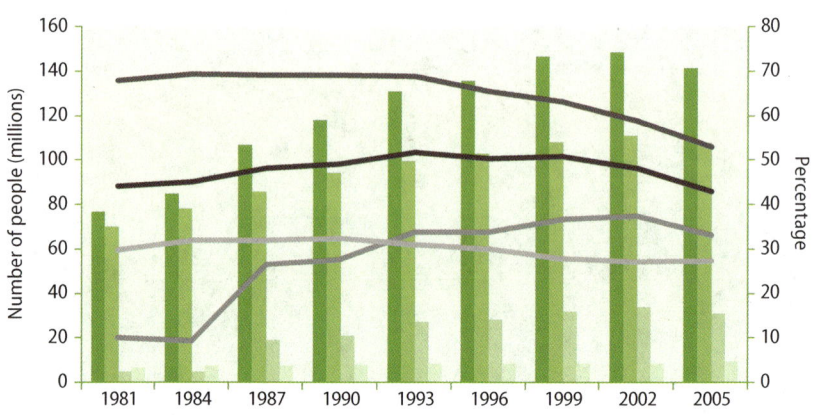

Left axis data:
- Landlocked developing countries
- Landlocked developing countries (Africa)
- Landlocked developing countries (Asia)
- Small island developing States

Right axis data:
- Landlocked developing countries (percentage)
- Landlocked developing countries (Africa) (percentage)
- Landlocked developing countries (Asia) (percentage)
- Small island developing States (percentage)

Source: World Bank, Development Research Group (2009).

maintain an annual reduction rate of 4.7 per cent to achieve the 2015 target. Small island developing States will also have to redouble their efforts, given the slackened pace of poverty reduction they experienced between 1999 and 2005, which was considerably slower than that experienced between 1990 and 1999. Given the trends as shown in table II.9, the least developed countries, landlocked developing countries, highly indebted poor countries and small island developing States will not meet the Millennium Development Goal target of halving poverty by 2015.

Countries of the European Union (EU) and other countries of the Organization for Economic Cooperation and Development (OECD)

The World Bank does not track progress on reducing poverty in developed countries, even though poverty is a major public policy concern in those countries. European Union (EU) members and the United States of America have a long-standing tradition and practice of collecting national poverty data as well as releasing official poverty estimates. The definition of poverty used for public

Table II.9
Proportion of the population living on less than $1.25 a day in least developed countries, landlocked developing countries, heavily indebted poor countries and small island developing States, 1990, 1999 and 2005, and the change needed to reach the 2015 target (*percentage*)

Country	Proportion living on less than $1.25 a day			2015 target	Annual rate of change (1990-2005)	Change needed to achieve the target (2005-2015)	Annual rate of change needed to achieve the target (2005-2015)
	1990	1999	2005				
All least developed countries	67.9	62.3	54.3	33.9	−1.5	−20.4	−4.7
African least developed countries	70.2	65.9	56.9	35.1	−1.4	−21.8	−4.8
Asia and the Pacific least developed countries	56.6	42.7	38.5	28.3	−2.6	−10.2	−3.1
Heavily indebted poor countries	63.8	57.5	48.9	31.9	−1.8	−17.0	−4.3
All landlocked developing countries	49.1	50.7	42.8	24.5	−0.9	−18.3	−5.6
African landlocked developing countries	69	63.1	52.7	34.5	−1.8	−18.2	−4.2
Asian landlocked developing countries	27.7	36.6	33.1	13.9	1.2	−19.2	−8.7
Small islands developing States	32.4	27.7	27.5	16.2	−1.1	−11.3	−5.3

Source: World Bank, Development Research Group (2009).

policy purposes and in public discourse is quite different from that used by the Bank. The prime concern is the standard of living relative to other people in the country; hence, poverty is a relative concept in the developed world. In the present section, therefore, the poverty estimates used are not comparable to those for developing countries as published by the World Bank.

Over the long run, there have been modest changes in overall poverty indicators in EU and other countries of the Organization for Economic Co-operation and Development (OECD), with levels of poverty growing in the recent past. For instance, with the poverty threshold defined as 60 per cent of a country's median income, in 2006, 72 million people in the EU were at risk of falling into poverty; and in 2001, more than half of all people in low-income households in the EU lived with the persistent risk of falling into poverty. In addition, it is estimated that one in five people in Europe lives in substandard housing and 10 per cent live in households where no one works (Commission of the European Communities, 2007).

Differences in poverty rates across Europe and North America are generally small. During the 1990s, poverty rates were highest in the United States, the United Kingdom of Great Britain and Northern Ireland, Ireland, Italy and Greece. As regards more recent trends, figure II.6 provides relative poverty estimates for various OECD countries based on the 40, 50 and 60 per cent median household disposable income levels. The graph shows large disparities across countries in the share of people with incomes less than 40,

Figure II.6
Relative poverty rates for different income thresholds in OECD countries, mid-2000s

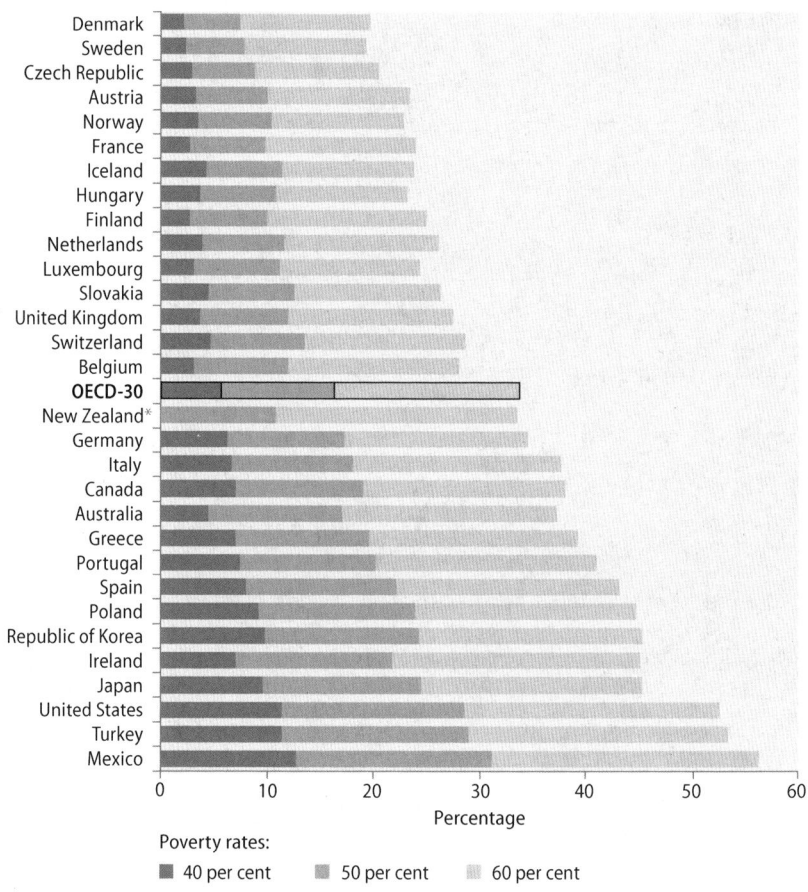

Source: OECD (2008a), computations from an OECD income distribution questionnaire.
Note: Poverty rates are defined as the share of individuals with equivalized disposable income that is less than 40, 50 and 60 per cent of the median for the entire population. Countries are ranked, from top to bottom, in increasing order of income poverty rates at the 50 per cent median threshold. The income concept used is that of household disposable income adjusted for household size.
* Poverty rates based on a 40 per cent threshold are not available for New Zealand.

50 or 60 per cent of the median income for the entire population. Relative poverty rates are lowest in Denmark, Sweden and the Czech Republic and highest in Mexico, the United States and Turkey. Cross-country differences in the mid-2000s range between 5 and 18 per cent when the income threshold is set at 50 per cent of the median, and between 11 and 25 per cent when the threshold is set at 60 per cent of the median (Organization for Economic Cooperation and Development, 2008a).

Although levels of poverty are generally low in OECD countries, the structure of poverty has shifted and has led to higher poverty risks among certain groups, particularly unemployed single parents and younger age groups (Förster, 2004). Poverty among young adults and families with children increased over the past 20 years as well. By 2005, the poverty rate for children and that for young adults were about 25 per cent above the total average, whereas they were close to and below that average, respectively, in 1985. Poverty rates are three times higher than the average among households with children; for single-parent families, they exceed 40 per cent in one third of OECD countries. In contrast, poverty among older persons has fallen (Organization for Economic Cooperation and Development, 2008a; European Commission, Directorate-General for Employment, Social Affairs and Equal Opportunities, 2008).

Some of the cross-country differences in the levels of poverty are accounted for by the nature and extent of public transfers and direct taxes that are aimed at reducing income poverty. The recent report *Growing Unequal Income Distribution and Poverty in OECD Countries* (Organization for Economic Cooperation and Development, 2008a) points to growing inequality and poverty in two thirds of OECD countries and finds that the economic growth of recent decades has largely benefited the rich more than the poor. Across OECD countries, the income of the richest 10 per cent of people is nearly nine times that of the poorest 10 per cent. In Mexico, Turkey, Portugal, Poland and the United States, the income gap is well above the OECD average. In Canada, Finland, Germany, Italy, Norway and the United States, the gap has also increased between the rich and the middle-class. The report also notes that countries with a wide distribution of income tend to have more widespread income poverty. It points out that the rise in cash-income poverty from the mid-1980s to the mid-1990s had been offset by increased government redistribution through public expenditures; however, between the mid-1990s and the mid-2000s, the redistributive effect of transfers and taxes slackened, leading to higher poverty rates based on disposable incomes.

Diversity within countries: poverty in China and India

The above discussion has focused on poverty trends at the global, regional and intraregional levels. Although such a focus is important, it is equally important to point out that spatial and inter-group disparities in poverty exist at the country level. For instance, the poor tend to be heavily concentrated in rural areas as well as in areas with limited access to public assets such as roads, schools and hospitals. In most countries, welfare disparities are reflected in the persistent gaps in living standards between rural and urban areas. Understanding and addressing these intracountry regional disparities are important in many ways. First, while some of these countries are on track to meet the first target of the Millennium Development Goals, namely to halve the proportion of people living on less than $1.25 a day at the national level, rural and remote areas, with their significant levels of extreme poverty, may still be far behind. Left unchecked, these disparities will likely worsen horizontal inequalities, that is, inequalities in respect of economic and political resources that exist among ethnic or religious groups (Brown, Stewart and Langer, 2007; Stewart, 2002).

In regions such as Asia and the Pacific, widening disparities between the well off and the poor and vulnerable groups are a major concern. The latter are falling further behind their urban counterparts (Economic and Social Commission for Asia and the Pacific, 2008b). To illustrate this point in detail, the present section will highlight the importance of regional variations by contrasting two countries, China and India, both large countries in terms of both geographical and population size and both regarded as quite successful in having reduced poverty at the aggregate level. As a result, however, of divergent regional patterns of economic growth and social provisions, one finds sharp differences in levels of living standards across provinces or states, as well as between rural and urban areas (Ravallion and Jalan, 1999).

For instance, in China, the slower pace of income growth in the central and western regions compared with the eastern coastal region has widened the intraregional income gap. This gap is related to structural changes in output and employment: the coastal regions have provided more opportunities for non-agricultural employment and income. By contrast, the distribution of agricultural income across regions has been more equal, reflecting the better quality of control over agricultural land. Notwithstanding China's substantial improvement in poverty reduction since 1978, new forms of poverty have arisen. This is accounted for by the deteriorating quality of growth in terms of its employment-generation potential and an increase in the degree of inequality (Hu, Hu and Chang, 2003). Trends in poverty have also been closely linked with trends in employment. In rural areas, slow growth in the agricultural sector resulted in almost stagnant employment after the mid-1990s. Rising unemployment had been a major driver of urban poverty in the post-1985 phase, a dynamic further strengthened by migration from rural areas.

It is known that reforms in China adversely impacted urban poverty by generating unemployment through the restructuring of the State-owned sector within a context where the social security system was weak or absent. It has been argued that urban poverty is closely associated with inability to find work, and that the increase in urban unemployment as a result of market-oriented reforms and withdrawal of financial support for ailing State enterprises had been a prime cause of the increase in urban poverty (Bouche and others, 2004).

Prior to the restructuring of the State-owned enterprises, there was no great variation in urban poverty among regions owing to guaranteed employment and the ubiquitous urban welfare system. This regional pattern changed when market-oriented reforms led to significant closures of State-owned enterprises, privatization and large-scale layoffs of workers, and a weakened urban social welfare system. Changes in the regional distribution of urban poverty were highly correlated with the original structure of industry and with regional economic growth. The incidence of urban poverty has tended to be higher in those regions where the heavy industries—set up during the era of central planning—were earlier concentrated and lower in the towns and cities of the south-eastern coast which have experienced more dynamic growth. However, overall, the prevalence of poverty is much higher in rural areas (26 per cent in 2005) than in urban areas (estimated at under 2 per cent in 2005), although income inequalities have grown faster in urban areas: the Gini coefficient increased from 26 to 35 per cent in urban areas and from 31 to 36 per cent in rural areas between 1990 and 2005.

Similar regional differences in levels of living standards have also been noted in India. While India's recent economic growth experience has been less spectacular than that of China, it has still been extremely impressive measured against that of most other developing countries in the same period and in comparison with its own past. Real GDP growth rates rose to a higher level over the last two decades and increases in per capita income were even more marked because of the falling rate of population growth. Official estimates of the extent of poverty, that is, the headcount ratio below the official poverty line, provide some food for speculation in respect of the slower rate of poverty reduction in the recent period of fast economic growth: poverty has been declining continuously in both rural and urban areas since the early 1970s, but between 1973-1974 and 2004-2005, the proportion of people living below the poverty line declined fastest in rural areas, from 56.4 to 28.3 per cent, while in urban areas the poverty rate declined from 49.2 to 25.7 per cent (India, Press Information Bureau, 2007; Sharma, 2004).

Levels of poverty have also varied significantly at the state level. The share of the total number of poor in the southern states of Andhra Pradesh, Karnataka, Kerala and Tamil Nadu decreased from 18 per cent in 1993-1994 to 15 per cent in 1999-2000. In contrast, the share in the total number of poor in the states of Bihar, Orissa, Madhya Pradesh, Uttar Pradesh and West Bengal jumped from 57 to 63 per cent during the same period (Sharma, 2004). Therefore, although there has been a steady decline in the incidence of poverty in India, the efforts of the Government have not resulted in a uniform impact across regions. There remain regions where the poverty is still deep and severe and hence they require greater attention.

These two countries demonstrate that, in spite of a country's strong growth, rural areas and other depressed regions often face bigger poverty reduction challenges. In several countries, the rate of rural urban or interregional convergence has declined over time as a result of widening income inequalities and pro-urban industrial and public investments policies. Hence, spatial poverty differentials are likely to persist into the foreseeable future.

Annex II.1

Poverty: indicators and their relationship

The *poverty headcount index* is the percentage of the population living in households with consumption or income per person below a commonly agreed poverty line. Trends in the poverty headcount index are determined by trends in the number of poor persons (the numerator) and by population trends (the denominator). If the growth (or decline) in the number of poor persons is proportional to total population growth (or decline), the poverty headcount index will remain constant. The headcount index will grow if the number of poor persons grows faster than the total population. Similarly, the headcount index will decline if the number of poor persons grows more slowly than the total population. Therefore, when the poverty rate (headcount ratio) falls, this means not that the total or absolute number of poor has declined but, simply, that the rate of growth of the number of poor persons is lower than the rate of growth of the total population.

The *absolute number of poor persons* by region given by the World Bank is obtained by applying the estimated headcount index to the population of each region, under the assumption that the estimated regional headcount index applies to countries with no data.

Income inequality, or the extent to which income is distributed in a more or less equitable manner, is measured using various summary indices. The most well-known is the Gini coefficient, a ratio with values between 0 and 1 (or between 0 and 100 per cent). A low Gini coefficient indicates a more equal income distribution and a high coefficient indicates a more unequal distribution. Another widely used series of indices compare the income of a given percentage of the richest population (most often the top 10 or 20 per cent) with that of the total population or of the bottom 10 or 20 per cent. Because different summary measures are sensitive to different parts of the income distribution, income inequality rankings depend on the specific measure used.

Poverty trends are arithmetically related to trends of economic growth per capita (mean income) and income distribution. The figure shows that an overall change in the proportion of poor persons can be decomposed into a growth component (area 1), resulting from higher economic growth per capita, holding distribution constant, and a distribution component (area 2), resulting from a more equal distribution, holding economic growth constant. According to this simple arithmetic identity, poverty reduction will be faster when the growth of per capita income is higher and/or when income distribution is improving. Since income distribution is far from equal in most developing countries, significant reductions in poverty are possible if distribution improves. Similarly, for any given growth rate of income per capita, poverty reduction will occur faster if incomes are more equally distributed.

The impact of these phenomena partly depends on the initial level of income, inequality and population growth; in highly unequal or very poor countries, an initial change in income levels or income distribution has a much stronger impact than in richer, less unequal countries. Empirically, their effects on poverty differ significantly across countries—even among countries with similar levels of income. Clearly, political, social and economic factors other than income per capita, income distribution and population growth are at play.

Decomposition of poverty reduction into growth and composition effects

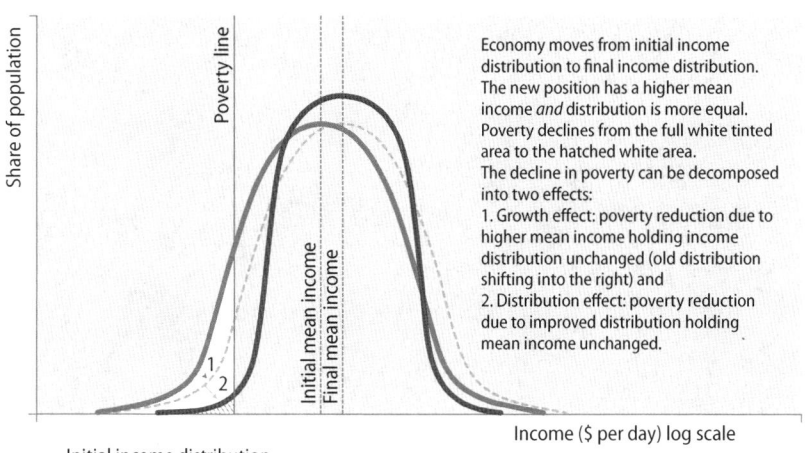

— Initial income distribution
— Final income distribution

Source: Khan (2009).

Chapter III
The poverty of poverty measurement

Measuring poverty accurately is important within the context of gauging the scale of the poverty challenge, formulating policies and assessing their effectiveness. However, measurement is never simply a counting and collating exercise and it is necessary, at the outset, to define what is meant by the term "poverty". Extensive problems can arise at this very first step, and there are likely to be serious differences in the perceptions and motivations of those who define and measure poverty. Even if there is some consensus, there may not be agreement on what policies are appropriate for eliminating poverty.

As noted earlier, in most developed countries, there has emerged a shift in focus from absolute to relative poverty, stemming from the realization that the perception and experience of poverty have a social dimension. Although absolute poverty may all but disappear as countries become richer, the subjective perception of poverty and relative deprivation will not. As a result, led by the European Union (EU), most rich countries (with the notable exception of the United States of America), have shifted to an approach entailing relative rather than absolute poverty lines. Those countries treat poverty as a proportion, say, 50 or 60 per cent, of the median per capita income for any year. This relative measure brings the important dimension of inequality into the definition.

Alongside this shift in definition, there has been increasing emphasis on monitoring and addressing deficits in several dimensions beyond income, for example, housing, education, health, environment and communication. Thus, the prime concern with the material dimensions of poverty alone has expanded to encompass a more holistic template of the components of well-being, including various non-material, psychosocial and environmental dimensions. Deficits within the other dimensions of well-being exist at levels of income well above the absolute—and even the relative—poverty lines.

More recently, the perspective in developed countries has widened further through the application of the concept of social exclusion. A hallmark of this approach is its emphasis on the relational dimension of deprivation. It is clear that these shifts of focus in discourse and practice—from absolute poverty to relative poverty, from income poverty to dimensional analysis, from poverty to well-being, and then to social exclusion—have profoundly altered the way deprivation is conceptualized, defined, measured, analysed, addressed and monitored.

In contrast, in developing countries, the field is still dominated by a definition of absolute poverty in terms of income. Little attention is paid to inequality beyond that of some empirical work linking growth and poverty trends and suggesting that inequality first rises with growth before it falls. However, this tends to breed policy complacency by imparting a kind of naturalness to the persistence, even the widening, of inequality in the phase of early growth

—the stage at which developing countries find themselves. There is no move to adopt relative poverty definitions as the new standard despite the widespread preference for it shown by developed economies.

The absolute poverty lines have seldom been revised, even in countries where there has been significant economic growth; hence, there has been a steady fall in the share of average per capita income represented by the absolute poverty line, a trend evident in India and China, for instance.

Instead of a revising of the norms upward, discussions of poverty in developing countries have shown a tendency to move in the opposite direction, as reflected in debates over caloric and nutritional norms, with some arguing in favour of reducing the standard norms in accordance with which poverty lines were generally constructed. Absolute poverty lines were drawn based on only a fraction of the basal metabolic rate, which refers to the energy required by the human body to survive in a state of inactivity. Distinctions were made between the different types of poor below the poverty line, resulting in the notion that redistribution from the poor to the very poor, for instance, would do good, while the imperative of redistributing from the very rich to the poor was not given much consideration. The emphasis on the permanently or the chronically poor again reflects this tendency towards manipulation of the scale and nature of the phenomenon so as to render it manageable.

What has finally emerged as the dominant instrument is the dollar-a-day money poverty line created by the World Bank for the purpose of measuring and monitoring poverty—but only in developing countries—within an internationally comparable framework.

There have been attempts, however, at reconceptualizing deprivation, for example, the capability approach (Sen, 1999). Capability deprivation goes beyond material wants to include lack of human capabilities, namely, skills and physical abilities, and self-respect in society. Sen's capability approach contributed to the launch of the human development approach and the human development index (HDI) by the United Nations Development Programme (UNDP) in 1990, within the context of which poverty is defined as the lack of opportunities in the areas of education, health and command over resources, as well as for participation in the democratic processes. The human poverty index (HPI), introduced by UNDP in 1996, measures deprivations in three of the four key dimensions of the human development index, namely (i) the capability to survive (measured, in developing countries, by vulnerability to early death defined as death before age 40), (ii) the capability to be knowledgeable (measured by the adult illiteracy rate) and (iii) having access to private income as well as public provisioning (measured by the proportion of malnourished children under age 5, and by the share of people without access to safe water). However, despite the philosophical underpinnings of this redefined point of entry, at an operational level, it tends to be summed up by a handful of social indicators. Since these indicators capture relative performances among countries, or population groups which are ranked and compared, the index does not help to define, identify or measure poverty;

furthermore, with this approach, inequality becomes visible in highly restricted ways among countries, and not at all within countries. Yet, in development discourse, the human development index has come to occupy a significant niche alongside the absolute poverty-line approach.

Thus, while the past decades have witnessed a wide acknowledgement of deprivation in developed countries, and a greater inclusiveness, the opposite tendency is clearly visible in poor and other developing economies. A simple example captures this divergence. In many rich European economies, the poverty threshold is defined as 50 per cent of average per capita income. In India in 1973-1974, the base year for current poverty-line estimations, the rural poverty threshold was 54 per cent of average per capita income for that year, a figure similar to that for the European economies. By 2004-2005, the average per capita income for the country had increased by a factor of 5 in real terms; however, the rural poverty line for 2004-2005 was just 16 per cent of average rural per capita income (Kannan, 2008). In fact, India's poverty line has not been substantively redefined at all, but only adjusted for inflation, which leads to an understatement of the real increases in the cost of living at the poor end of the distribution scale.

The World Bank $1-per-day line

The dollar-a-day poverty line has its roots in the purchasing power parity (PPP) exchange rates generated by the International Comparison Program project, undertaken jointly by the United Nations Statistics Division, the World Bank and the University of Pennsylvania. The PPPs were used first to construct an "average" poverty line for a group of countries for which the International Comparison Program provided information and then to convert this common line into national currencies in order to estimate the incidence of poverty using national distributional data. The Program has produced three rounds of estimates: in 1985, when the Program covered 22 countries, with a poverty line of $1 per person per day; in 2000-2001, when the estimates were revised using the PPP exchange rates of the Program's 1993 round with a poverty line of $1.08 per person per day; and in 2005, when the Program produced new estimates using its 2005 PPPs, with the poverty line raised to $1.25 per person per day. Each subsequent round leads to a re-estimation of the incidence of poverty. According to the last round, the number of people living below the international poverty line in 2005 was 1.4 billion, or close to 500 million (or more than 50 per cent) more than previously estimated. In the view of the World Bank, the world is still on track to meet the Millennium Development Goal poverty target, although if one excludes China, much of the rest of the developing world seems well off course (Chen and Ravallion, 2008).[1]

---

[1] These estimates were made before the onset of the global financial and economic crisis; thus, they do not reflect the impact of the crisis on global poverty trends. Preliminary

These estimates have been widely publicized, even though many analysts (Reddy and Pogge, forthcoming; Sala-i-Martin, 2006; Kakwani and Son, 2006; Bhalla, 2002) have noted their shortcomings. A focus on the last round reveals that there are several persisting or new problems that can be singled out for criticism.

The main problem concerns the intrinsic worth of the poverty line as a meaningful representation of poverty. There is evidence to suggest that the poverty lines underestimate the actual extent of poverty. Reddy (2009) has suggested the possibility that some of the recent poverty lines might themselves have been expediently put at the dollar-a-day mark. In the new round, the new World Bank line of $1.25 per person per day has been based on the average poverty line for the poorest 15 countries; alternatively, the Asian Development Bank chose to base its estimates on the poverty line of the median country in the sample, and arrived at significantly higher numbers living in poverty for countries such as India. Furthermore, the new World Bank line is not based on the United States rate of inflation; had it been taken into account, the original $1.08 would have become $1.45 for 2005, with obvious implications for the corresponding estimates of numbers of persons in poverty, and hence for the achievement of the Millennium Development Goals poverty target by 2015.

Himanshu (2008) and Reddy (2009) demonstrate that the new round remains subject to the same criticisms that had been levelled by Pogge and Reddy (2006) at the original edition. In addition, the new round follows an inconsistent procedure with regard to correcting for rural/urban price differences, applying it only to the cases of India and China and there, too, essentially using urban prices, thereby introducing what Himanshu calls an urban bias. Tellingly, Himanshu (p. 410) concludes:

> As it stands, the present World Bank estimates for India and China are not comparable to poverty estimates for the rest of the developing world, and either grossly underestimate the relative poverty in these two large countries compared to other countries or overestimate poverty elsewhere. In either case, the present world poverty estimates are flawed and an odd aspect of this is that the selective urban-rural adjustment now made reduces measured world poverty, whereas in an earlier paper Chen and Ravallion (2007) had reported that world poverty at 1993 PPP $1.08 increases by about 2 percentage points when such a rural-urban distinction is made.

One might also wish to question the motivations behind the undertaking of international comparisons of poverty. Those motivations are traceable to the compulsion to systematize of the originators, who in the process acquire an instrument for making periodic statistical pronouncements which then in-

---

assessment indicates that between 55 million and 90 million more people will be living in poverty in 2009 than had been anticipated before the crisis, stalling progress towards achieving the Millennium Development Goals (United Nations, 2009a).

fluence the discourse on poverty. Thus, with their serious distortions arising from known methodological problems, the numbers provided often have little utility and may actually serve to mislead, albeit unwittingly, as highlighted by a pioneer in poverty studies:

> The World Bank's adoption of the crude criterion of $1 per day at 1985 prices for the poorest countries, $2 per day for Latin America, and $4 per day for the transitional economies, without regard to the changing conditions of needs and markets, affronts science as it affronts reasoned development of priorities in international policies. In 1997, UNDP topped this absurdity by suggesting that the US criterion of $14.4 per day might be applied to the OECD countries. If measurement is arbitrary and irrational, it is impossible either to concoct the right policies for the alleviation or eradication of poverty, or monitor their effects closely (Townsend, 2002, p. 5).

The poverty of poverty lines

The potential strength of the monetary poverty-line approach, entailing, for example, the dollar-a-day line, is considerable: it defines absolute poverty in a simple manner which is intuitively attractive and seems to provide a universally applicable definition for making comparisons among countries cross-sectionally as well as (for single countries) inter-temporally; moreover, the measures of incidence derived by using it have some desirable axiomatic properties. Thus, it is understandable that the dollar-a-day poverty-line approach has become the dominant one. However, it has significant weaknesses and there are several types of problems connected with its use that need to be reviewed.

Food and the basic needs basket

There are several assumptions involved in determining what should constitute the food component of the basic needs, or poverty threshold, basket, many of which have ethical implications. Depending on how the constitution of the basket is determined and what is included, the poverty line can be pushed down to what many might feel is too low a threshold, or raised to what others might question as being an overly generous one.

The customary approach, albeit a controversial one, has been to specify the food component of the poverty line in terms of calorie requirements. However, such requirements are not fixed. Debates have been fuelled by the finding that the incidence of poverty obtained using a calorie-based poverty line was a small fraction of the prevalence of malnourishment as estimated from nutrition surveys (Dev, 2001; Ray and Lancaster, 2005). While many analysts have attributed this to the deficiencies of the monetary poverty-line methodology itself, others have argued that the food poverty line was not low enough and that caloric intake was not relevant as a criterion of nutrition (Sukhatme,

1988): if the poor do not meet their nutritional needs because of suboptimal expenditure patterns, then this is their own fault and need not be factored into the creation of the poverty line. Such suboptimality could involve the intake of more expensive calories, the search for a more balanced or a more tasty diet, or the inability to forgo compliance with social demands.

Another fundamental issue concerns the assumption made about the needs for energy expenditure. The prescribed calorie norm is far below what is deemed necessary for a full day of the strenuous manual labour expected in the rural works programmes that are a part of many anti-poverty interventions. In such a situation, workers would experience significant nutrition deficits, which over time would result in higher rates of morbidity and mortality. Sukhatme (1988) has argued that variations between individuals, and processes of adaptation, could contribute to making persons into more efficient workers, while Deaton and Dreze (2009) have maintained, in the light of declining calorie consumption trends in India over the past decade, that changing work patterns over the period might have resulted in less energy expenditure and therefore lower caloric needs. Both propositions remain the subject of intense controversy, especially in view of their weak empirical basis and the mounting empirical evidence on the consequences of malnutrition.

Non-food basic needs

How should non-food basic needs be specified and aggregated in monetary terms? This task is as difficult as defining the food component of the income poverty line. The standard methodology for the estimation of the non-food items is based on the platform set by the threshold adopted for food needs. Three routes could be taken.

The first method is to try to list the basic non-food items and then quantify and value each of them at market prices. However, the procedure is virtually impossible to operationalize for any large and diverse population group inasmuch as the number of factors and variables that influence these needs is very large. In this regard, imagine attempting to specify the needs of a family for linen and clothing: issues of free choice and preferences would also arise. Hence, the exercise is not realistic.

The second method sidesteps all such difficulties by arbitrarily setting expenditure on non-food items as some proportion, say, 50 per cent, of food needs, on the general assumption that the poor "usually" spend about two thirds of their income on food. This method was used by the International Labour Organization in its early discussions on basic-needs lines.

The third method, which is essentially a methodological refinement of the second, is most often used in specifying the income poverty line. It basically applies the logic of the second approach to non-food basic needs. Any household with an income above the poverty line should be able to meet its basic food and non-food needs and is not deemed deprived in terms of nutrition or health. Implicit in this method is the acknowledgement that everyone, including the poor, is free to make bad choices, but must then face the consequences of his or her decisions. The ramifications of, and possible objections to, such an assertion have been taken up above in the context of the composition of the prescribed, as opposed to actual, food expenditures and intakes, and they apply here as well (see box III.1).

Box III.1
Problems in estimating basic non-food needs

Different procedures are used to estimate the food and non-food components of the poverty-line basket. While dietary requirements are calculated on a "scientific" basis according to bodily needs, the non-food component of the poverty threshold is not calculated on such a *needs* basis. Instead, the procedure essentially identifies households whose expenditure on food exactly matches the cost of the food component in the poverty-line basket, and then checks how much such households *actually* spend on non-food items. Thus, the food component is needs-based, whereas the non-food component reflects the poverty of the poor with no guarantee that all basic non-food needs are in fact, or in principle could be, satisfactorily met.

This is a very serious shortcoming, and could have the effect of suppressing the visibility of such crucial basic needs as health, education, housing, transport and communications, fuel, information, and social and political participation. What such benchmark poor households actually spend on non-food items is assumed to substantively meet the non-food basic needs, but there is no verification process to confirm this assumption in any manner: it remains an assumption, and one with respect to which there are overwhelming prima facie grounds for rejection. Thus, after spending on food basic needs, poor households might not be left with enough to meet the real basic needs of education and health. Children might not be going to school or might not be well provided for in terms of educational accessories, and many health needs might be postponed or overlooked; these deficits might then be absorbed in the form of vulnerability to disease, or illiteracy.

In fact, in many cases, the methods for imputing non-food needs for inclusion in the poverty line are even more restrictive. The non-food component is in some cases taken to be the non-food expenditure of households whose *total* expenditure is equal to that required to be on the *food* poverty line (Klugman, 2002). This procedure is remarkable, in that it guarantees that such households cannot under any circumstances meet both food and non-food basic needs simultaneously. Why then should it be adopted at all? The underlying motivation seems to be obsessive zeal with regard to making absolutely certain that no non-necessity enters the poverty-line basket. Explaining this methodology, a World Bank sourcebook notes that in this case "the non-food expenditures of the households ... must be necessities, since the households are giving up food expenditures considered necessary to buy non-food items" (ibid., pp. 409-410). A monetary poverty line postulated by such a methodology cannot by definition be a basic-needs line: it is guaranteed to short-change the poor.

Economists can solve difficult problems with convenient assumptions. For example, in 1962, a pioneering study group of India's Planning Commission set a monthly per capita consumption level of rupees (Rs) 20 in 1960-1961 prices as the bare minimum level-of-living threshold. This excluded expenditure on health and education, since it assumed that such needs would be covered directly for all and for free by the State, as enjoined upon it by India's Constitution. The State's obligation has not been fulfilled but the assumption of its fulfilment has nevertheless survived.

Source: Saith (2005).

Some empirical studies confirm the tendency of the methodology to suppress the visibility of non-food needs in the poverty line. In India, the official poverty line does not cover education and health needs. Factoring these in on the basis of the actual expenditure pattern of the median household reveals that the poverty line would need to be raised by 10.4 per cent for rural areas and by 15.6 per cent for urban areas.[2] The rates of rural and urban poverty would increase from the official estimates of 28.3 and 27.5 per cent to the revised estimates of 36.4 and 35.8 per cent, respectively (Ravi and Dev, 2008, pp. 8-9). Another study estimates the cost of all major non-food needs—including food, health, insurance, clothing, fuel and electricity, transport, rent, etc., but excluding education—and arrives at a poverty threshold of Rs 840 per person per month, compared with the official poverty-line figures of Rs 368 and Rs 559 per month for rural and urban areas, respectively. This yields headcount poverty rates of 84.6 and 42.4 per cent for rural and urban areas, respectively, and a weighted average of 68.8 per cent for the country—close to three times the official headcount rate for 2004 based on the official poverty line (Guruswamy and Abraham, 2006). Similar findings also emerge in the context of China (Caizhen, 2009). While it is stated that official monetary poverty affects about a quarter of the population, direct evidence confirms the existence of a wide range of human development deficits for a much higher share of the population.

Ranking households by expenditure

Using the distribution of consumption expenditure per adult equivalent per household as a measure of a household's capacity to meet its basic needs can have perverse consequences. Consider two paradoxical examples, one dealing with health and the other with education.

In the first case, assume two households have identical demographic profiles and identical expenditure levels; the difference lies in the fact that the first household has a couple of seriously ill older persons who receive no treatment, whereas in the second there is no such problem of ill health. Both households, based on this methodology, are equally deprived. Now imagine

---

2 There are no a priori grounds for believing that the median household in either sector is able to meet its basic education and health needs; this exercise merely takes into account the actual expenditures. Offhand, it would be remarkable if all health and expenditure needs could be met by an outlay of 10-15 per cent of total expenditure. For instance, in 1999-2000, 71 per cent of children in age group 15-19 had not completed a secondary education; and 4 out of 5 households did not have access to public-health facilities. Household consumption data for India reveal that 62 per cent of the population do not have an intake of 2100 calories per day! Using the international poverty lines employed by the Asian Development Bank in the recent revised estimates of poverty based on PPPs for 2005, headcount poverty is estimated to be in the range of 54.8-65.3 per cent using a $1.35 poverty line; and at 60 per cent using a $1.25 line without a distinction between rural and urban (Himanshu, 2008, p. 42). The use of the median is utterly unjustifiable in such circumstances.

that the first household decides to sell off its land and thereby obtains the cash needed to meet the heavy medical expenses arising from dealing with the serious illness of its aged members. As most poor households do not have any land to sell, they might sell off their possessions or enter into a dangerous state of debt or, in an extreme situation, of debt bondage. Paradoxically, this household will now move above the other and, should the medical expenses for the illness be high enough, it will move even *above* the poverty line: its status will have *improved* relative to the other household's. The fact that it might have fundamentally jeopardized its long-term viability would go unnoticed in the methodology. All that would be recorded would be the higher expenditure, inducing the false deduction of an improvement in the status of the household on the poverty scale. If the medical expenditure was greater than its poverty gap, the household would appear as having improved its status and moved above the poverty line.

Consider the situation—tragically all too common in developing economies—where parents keep children out of school or prematurely withdraw them and send them out into the labour market. Child earnings would boost the family income and expenditure and, based on this methodology, might help the family move above the poverty line. The fact that a lack of education is a constitutive component of poverty somehow seems to elude this methodology and its practitioners. In short, the expenditure variable cannot be used automatically as a proxy for the fulfilment of the basic needs of a household.

Household size and composition

The only characteristics that the poverty-line method explicitly takes into account are urban or rural residence and total household size. This is an important methodological flaw. Households have different numbers of children at potentially different stages of schooling. Many poor households also engage in strenuous manual labour which requires the expenditure of more energy than is generated by the diets on the basis of which the average poverty line is constructed.

While adult equivalence scales adjust for the demographic structure of the household, and while further adjustments can be made for the additional needs of lactating mothers and pregnant women, the prevalence of illness, with its potentially debilitating impact on the economic well-being of the household, is not taken into account. Health expenses are increasingly coming to be recognized as a common cause of families' falling into poverty.

Adult equivalence scales may not be sufficient for normalizing household expenditure. Other elements, such as sex composition, could be very important. For instance, the villagers of northern India perceive the overall strength or vulnerability of a household as depending partly on whether the family has girls, for whom a dowry would have to be accumulated, or sons, who would provide both additional labour and dowries.

The list of household-specific diversities can be expanded. The relevant point is that none of those diversities, apart from rural or urban, and total household size, are explicitly taken into account. An exceptional case, however, is provided by the United States practice of targeting poor households, where such diversity is extensively taken into account. Ignoring household-specific diversities constitutes a fatal methodological flaw if poverty lines and gaps are to be used.

Public provisioning

The expenditure profile should include the imputed cash value of goods and services received in kind as gifts or transfers, but it is typically limited to private expenditure. Public transfers of goods and services are usually excluded. This produces a significant gap when it comes to health and education services, particularly in developing economies, where the role of public provision is usually substantial. In the absence of such information, one can only speculate over actual outcomes with respect to these key basic needs. Since access to such public provision is often heavily unequal across locations, and within communities, this gap constitutes a significant weakness, especially in the context of cross-sectional or inter-temporal comparative analysis. In many situations, even households that have the financial capacity might find it impossible to obtain adequate education and health services simply because those services are not available locally. The poverty-line approach implicitly assumes that money can buy health, education and other services at any time and in any place, or that these are provided by the State.

Problems of comparison arise also when public provisioning systems shift from subsidized to non-subsidized access. As a general rule, poverty-line estimates have not taken this crucial change on board. The reason for this lapse is that such publicly provided non-food goods and services are not assessed separately, as discussed earlier. The implications of this are potentially very damaging: if these services were earlier subsidized or provided virtually free of charge and later on are privatized, or provided by the State against user fees,[3] increases in poverty are likely to be underestimated.

Household assets base

The economic strength of a household, family or individual depends not just on its income but also on its asset base. If there were a uniform and stable relationship between asset ownership and income, additional information

---

[3] The case of basic health services in China's rural villages is relevant in this regard. Rudimentary health care provided by an army of "barefoot doctors" was free to villagers before the economic reforms of the last three decades, with financial support from rural collectives. The rural household responsibility system (family unit-based agricultural production) of the post-reform era eliminated the financial bases for maintaining the services of these rural health-care workers. As a result, rural households now incur greater out-of-pocket expenses for health services (Grigoriou, Guillaumont and Yang, 2005).

on assets could be redundant. However, levels of asset ownership vary and many unproductive assets are also held as stores of value. The level and pattern of assets also determine the staying power of the household unit in the face of fluctuations in incomes. Many poor households are deeply in debt, and the profound implications of this fact are ignored. Poverty lines are typically drawn in terms of expenditure, not income levels, and, this being the case, they do not take into account how this expenditure was financed, that is to say, whether there were positive or negative savings. The issue of sustainability is therefore overlooked.

Intra-household disparities

By adopting the household as the basic measurement unit, the method ignores intra-household disparities in access, consumption and other entitlements. Thus, the welfare of women, children and older persons might not be adequately reflected in the average level for the household.

Marginalization and exclusion

The poverty-line approach treats each household independently and scales it on the basis of its average per capita expenditure level; hence, all relational dimensions go missing. The fact that poor households suffer from high levels of social exclusion and marginalization is omitted. There is no reference to the issues of inequality and to power relations in the community within which the poor live. The approach ignores the socio-political dynamic that underlies the persistence and the reproduction of poverty. Thus, the claims of the poor with regard to community or social resources, or in the domain of access to government services, are rendered invisible. Lineage and social networks, which also influence vulnerability, are not taken into consideration either.

Self-perception of the poor

Those who experience poverty usually have a perspective on the sources, forms, nature and intensities of their various deprivations and deficits that is somewhat different from that of the analyst studying a particular indicator, especially absolute income or the food poverty line. These insights remain silent and invisible. Notwithstanding the fact that the methodology of self-perception-based approaches to poverty identification and analysis is not without its own problems, the relevance of such subjective information cannot be overlooked.

Inequality

The issue of inequality is increasingly absent from poverty debates. Given the rise in inequality in recent decades, this suppression is all the more worrisome. Furthermore, since inequality and resource availability are closely related, legitimizing the absolute poverty line as a targeting instrument also distorts discussions concerning the existence and extent of budgetary constraints. Thus, the approach to poverty reduction that ignores inequality actually hides, condones, legitimizes and perpetuates it. The more widely used measures of poverty, for example the Foster-Greer-Thorbecke index and the Sen poverty measure, are lauded for being sensitive to the degree of inequality among the poor; however, they neglect the issue of inequality between the poor and the rich.

Problems of use and interpretation

Chronic income poverty or socio-economic vulnerability?

The poor are especially vulnerable to shocks, and this is reflected in fluctuations in their annual levels of income. Thus, while the poverty line itself is held constant, and even if the statistical incidence of poverty remains the same over two periods, the composition of the poor population can change, with some of the poor climbing above the poverty line as others slip below it. For the sake of illustration, let us say that the incidence of headcount poverty was estimated to be 30 per cent in each of three successive years. These annual estimates cannot, however, indicate what proportion of the population experienced poverty, say, in any one or two or each of the three previous years. Was poverty a permanent condition for all 30 per cent, with the same households, and no others, experiencing poverty? Or was it also a transitory state experienced by, say, 60 per cent of the population?[4] These are crucial questions which remain unanswered by stock data. Similarly, the annual average for consumption hides the possibility of extended periods of hunger which cannot be compensated by possible consumption above the norm in the plentiful season.

Sound answers call for careful and systematic panel data monitored over several years. Such panels are rare, and hence such empirical evidence as is available is scattered and sketchy; but some synthetic, indicative conclusions are nevertheless possible. The report of the Chronic Poverty Research Centre for 2004-2005 (Chronic Poverty Research Centre, 2004) uses a definition of chronic poverty as "still being poor after five years". The data are based on a two-point comparison and discount for any mobility out from and (back) into poverty in the interim years; it is thus possible that they might well overstate the dimensions of chronic poverty considerably. For South Asia, the report es-

---

4 For instance, a two-point comparison of the same households in rural India, for 1970-1971 and 1981-1982, revealed that about a quarter of the households had been poor in both periods, while 22.8 per cent had escaped poverty and 13.3 per cent had descended into it, thereby implying that while about 25 per cent had been poor in both periods, about 60 per cent of the households had experienced poverty in one period or the other (Chronic Poverty Research Centre, 2004, p. 94, table 11.1i). Clearly, if all annual flows to and from poverty had been recorded in the panel, the proportion of households that had never experienced poverty in the period from 1970-1971 to 1981-1982 might have represented a slender minority.

timates that while 536 million persons were below the $1-per-day poverty line for its reference year, the number of those in chronic poverty ranged between 134 million and 188 million, representing between one fourth and one third of the annual rate; for East Asia, the ratio ranged between one sixth and one fourth; for Africa, with its lower level of income, the ratio ranged between 30 and 40 per cent.

Based on panel findings for a small group of countries, Baulch and Hoddinott (2000) present proportions of households that are "always poor" (AP), "sometimes poor" (SP) and "never poor" (NP).[5] In India, in the late 1970s and early 1980s, for every household that was always poor, there were another three households that were sometimes poor; only 12.4 per cent were reported as having been never poor. For Zimbabwe, the ratio of AP to SP in the first half of the 1990s was 1 to 6; for China in the second half of the 1980s, it was 1 to 8. Panel data for 379 households in 21 villages in rural Bangladesh show that 31 per cent of households in the sample were poor in both 1987-1988 and 2000 and 25 per cent of households were never poor, that is to say, not poor in either 1987-1988 or 2000, while 26 per cent of the households who had been poor in the base year (1987-1988) were no longer poor in 2000, and 18 per cent fell into poverty between 1987-1988 and 2000 (Sen, 2003). In that sample, the chronically poor constituted only 31 per cent of households, which demonstrates that by focusing on the chronically poor as their target, policies miss many of the other poor.

The exclusionary tendency of the focus on chronic poverty is actually stronger than these data suggest, the reason being that the comparison is with the part of the population deemed to be poor according to the $1-per-day line, or one based on nationally specified poverty thresholds. It has been argued above that these lines are already very restrictive in their definition.

Why narrow the target?

First, the chronically poor households are the households that face the most acute forms of poverty, that is, they are the "poorest of the poor", and as such deserve to be given priority. However, not all chronically poor households are among the poorest of the poor. A study of rural India using panel data showed that of those households that were poor in each of a string of three years, only a fraction belonged to the category of the poorest (Gaiha, 1989).

A further issue arises, namely, whether identification of "the chronically poor" is carried out only to provide a means of ranking the poor so as to ensure that relief can be prioritized and rushed *first* to those found to be poorest. If so, prioritization would hardly matter except in extreme situations, for example, in famine-stricken camps where aid workers have to resort to weighing scales to determine the neediest in the face of impossible constraints.

---

5 The data are reported in Holzman and Jorgensen (2004, p. 33, table 2.1).

Or is it simply that narrowing the focus makes the project of anti-poverty more manageable, even if it comes at the cost of excluding the majority of those in poverty or vulnerable to it? When the focus is on the duration and depth of poverty, limited resources can be devoted to the chronically poor, while other people living in poverty are left out.

Such exercises and methodologies perhaps reflect the ethical dilemmas of the members of the aid-fatigued donor community who feel they need an allocation criterion in situations where available resources cannot match the need. It is commonplace to justify and legitimize such targeting strategies—such as identifying the "poorest of the poor", or the "chronically poor", by ingeniously—but disingenuously—adducing Rawlsian or Gandhian ethical criteria as their foundation.[6]

Is poverty a discrete concept?

The utilization of the income poverty line fosters the impression that a statistical test is capable of identifying who is and who is not suffering from the impact of the phenomenon of poverty. The substantive issue concerns the discriminatory power of poverty lines in separating the poor from the non-poor. In reality, the experience of poverty is multifaceted, multidimensional and subject to volatility; it also has time and relativity dimensions.

This being the case, poverty cannot be defined by a straight line that divides a population into two segments based on an expenditure criterion. Deficits in various specific dimensions, for example, those of education, health, housing, etc., commonly persist at expenditure levels well above the stipulated poverty line. Therefore, multiple indicators besides money-metric income and expenditure measures are needed to capture the scale and dimensions of poverty. While monetary poverty might affect just a minority, only a few might escape poverty in any form.

There are usually high proportions of the population in most developing countries at expenditure levels concentrated around the poverty line. Shifting the line up or down could make a dramatic difference with respect to the estimated incidence of monetary poverty. Since the methodological and statistical bases of the money-metric approach are so seriously compromised, there has

---

6 The contemporary philosopher John Rawls has elaborated what he calls the difference principle, according to which the arrangement of social and economic inequalities is such that they benefit those who are least advantaged. In other words, differences in wealth and social position are acceptable as long as they can be shown to benefit everyone and, in particular, those who have the fewest advantages. This principle also requires that systems allow for all people to have access to goods and positions under conditions of fair equality of opportunity based on both need and merit. Gandhi's yardstick for action was simple: "Whenever you are in doubt, or when the self becomes too much with you, apply the following test: Recall the face of the poorest and the weakest person whom you have seen, and ask yourself if the next step you contemplate is going to be of any use to that person" (see Barker (2007)).

been interest in measures of the "depth" of poverty (below the poverty line) as well as attention to measures of vulnerability to poverty.

How significant are these issues empirically? The case of India provides some clues (see also box III.2; and Sengupta, Kannan and Raveendran, 2008, pp. 50-51). In 2004-2005, someone on the national poverty line had a daily consumer expenditure of Rs 12; a level below Rs 9 was classified as extreme poverty; that between Rs 12 and Rs 15 was deemed marginal poverty; and a level below Rs 20 was taken to define those vulnerable to poverty. Across these four levels, the range was from $1 to $2.2 (PPP) per day. While only 6.4 per cent of households were found to be extremely poor, as many as 76.8 per cent were below the vulnerability line. In 1993-1994, those below the vulnerability line had constituted 81.9 per cent of the population. If other households experienced poverty or vulnerability in the interim, a large majority of the population lives in poverty or in its shadow.

When compared with those clearly above this band, most households within and below it might appear relatively similar, in that they usually display similar social, visual and behavioural characteristics, irrespective of the differences in their expenditure levels. After all, the gap between the income that defines the extremely poor and that defining the vulnerable, Rs 11 per day, is approximately equivalent to the price of any of the following: a ticket in a municipal car park, half a litre of bottled water, a bus ride or a mini-sized snack from a street food vendor. This offers little justification for discriminat-

---

Box III.2
Does the choice of approach matter? Soundings from rural China

Who is poor in rural China? There are many answers to this question. The incidence and pattern of rural poverty are highly sensitive to the measurement approach taken.

A recent study of an administrative village in Wuding County in rural Yunnan applied multiple methodological and measurement approaches to the 473 households in the village. The use of the national official poverty line of 668 yuan yields an incidence of headcount poverty of just 3.4 per cent of households. Re-estimating the incidence of poverty on the basis of two other specifications of the poverty line yielded different results.

First, the national poverty basket was estimated using local prices; this led to a poverty line of 1,296 yuan; the incidence rate was then 18.0 per cent. Second, a notional basket of items that would correspond to the poverty threshold based on local perceptions was composed through participatory interactions with village folk. This basket, valued also at local prices, was calculated as 2,315 yuan; through use of this local poverty line, the conclusion was reached that 59.6 per cent of the households were in poverty. The spread was enormous: for every 1 household that was classified as being poor using the official poverty line, there were nearly 18 households that would have been deemed poor using a poverty line based on local perceptions of basic needs valued at local prices.

This being the case, the incidence fluctuated widely from year to year, with the pattern of these fluctuations often running contrary to what should reasonably have been expected based on trends in the real economy of the village for the years in question. For the reference year of research, the incidence rate, based on the local list, turned out to be 40.2 per cent.[a]

> **Box III.2** *(continued)*
> **Does the choice of approach matter? Soundings from rural China**
>
> The same population of 473 households was then investigated through the field application of participatory poverty assessment methods. This exercise revealed a poverty incidence of 33.8 per cent.
>
> Finally, India's recently established multidimensional poverty household indexing template was adapted to calculate household scores which were then used to rank households. This ranking was then compared with the one obtained using the other criteria. The lesson that emerges from this multi-method field research is that different approaches lead to very different estimates of poverty for the same set of households.
>
> Only 4 households of 473 were poor on all criteria. This no doubt reflects the very low poverty line. However, when the high local money poverty line was used, the number rose to 34, or to only 7.2 per cent of all households. Using the low official poverty line, 170 households, or 35.9 per cent, were found to be non-poor on all criteria; the number was 90, or 19.0 per cent, if the much higher local poverty threshold was used. Four of every five households were found to be in poverty on at least one criterion, using the local poverty line.
>
> Applying diverse methods to estimate the incidence of rural poverty for a fixed population for the same reference period yields very different results, with regard to both the overall rate of incidence and the rankings of and the overlaps between the groups of "households in poverty". These findings provide revealing insights into the conceptual and methodological ambiguities of the empirical estimation of poverty, which have powerful implications for the design and implementation of anti-poverty interventions.
>
> Source: Caizhen (2009).
>
> a   The local list was prepared by local officials and included households identified as slated to receive support from public resources. In this regard, it was heavily influenced by the guidelines and budgets set by authorities at higher administrative levels. This accounted both for considerable fluctuations in the length of the local list from year to year and for the divergence in the incidence of poverty based on this criterion from the estimate derived from the application of the official national poverty line.

ing between such groups at a policy level but strong justification for exploring anti-poverty strategies based on the principle of universal coverage.

Towards universalism: life without poverty lines?

The fundamental question is whether the poverty-line approach is useful in addressing poverty, or whether its methodological problems have proved fatal to its utility in efforts to significantly reduce poverty. While the methodologies used are the subject of much criticism and debate, States Members of the United Nations and international development agencies have agreed to halve the incidence of poverty by 2015 despite such problems of measurement. The current techniques for measuring poverty undoubtedly have serious flaws. Conceptual and methodological improvements that address the limitations of the current approach should continue to be explored and pursued, as so many lives and livelihoods are at stake.

Reverting to national poverty lines and improving their methodology may be one way of dealing with the limitations of the global poverty-line approach (Reddy, 2009). This approach has begun to take hold over the past few years

(Saith, 2005, 2007; Srinivasan, 2007; Reddy, 2009) and official methodologies are under expert review in places. Another advance has been to replace money poverty lines by multidimensional scoring criteria; promising as this is, the initiative introduces its own methodological problems and questions neither the intrinsic nor the operational worth of targeting. It is against this backdrop that the alternative of universalism has to be viewed.[7]

If the objective is to reach the poorest in any given population, where being poor is defined in the usual terms of private consumption expenditure per adult equivalent within each household, all that would be needed are the data on the distribution of this expenditure variable across households. For the purpose of reaching the poorest first, the poverty line is redundant; it becomes necessary only when a cut-off point is being defined indicating where to stop, not where to begin. But why is such a cut-off point needed at all?

One alternative to targeting based on the income poverty line would be to widen the frame of reference to include all sections of society at risk of sliding into poverty, instead of moving in the direction of limiting action only to the chronically poor, who often form a small fraction of those in poverty or those seriously vulnerable to it. It was observed earlier that including this dimension of vulnerability to poverty for a country such as India could widen the net, expanding the proportion from one quarter to about four fifths of the population. If one adopted the strategy of excluding never-poor households, the coverage could well expand to all but the top 10 per cent of the population. This course of action remains, of course, within the money-metric approach itself.

An alternative strategic perspective emerges within from the universalizing framework of the dimension of socio-economic security (United Nations, 2008). This involves a rejection of targeting the poor, in favour of profiling and addressing deprivations for the entire population in each of a wider range of specific dimensions of well-being.

There are profound differences between the reductionist monetary approach based on an expenditure poverty line and an alternative strategy that defines and addresses deprivations in multiple dimensions, regardless of the income of the household. The monetary approach assumes that all dimensions can be measured and accessed in money terms. It is then assumed that if a household has enough money to procure its basic needs, it is up to that household to make its own consumption choices. Thus, if the household over-consumes but has deficits in other dimensions, that becomes a reflection of consumer preference and the exercise of agency by the household and the ensuing deficits need not be a matter of policy concern. This approach therefore holds households responsible for poverty.

This view has several shortcomings. **First**, whether the poverty-line budget of the household is enough to cover stipulated basic needs at set levels and in

---

7 See, for instance, Mkandawire (2007); Robeyns (2008); Chhachhi (2008); and Saith (2008).

terms of quality norms remains unclear. Being above the poverty line should be enough to prevent primary poverty, but given the way in which the non-food component of the poverty-line budget is estimated, this is not assured. **Second**, not all secondary poverty is necessarily the responsibility of the household: for instance, there might be a supply-side failure which prevents the children of the household from going to school or receiving medical attention when necessary. The monetary poverty-line approach seems to assume that money in the pocket automatically secures access to goods and services. **Third**, ascribing accountability for under-nutrition to the household, for instance, is ethically questionable. There is casuistry at work in setting a budget to meet basic needs based on questionable assumptions and then blaming the household for the subsequent deficits in key dimensions. **Fourth**, the household member who makes the decisions leading to secondary poverty may not be the one who suffers from the ensuing deficits. Thus, the choices of the parents might affect outcomes for the children or older persons, for which there can be little ethical justification. **Fifth**, there could be parental biases that interfere with the rights of the children, resulting, for example, in the withholding of education from girls. Data on dimensional poverty with respect to children firmly reveal that deficits in specific dimensions, such as health and education, exist at income levels far exceeding the poverty-line cut-off point.

The alternative strategy of addressing all deficits in specific dimensions, entailing the provision of access to all in the form of rightful entitlements, at socially determined norms and levels of quality and assured supply, calls for a multipronged approach. The first step is to ensure that these entitlements are provided through adequate resources. Second, physical availability has to be coupled with guaranteed and unrestricted social access. Third, there have to be mechanisms for financial access, which could take various forms, including mobilizing resources away from inequitable provisioning programmes towards underwriting more universal ones. It is worth emphasizing, however, that not all initiatives for advancing well-being require financial resources.

In adopting such an approach, it is necessary to extend the net so as to cover wider dimensions of well-being using non-conventional indicators of psychosocial and mental health, and environmental, relational and subjective components. As noted earlier, the approach adopted in both academic discourse and policy practice in developed countries has long represented a shift in perspective from monetary poverty to a holistic appreciation of well-being. Taking this step, which is being done increasingly in developed countries, immediately broadens the focus to include all persons, whether in a state of money poverty or not, who are faced with deficits within any of these additional dimensions of well-being. There is a clear case to be made for promoting an integrated, more universal, more inclusive and more holistic approach to deprivation. This is attempted in chapter IV.

Chapter IV
Deprivation, vulnerability and exclusion

The need for a new approach

The critique of conventional monetary-based measurement using poverty lines suggests some imperatives with regard to approach and method.

It is not enough to define and aggregate "poverty" in the abstract, as if it were a commodity measurable in dollars and cents. What is essential is to progress from an abstract focus on the incidence of poverty to an empathetic understanding of the lived experience of poverty. To do this, it is necessary to identify people who are in poverty.

It is also necessary to recognize the multiple and distinct dimensions in which people—both those above and those below any stipulated poverty line—experience deficits in well-being, whether or not they can be quantified in monetary terms. Conventional basic needs are critical, but do not exhaust the necessary areas of concern.

Furthermore, it is essential to move away from approaches dominated by a focus on outcomes to those where monitoring the outcomes is just the starting point for an exploration of the structures and dynamic processes that produce them. In other words, diagnoses of the problems are needed, not just snapshots of outcomes.

Investigation of these social dynamics using the individual as the essential unit of study is not sufficient, and often leads to a serious misinterpretation. It is necessary to go beyond—indeed to replace—such an individual-based view and to recognize the relational and group affinities and affiliations of individuals and then rise to the challenge of devising a workable conceptualization of group identity.

The use of the poverty line inevitably leads to the simplistic division of the population into two mutually exclusive segments: those below the poverty line (BPL households); and those above (APL households). This ignores diversities and differentiation and thereby introduces distortions marring policy intervention and collective action.

The poverty-line approach limits the field of vision to individuals and households below the prescribed poverty line, ignoring the fact that there is a large share of the population above the poverty line who are highly vulnerable to poverty. Many households enter and exit poverty as defined by a poverty line as their circumstances and fortunes fluctuate, such fluctuations being a hallmark of deprivation. This calls for a dynamic analysis that investigates vulnerability, household socio-economic mobility, and movement of households into and out of specific states of deprivation.

Taken together, these observations constitute an effective critique of the conventional dollar-a-day poverty-line approach—whether as a tool for conceptualization, definition or monitoring of poverty, or for instrumentalizing targeted interventions, impact assessment and priority-setting—and underscore the value of more universal approaches to human and social development. However, the case to be made for more universal approaches cannot limit itself to a rejection of the narrow monetary-based approach; nor is it sufficient to identify an alternative universalist paradigm. It is imperative to go further and develop alternative conceptual perspectives and corresponding strategies encompassing alternative forms of policy intervention and collective action.

Where does this exercise in creative destruction lead: which is the way ahead?

Thinking constructively, an analytical framework suitable for a social analysis of deprivation must be broad and flexible enough to absorb considerable diversities across economic structures, development pathways and experiences, and sociocultural specificities. As such, the approach is understandably—and unavoidably—eclectic, synthetic and unorthodox. This having been said, the approach followed does at the same time need to possess certain features. Ideally, in the recognition of deprivation, it should: be aware that while measurability can be a virtue, it is neither necessary for, nor a guarantee of, relevance and meaning; be sensitive to absolute and relative deprivations and disadvantages as well as to inequality in both the developing and the rich countries and be able to recognize the relevance of groups as units of social analysis; explore multifaceted well-being and human development in a holistic manner; conceptualize the issue in a dynamic framework that encompasses questions of mobility; investigate outcomes as well as the structural factors, the process and the causal mechanisms that generate them; incorporate participatory perspectives into the theoretical approach and avoid targeting; and embrace the universality of rights and needs, uncompromised by calls for pragmatic expediency or resource constraints which serve as excuses for continued exclusion.

The need for combining these desirable features enjoins the adoption of a broad approach rather than a single-concept strategy. These considerations provide the rationale for moving from a narrowly defined monetary-based concept of poverty to a broader analytical framework grounded in the concept of social exclusion. This approach, if adopted, would be free of the weaknesses identified in the poverty-line approach, while also incorporating many of the desirable features mentioned above. Nevertheless, such an approach would still be scrutinized for its ability to provide a better understanding of the nature of the problem.

Alternative points of entry

In response to the inherent weaknesses of the monetary approach, several alternatives were spawned. In this regard, Morris D. Morris (1982) prefaced his presentation of the Physical Quality of Life Index with an explicit critique of the aggregated gross national product (GNP) or money-metric approach; Amartya Sen launched his capability approach and the human development index with a powerful critique to the effect that the basic needs approach was trapped in commodity space; Robert Chambers (1997) argued for a participatory approach to poverty.

While these approaches provide alternative points of entry for developing a framework for a social analysis of deprivation, they all have features that tend to significantly limit their usefulness for this purpose. The human development approach, whether it utilizes the human development index or the earlier Physical Quality of Life Index, is explicitly outcome-based and focuses on a set of chosen indicators. This inevitably leads to the use of methods of cross-sectional and comparative statistics in evaluating alternative situations, without any emphasis on the societal structures, dynamics, processes and policies that generate these outcomes. Further, there are usually large group averages hiding inequalities.

The participatory approach, in contrast, does provide an understanding of the multidimensional background of deprivation, especially its subjective dimensions, but loses analytical power at higher levels of aggregation. There are nonetheless significant arguments to be made in support of this approach, some of which are identified in the discussion below.

Social exclusion: a new approach to poverty analysis

The grim realities that underlie and concretize the concept of social exclusion are ubiquitous and global. Virtually no country, rich or poor, "traditional" or "modern", can credibly claim to be unaffected by them. They seem to be woven into the fabric of societies, embedded in the system, with deep roots which lead to their continuous reproduction.

The various manifestations of social exclusion can be categorized within four dimensions. The first pertains to endowments and the ownership of and access to assets; exclusion from those forms the basis of other forms of exclusion. Not enough attention has been paid, however, to the structural inequalities and exclusions embedded in the initial conditions from which processes originate and which also set the relational parameters. This oversight might be attributed partially to the fact that, under the conventional paradigm, asset ownership structures are ignored when considering policy options. This reluctance has to be overcome if meaningful alternatives are to developed, not just ex post facto Band-Aid interventions.

The second dimension covers processes generating productive, or primary, entitlements secured by individuals, households and groups through their engagement in the economy on the basis of their control over productive endowments. It is essential not to reduce this to an enumeration of alternative "livelihoods", but instead to analyse the structure and dynamics of these activities within the context of wider policy parameters that causally govern the outcomes for individuals, households and groups and at the local level.

The third dimension is that of social provisioning, covering claims and access to the necessary range of basic needs and social services at appropriate levels and with quality assurance; this is the area where the most commonly discussed forms of social exclusion are located, for example, those related to nutrition, education, health, housing and so on. More widely, this area covers the various aspects of the secondary process of entitlement generation, highlighting transfers, subsidization and other forms of social provisioning and claims.

The fourth and final dimension is that of full and equal citizenship; this puts the spotlight on the institutional framework for ensuring political and socio-economic rights, on issues of identity-based discrimination, and on democratic participation in local and wider decision-making political structures and processes.

There are multiple feedback loops among these four dimensions. Yet, some dimensions dominate others in terms of causation. For instance, while incomes generate savings and investments that increase the original stock of household endowments, it is the total level of the latter that primarily governs the level of savings and investment possible in the first place. Likewise, while incomes form the basis for meeting household basic needs, there are often important supplements from the State through various forms of subsidized social provisioning and income transfers addressing gaps in meeting basic needs. The fourth dimension influences the manner of functioning of all others.

A distinction has been made between passive and active exclusion: the latter occurs when there is a wilful act leading to exclusion; the former is deemed to occur in the absence of such an act, through the workings of larger economic processes or the system as a whole (Sen, 2000).

Social exclusion has remained a regularly contested concept. Some analysts have seen little value in the notion of social exclusion, decrying its limited theoretical or researchable content (Oyen, 1997). Others have pointed out that it perhaps reflects the attempt to address the old agenda of poverty, albeit with reduced power and precision (Townsend, 2002; Levitas, 2000).

However, through its focus on the non-material dimensions of deprivation, and through incorporating subjective and experiential perspectives, the social exclusion approach expands the final outcomes that signal development objectives. Dimensions of self-esteem, dignity and recognition of mutual social acceptability enter the expanded societal frame.

The social exclusion concept encompasses processes, social relations, causality and dynamics in analysing outcomes, while taking into account initial conditions such as asset ownership. It also extends the analytical focus beyond just individuals to social groups. Thus, the social inclusion approach can effectively complement other poverty reduction strategies.

Social exclusion: ubiquitous presence, multiple forms

Forms of social exclusion can be defined in terms of the final outcomes of the development process. Here, the focus is generally on the elements of basic needs, or a wider set of elements that include non-material dimensions of wellbeing. They could also be defined in terms of the features of the structures, processes and policies that generated these final outcomes; this would link up with the various instrumental elements of causal processes: exclusion from employment, from credit, from access to land, etc. The concept of social exclusion could also be applied to social constituencies that have been excluded on account of relatively immutable attributes of their identity, implying the existence of discrimination.

The following sections present selected illustrations of poverty and social exclusion, with a wide range of examples drawn from various regions, countries and social groups. The diversity of these examples highlights the pervasiveness of poverty and social exclusion—in developed as well as developing countries and among people of all ages and ethnic groups.

Regional diversity in its manifestations

In Africa, social exclusion is mostly seen as a direct consequence of poverty, and they both stem from discrimination on the basis of race, ethnicity and gender, inequality, unbalanced rural/urban development, unequal distribution of assets or unequal access to services. Persistent conflicts and instability, often resulting from long-term exclusion, impede poverty reduction efforts. Close to 12.7 million people were internally displaced on the continent in 2007, including 1.6 million additional in that year alone.

Besides protracted conflict situations, the prevalence of HIV/AIDS is a major obstacle to inclusion and poverty eradication in Africa. Children who have lost their parents to AIDS often become street children relying on begging and petty crime in order to survive; with little chance of going to school, they will continue to suffer from exclusion and poverty as adults.

In Latin America and the Caribbean, social exclusion often denotes a specific problem, such as the existence of an underclass or the long-term unemployed. It is often seen as a major concern in the context of high inequality, as well as ethnic and racial discrimination. Both indigenous people and Afro-descendants are the poorest in the region. In Colombia, the poverty rate for ethnic and racial minorities is 1.6 times higher than that for the rest of the population, and in Paraguay, it is 7.9 times higher. The gap between indigenous and non-indigenous populations is especially persistent. Such disparities are reflected in educational attainment. For instance, in Brazil, in the early 1990s, illiteracy rates for the black population were more than double those of the white population (Hopenhayn, 2008). The causes of discrimination in Latin America relate mostly to being poor, old or uneducated or belonging to an ethnic minority. Recent data indicate that only 34 per cent of indigenous children attend secondary school as compared with 48 per cent in the general population (Economic Commission for Latin America and the Caribbean, 2008).

In Asia and the Pacific, the region with the highest number of older persons in the world, income security, employment, health, nutrition and social services for older persons are of major concern. Migrant workers, facing exploitation, abuse and discrimination, experience significant exclusion. Prolonged migration has been found to cause the break-up of families and violent behaviour and delinquency in the children left behind (Economic and Social Commission for Asia and the Pacific, 2008a).

In Western Asia, conflict and displacement intensify exclusion, with minorities being at a greater risk of displacement. There are close to 7 million refugees and 3.5 million internally displaced people in the region. Many migrant workers in the region lack the status of citizens and are thus excluded from the poverty eradication programmes.

In respect of exclusion, the focus of developed countries is on marginalized groups. This is especially warranted considering that some of these groups are affected by exclusion and poverty more than others. For instance, in the Organization for Economic Cooperation and Development (OECD) member countries in 2005, children and young adults had poverty rates that were about 25 per cent above the population average, while those rates had been respectively close to and below that average 20 years ago (Organization for Economic Cooperation and Development, 2008a). Consequently, focusing on reducing child poverty is considered a very important component of overall efforts to combat poverty in Europe and prevent intergenerational transmission of poverty.

Everywhere, a key feature of social exclusion is the relative powerlessness of those excluded. The ability of a person living in poverty to improve his or her material and non-material well-being depends on the socio-political structure of the society he or she lives in. It further depends on the institutions fostering economic opportunity and local democracy. Regrettably, divisions in a society diminish the possibilities of accessing economic and political opportunities. Another dimension is the individual and collective agency of people living in poverty.

As noted by Narayan, Pritchett and Kapoor (2009, pp. 115-116):

For the most marginalized people, their collective agency in organization, representation, voice, and identity is critical in overcoming social discrimination that leads to economic, social, and political exclusion and inequality. Without this collective capacity to negotiate, control, and bargain, individual initiative on its own may not be sufficient.

Individual and collective agency can improve access to new economic opportunities or lead to greater mobility through the practice of democracy.

Local democracy is especially important in overcoming poverty, although it may function as a zero-sum game where some poor people gain while others lose. Sometimes, local democracies become corrupt and are exploited by the elites, with the possibility of exclusion and corruption being more likely in more socially stratified societies. The negative effects of corruption were measured in Uttar Pradesh, India, where a unit increase in corruption decreased the probability of moving out of poverty by 10 per cent and negated the positive effects of increasing landownership and reducing illiteracy (ibid.).

Social schisms beneath the averages: disparities in life expectancy

Life expectancy is a fundamental indicator of both well-being and poverty. Globally, life expectancy increased from 46 years in 1955 to 66 years in 2005. Among more developed regions, it increased by 10 years over the same period, from 66 to 76 years. In less developed regions, it increased by 23 years to 64 years, while in the least developed countries, the increase was only 18 years, from 36 to 54 (United Nations, 2009a).

Notwithstanding the continuing improvement of overall life expectancy among the wealthiest countries, significant inequalities are persistent and widening.

In the United States of America, between 1980 and 2000, the gap in life expectancy between members of different socio-economic groups widened as a result of larger gains in life expectancy for those in higher socio-economic groups relative to those in more deprived groups (Singh and Siahpush, 2006). The gap in life expectancy between the most and least deprived deciles grew from less than 3 years in 1980-1982 to 4.5 years in 1998-2000. Life expectancy at birth varies significantly by race in the United States; white Americans are expected to live about five years longer than black Americans on average (United States Department of Health and Human Services, Centers for Disease Control and Prevention, National Center for Health Statistics, 2009). The gap is wider for men, and wider when economic disparities intersect with race. In Montgomery County, an affluent white community near Washington, D.C., life expectancy is 80 years. In Washington, D.C., itself, a less well-off, predominantly African American community, male life expectancy is 63 years —similar to that for India and the Philippines (Commission on Social Determinants of Health, 2008).

In Australia, the Aboriginal and Torres Strait Islander (indigenous) population has a life expectancy of about 17 years less than that of the Australian population as a whole (Australian Bureau of Statistics, 2004). The main contributors to the gap were found to be non-communicable diseases and conditions such as cardiovascular, respiratory and genito-urinary disease and diabetes, which highlights the importance of inclusive access for all segments of society to primary health programmes designed to address prevention, early diagnosis and treatment.

Recent research reveals that inequality in life expectancies among countries is also increasing (see figure IV.1). After having declined between 1962 and 1987, health inequality among countries began to increase, and by 2002 had reached the same levels as in 1967. As of 2002, life expectancy among the countries with the poorest survival prospects had returned to the 1977 level of 44 years on average (McGillivray, Dutta and Markova, 2009). Many of the countries with the shortest overall life expectancy are in sub-Saharan Africa and they have been hard hit by the HIV/AIDS epidemic. Other factors that have contributed to poor survival outcomes in sub-Saharan Africa include armed conflict, economic stagnation and infectious diseases such as malaria and tuberculosis.

Years of life are among the most basic indicators of well-being. Large, and often growing, gaps in life expectancy among and within countries indicate that large segments of the population are not sharing equally in the benefits of economic growth, that more attention must be given to the most marginalized individuals in terms of health and well-being, and that the social determinants of health outcomes should be given more attention in policy formulation.

Figure IV.1
Inequality in life expectancy has been increasing, 1962-2002

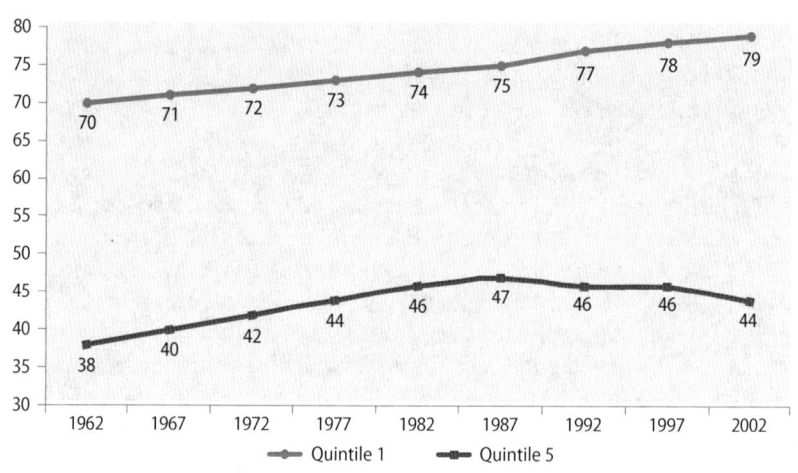

Source: McGillivray, Dutta and Markova (2009).

Identity, exclusion and poverty

The social exclusion approach is especially valuable since it enables an acknowledgement and analysis of the dimension of identity. Within this dimension, a distinction can be made between features of identity deriving from attributes that, in principle, could be temporary, and those aspects of identity that are inherited and remain relatively immutable through life. Examples of the former are the status of migrants and refugees, and the categories of youth. In these cases, the disadvantages of social exclusion that are attached to these categories are suffered by individuals as long as they continue to be associated with them; on the other hand, it is entirely possible—and a plausible explanation—that such individuals will acquire the mobility that enables them to leave their disadvantages behind.

In contrast, there is only very limited mobility, and often none, out of domains where the elements of identity, such as gender, race, ethnicity, indigeneity, caste and disability, are immutable. Here, socially constructed disadvantages attach to individuals virtually from birth and stigmatize them throughout their lives. These forms of identity-based exclusion typically characterize individuals constituted as social groups. Such exclusion expresses itself explicitly in the form of social prejudice and discrimination and is not often dispelled by a higher economic status achieved by the individual or the group affected. It becomes an overarching factor which tends to perpetuate the material poverty and low socio-economic status of such excluded marginalized groups.

Such discrimination is not a phenomenon unique to poor countries; regrettably, it is all too ubiquitous in every society, rich or poor, as is confirmed by the selected illustrations that follow. The crucial policy significance of this aspect of social exclusion lies in the fact that rather than melt away with the elimination of poverty, it actually tends to undermine the effectiveness of efforts at poverty reduction in the first place. Another important insight produced by the social exclusion approach in this regard concerns the salience of social norms and behaviour, since much of the social exclusion of this type arises not from governmental failures but from societal fractures. This underlines the need not just for good public policies, but for new social norms conducive to better social integration.

Ethnicity and poverty: the cases of Native Americans in the United States of America and Roma in Europe

Ethnicity is one of the immutable components of identity. Ethnic minorities often find themselves marginalized by the mainstream societies they live in. For example, indigenous peoples in many developed countries disproportionately suffer from exclusion and poverty. They live shorter and less healthy lives, are more likely to be unemployed, and earn less than the general population. Rates of poverty, substance abuse, suicide and incarceration are also higher than those for non-indigenous people.

Native Americans[1] in the United States suffer poverty at a rate three times higher than that of the non-Hispanic white population. The situation of Native Americans who live on reservations is particularly dire (box IV.1).

The situation of Roma in Europe clearly illustrates the fact that discrimination and racism are linked to poverty. Roma are discriminated against in educational and health-care systems and in their access to labour markets and social services. The situation of Roma within new member States of the European Union (EU) remains a cause of special concern, given the evidence of racism and discrimination in employment, education and health-care provision, the failure of criminal justice systems in cases involving Roma, and the incidence of acts of violence perpetrated against Roma (European Commission, Directorate-General for Employment and Social Affairs, 2004). While only 6 per cent of EU citizens would feel uncomfortable having a person with

---

Box IV.1
The Oglala Sioux people on the Pine Ridge Reservation

The Pine Ridge Reservation in South Dakota is one of the poorest places in the United States. The Pine Ridge Reservation, home to the Oglala Sioux people, is characterized by both deep poverty and a high degree of vulnerability to poverty. More than half the population live below the poverty line and nearly one third live below half the poverty line, five times the national average (United States Census Bureau, 2000).

The Reservation's weak ties to the market economy are reflected in an unemployment rate of nearly 30 per cent, about five times the national average. Wage employment is limited and insecure: only about half of all households had wage income in 2004, and of those households about 25 per cent had not had wage income in the previous year (Pickering and Mizushima, 2007). The majority of those employed are in education, health and social services (40 per cent) and public administration (18 per cent).

Half of the households engage in home-based enterprises; however, the limited access to financial services is a barrier to entrepreneurship. As there are no banks on the Reservation, residents must travel between 40 and 180 miles (round trip) to meet their banking needs (Mushinski and Pickering, 2007). Lakota Funds, a community development organization on the Reservation, offers small loans to tribe members ranging from $200 to $200,000.[a] While Lakota Funds has contributed to many success stories, it estimates an unmet need for small business capital at over $10,000,000.

The extreme poverty on the Pine Ridge Reservation is reflected in the poor health of the population, which exacerbates and perpetuates poverty. The mortality rate in Shannon County, which lies entirely within the Reservation, is more than double the rate for the United States. The infant mortality rate is almost twice that of the State and national averages. At 13.55 deaths per 1,000 live births, the infant mortality rate is higher than in some countries in less developed regions such as Viet Nam (12.93 per 1,000), Mauritius (12.8 per 1,000) and Uruguay (12.4 per 1,000). Rates of death from accidents, diabetes and chronic liver disease and cirrhosis are several times higher than the national average (see figure). Poor living conditions contribute to ill health on the reservation. Clean water, health services and electricity are not consistently available (Mushinski and Pickering, 2007; United States Census Bureau, 2000). Complete plumbing and kitchen facilities are lacking in 12 per cent and 8.6 per cent of housing units, respectively. These figures are considerably higher than the national average (United States Census Bureau, 2000).

---

1 Native Americans referred to in census data are people who self-identified as American Indian or Native Alaskan only in the 2000 United States Census.

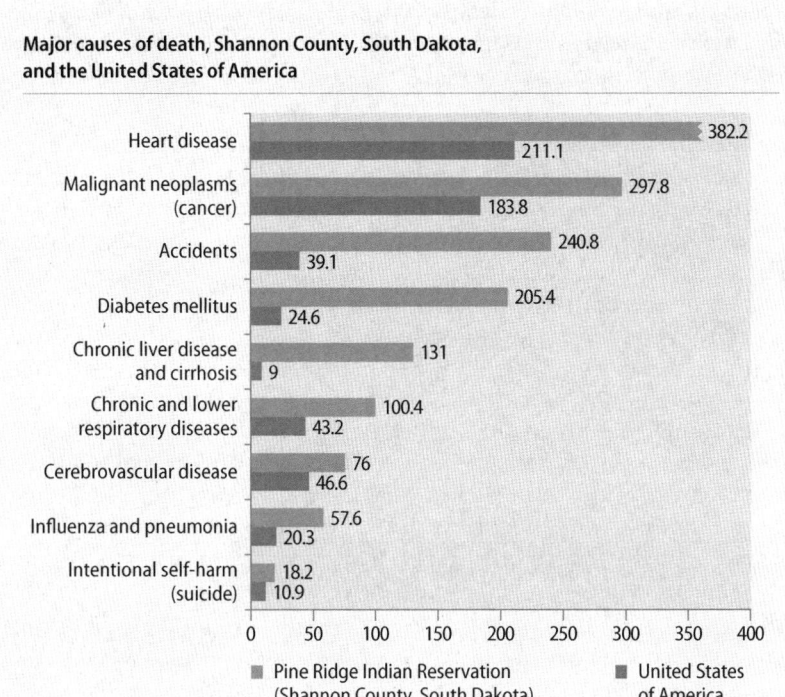

Major causes of death, Shannon County, South Dakota, and the United States of America

- Heart disease: 382.2 / 211.1
- Malignant neoplasms (cancer): 297.8 / 183.8
- Accidents: 240.8 / 39.1
- Diabetes mellitus: 205.4 / 24.6
- Chronic liver disease and cirrhosis: 131 / 9
- Chronic and lower respiratory diseases: 100.4 / 43.2
- Cerebrovascular disease: 76 / 46.6
- Influenza and pneumonia: 57.6 / 20.3
- Intentional self-harm (suicide): 18.2 / 10.9

■ Pine Ridge Indian Reservation (Shannon County, South Dakota)   ■ United States of America

Source: South Dakota Vital Statistics (2007).

A recent longitudinal study on health and poverty on the Reservation found that health problems place a significant demand on the limited resources of households (Pickering and Mizushima, 2007). The Lakota people interviewed for the study described ill health as a tremendous burden, and about 1 in 5 reported personal or family health conditions as a reason why a job had ended. Access to health care is very limited, resulting in extensive use of unpaid family care, which limits opportunities for wage employment. Only 7 per cent of households report having health insurance. The study also found that Indian Health Services, a severely underfunded federal agency, is the only source of health care for 90 per cent of the Reservation's population.

---

a See www.lakotafunds.org.

a different ethnic origin as a neighbour, 24 per cent of them would feel uncomfortable having a Roma as a neighbour.

It is sometimes noted that, while racism and discrimination directed towards ethnic minority groups in Europe is widely seen as offensive and unacceptable, racism towards the Roma is often seen as justified. The media as well as local and national politicians fuel the prejudices of the population at large.

Roma face wide-ranging and mutually reinforcing inequalities. They have shorter life expectancy, experience poorer health, and are less likely to receive health care than the population at large. Children have a lower educational attainment and are highly unlikely to enrol in secondary schools owing to discrimination and abuse from fellow students and teachers alike. Disaffected Roma youth are more likely to suffer from substance abuse and have higher rates of suicide and criminalization at a young age.

Insecure accommodation remains a severe problem, with continuing cycles of eviction associated with homelessness among caravan-dwelling Roma, some of whom do not have access to the due process needed to challenge the evictions. To avoid evictions, Roma families often find accommodation in the most neglected areas, facing, in consequence, not only environmental disadvantages but also hostility from neighbours.

Gender and poverty: multiple and multiplied discriminations

Women experience structural exclusion in societies that perceive them as inferior and subordinate to men. In developing and developed countries alike, a disproportionate number of women experience relative poverty. Social exclusion of women in some societies is related to several factors, including their marital, health or employment status. The unequal possession of power and ownership of resources result in a greater risk of poverty among women.

Women are overrepresented among people living in poverty and suffer from exclusion from basic education, landownership and employment. It has been argued, however, that although anti-poverty policies focusing on women are often seen as attaining development objectives, they may not be very effective in tackling gender-related issues because the subjugation of women is not caused by poverty alone. That is why equality issues should be considered in development programming (Jackson, 1996).

Social exclusion of women is linked to the cultural perceptions of their role and potential contribution to society. The social exclusion perspective compels us to look beyond gender gaps in education and health. Voice and participation are vital and the cultural perceptions of women that keep them in subordinate status need to be challenged. Creating the conditions that allow women to demand change and influence priorities of State institutions is vital if gender equality and the empowerment of women are to be advanced.

Gender identities leading to specific outcomes need to be examined as well. For instance, in many South Asian countries, there is a high mortality among girls, who are subject to aggressive neglect, not to mention foeticide and infanticide. To understand the causes of this phenomenon, a comprehensive analysis of gender identities and relations over the life course is required, exploring forms of marriage exchange and the gendered hierarchies within belief systems (Jackson, 2002).

It is often argued that the best way to address women's poverty is to improve women's citizenship status. Since they lack political and economic resources, it is more difficult for women than for men to overcome poverty. For example, it has been noted that the call in India for citizenship for women should entail a shift in focus: rather than a concentration on women as poor people, there should be a study of the processes that relegate women to a secondary place in Indian society.

In South Asia, social exclusion issues often relate also to ethnicity and caste. The Hindu caste system in India and Nepal, as well as caste-like identities in Pakistan, "exclude lowest caste groups from ownership of land and key productive assets and assign them to various forms of labour and services which are considered to be menial, degrading and dirty" (Kabeer, 2006b, p. 9). There are major differences in respect of poverty by caste and ethnic group. For instance, per capita household consumption in the highest castes is 42 per cent larger than in a Dalit household (a Dalit is a member of the lowest caste). In India, 54 per cent of children among the Dalits were underweight as compared with 44 per cent in the rest of the population. The infant mortality rate was 83 per 1,000 live births compared with 68 per 1,000 live births for the rest of the population. In addition, under-five child mortality was 119 per 1,000 live births, compared with 92 per 1,000 live births for the rest of the population (ibid., also see box IV.2).

Moreover, in India, people living in poverty in urban areas are often trapped in patron-client relations with a broker (*mastaan*) who manages shelter and key services and charges for water, electricity and protection. Those patrons also manage the links to jobs for migrants and the urban poor (Mosse, 2007). Such oppressive social relations perpetuate poverty and exclusion.

Box IV.2
Dalit women: exclusion and violence

Dalit women in India are at the bottom of India's caste, class and gender social structure and their situation constitutes an extreme case of *active exclusion*. They suffer from endemic gender and caste discrimination, violence and exploitation. Pervasive violence against Dalit women in India is the core result of gender-based inequalities enforced and intensified by the caste system. Despite constitutional guarantees of non-discrimination on the basis of caste and gender as well as a series of laws aimed at protecting Dalits, discrimination, exploitation and violence continue. The societal acceptance of discrimination directed against caste, class, community and family is at the root of the persistence of the problem.

A study examining the forms and manifestations of violence against Dalit women in India revealed that they endure violence in the community and in the family, from state and non-state actors. Forms of violence include physical assault, verbal abuse, sexual harassment and assault, rape, sexual exploitation, forced prostitution, kidnapping and abduction, forced incarceration and medical negligence regarding female foeticide and infanticide, child sexual abuse and domestic violence from family members.

Exploitation built into the caste system often relates to economic resources, including land, wages and payment for services. Violence is especially pronounced when Dalit women try to assert their right to own or utilize resources or protest against forced labour or challenge working conditions; for example, Dalit women provoked violence when they asserted their right to access housing and services (Irudayam, Mangubhai and Lee, 2006).

Migrants and migration: aspirations and exclusions

Migration, social exclusion and the impact on poverty and inequality

For some poor people, migration can be a practical strategy for escaping poverty. However, migrants in the industrialized world face compounded forms of discrimination in the labour market, and in access to housing and services. Migrants from ethnic minorities face even greater disadvantages. Many migrants have no or very restricted work permits, making them highly dependent on employers and causing them to live in constant fear of losing their jobs and/ or being deported. Their qualifications often go unrecognized. Undocumented migrants are especially affected by social exclusion and discrimination, as they have no access to any social services. They suffer from acute civil disenfranchisement combined with legal disempowerment. Such exclusions undermine migrants' capacity to escape poverty through migration, implying the weakening of potential positive gains for the migrants themselves, for their families at home, and for their communities and countries of origin.

Voluntary migration, both international and internal, allows migrants to save and, in many cases, to remit part of their earnings home. Existing evidence suggests that remittances contribute to household welfare. They are often used for the consumption of basic subsistence goods, including food, but they have also been found to encourage investments in education, health and other productive spending (Ghosh, 2006; United Nations, 2005b). Because they tend to be counter-cyclical, remittances can protect families from income shocks during economic crises and help migrant households spread income risks. In general, households with migrants have a higher propensity than non-migrant households to save and invest.

Remittances often alleviate the hardship of poverty, but they rarely allow for significant accumulation or foster upward economic mobility. For internal, seasonal and temporary migrants in particular, migration is simply a coping strategy for combating extreme economic vulnerability and does not constitute a consistent way out of poverty. At the aggregate level, the existing evidence suggests that the impact of migration and remittances on poverty reduction is positive but generally small in magnitude (Acosta and others, 2007; Ghosh, 2006).

However, migration does not necessarily reduce income inequalities across households or regions. While some studies suggest that highly skilled and richer migrants are less likely to remit than unskilled migrants, the amount remitted increases with earnings.[2] Most of the existing evidence indicates that transfers by internal migrants, who generally come from poorer households than those of international migrants, tend to reduce income inequalities, while international remittances tend to increase them (King and Vullnetari, 2003;

---

2 For a summary of the findings on the impact of remittances on urban rural disparities, see Jones (1998). For findings on their impact on inequalities among households, see Taylor, Mora and Adams (2005) and Black, Natali and Skinner (2006).

McKenzie and Rapoport, 2007; Adams, Cuecuecha and Page, 2008). Thus, the overall effect of migration on inequality depends on the composition of migrant flows and on the propensity of each group to remit.

Most evidence on the relationship between migration and poverty, however, is based on one single snapshot of the migrant population. There are few longitudinal studies of the dynamics between migration and poverty, from the time of the departure of migrants to that of their eventual return. Descriptive studies of migrants' journeys suggest that migrants probably endure frequent spells of poverty along the way. The costs of migrating, that is to say, the funds (and goods) that go with migrants when they leave, and that go to them from their origin countries or regions afterwards, are rarely taken into account when assessing the impact of migration and remittances on those left behind.

Central to the outcomes of migration are the actions of a variety of political, economic and social institutions that determine the extent to which migrants can integrate successfully in the region or country of destination. For international migrants, key in this regard are government policies and the social and economic conditions in the host society.

Policies determine the status of migrants in the host society, their human and labour rights, whether they are entitled to social protection, whether discriminatory practices are sanctioned, whether they can maintain their cultural traditions and practice their religion, etc. As labour migration policies are becoming increasingly selective both in developed countries and in the main receiving countries of the developing world (favouring highly skilled migrants), migrants with low skills have very limited legal access to labour markets: most are allowed in only as temporary or seasonal workers. Currently, temporary programmes are far too narrow to meet the domestic demand for migrant labour and to then create space for a continued flow of irregular entries, stays and employment. In general, these policies fluctuate with economic conditions, becoming less receptive during economic downturns.

In the EU labour market, foreigners face limitations in taking on self-employment and are barred from certain jobs, including most public sector jobs. Regarding employment security, few foreigners can expect the forms of protection enjoyed by national workers if they lose their job: only selected groups of long-term migrants in European countries have access to unemployment benefits (Taran and others, 2009). In some countries, work and residence permits are combined, so that losing a job means losing the right to reside in the country. As educational credentials and skills acquired abroad, particularly in developing countries, are rarely recognized, migrants often fill jobs for which they are overqualified. In 10 countries studied by OECD, for instance, nearly 50 per cent of all skilled foreigners were found to be unemployed, non-active or confined to jobs for which they were overqualified[3] (Organization

---

3 Where they do exist, concerted placement and adaptation policies have shown positive results. In Canada, where the Immigrant Settlement and Adaptation Program (ISAP) assists

for Economic Cooperation and Development, 2008b). Similarly, unemployment levels are higher among migrants than among natives in most developed countries. For OECD, the gap between migrant and native unemployment exceeds 10 percentage points in Finland, the Czech Republic, the Netherlands, Norway and Switzerland. In Austria, Belgium, the Netherlands and Switzerland, the proportion of migrants among the unemployed is twice their proportion in the active population (Organization for Economic Cooperation and Development, 2007).

The granting of nationality is the most important policy measure for the social integration of international migrants, as it ensures full membership in the country of residence; however, it is not a sufficient condition for social inclusion. In many receiving countries, individuals of migrant origin—regardless of their citizenship status—endure more deficits in well-being and exclusions than do natives of comparable educational level in the form of unemployment or underemployment, insecure income, denial of rights at work, discrimination, inadequate social protection, lack of social mobility, etc. (Stalker, 2000; International Organization for Migration 2008; Taran and others, 2009). In Spain, for instance, more than 50 per cent of foreign-born workers had temporary work contracts in 2006, as compared with 25 per cent of the native population (Organization for Economic Cooperation and Development, 2007).

Similarly, the situation of internal migrants, whose status is not influenced by citizenship laws, is often not comparable to that of non-migrants.[4] In the urban areas of many developing countries, for instance, internal migrants are poorer and more often employed in unskilled manual jobs than urban natives of similar educational levels (Roig and Singelmann, 2009).

Where they exist, such well-being deficits have long-lasting effects. In Europe, most research has found that children of immigrant parents (the so-called second generation) have an educational attainment that is below that of native children of comparable family background and are more often unemployed.[5] However, results differ by country and by group, with some groups of immigrant children systematically underachieving and a few doing as well as natives. Historically, these differences have been attributed to differences in social capital, values and skills and to residential segregation.

---

migrants in searching for jobs and provides job-specific training and job placement, up to 75 per cent of immigrants with a university degree were working in jobs that required more than a high school diploma in 2005 (Migration News, 2005).

4 Internal migrants usually enjoy the same political and social rights as non-migrants, but there are some who do not. Most notable are those in China affected by its household registration (*hukou*) system, according to whose rules individuals wishing to change their place of residence must obtain approval from the authorities. Those who move without registering have no access to public services, including health, education or housing, at subsidized prices.

5 For a summary of research on the second generation in Europe, see Crul and Vermeulen (2003) and Organization for Economic Cooperation and Development (2008a).

Social networks affect opportunities and perceptions. In certain contexts, migrants and their children may perceive that the paths to social mobility available to them are limited, and that such paths as do exist do not require educational credentials. Inherited cultural values influence such perceptions, as well as the social and economic contexts that migrants and their children find themselves in. Because of discrimination, education may actually be a less valuable asset for some groups.

Discrimination plays an important role in maintaining segmentation in the labour market and contributes to the relegation of certain groups to certain sectors of the labour force. The pressures of higher unemployment rates among immigrants and their children make them less prone to unionize, especially in sectors with precarious and non-standard forms of employment.

Finally, residential segregation is the outcome of a natural tendency for spatial concentration of ethnic or national communities after arrival but also of discrimination in the housing markets and, sometimes, of deliberate housing policies. For migrants, spatial clustering can be beneficial initially, as it can give rise to successful ethnic enclave economies. However, in the long term, spatial segregation, often into isolated and substandard residential areas, prevents the contact and interaction that facilitate familiarity, mutual understanding and upward social mobility.

Patterns of mobility and settlement have been quickly evolving. Improved travel and communication systems permit more frequent mobility (the terms "circular migration" and "repeat migration" are often used) and the maintenance and expansion of transnational networks. The fact that migrants increasingly maintain multiple social and economic ties that transcend borders and sometimes keep dual citizenship—from the home and host countries—can be beneficial not just to migrants but also to the home and host countries. However, the emergence of these patterns is often a consequence of restrictions to settlement in the host country and of policy approaches based on economic and social exclusion, which leave migrants no choice but to move between societies that reject them (Pecoud, 2006, p. 63). All in all, these evolving patterns pose new challenges and bring new imperatives for integration.

International migrants and the current economic crisis

Between 2000 and 2008, several countries with booming economies eased restrictions to legal immigration and expanded immigrants' rights. Spain's 2005 extraordinary regularization process, for instance, granted work permits to some 650,000 previously undocumented foreign workers (Arango and Jachimowicz, 2005). For the first time, the programme was designed by consensus among employer organizations, unions and immigrant organizations. In 2004, the United Kingdom of Great Britain and Northern Ireland started to grant immediate access to the labour market to nationals from the new member States of the EU, thereby regularizing the situation of more than half a million Eastern Europeans (Migration Policy Institute, 2008).

The current economic downturn has made many destination countries less open to the welcoming of migrants, with some of those countries expressing remorse over earlier policies and adapting them to economic circumstances. In 2008, Spain announced a voluntary return programme which would give unemployed legal resident migrants compensation for leaving Spain and agreeing not to return for three years. Spain, the United Kingdom, Australia and other developed countries have announced that they will issue few new immigrant visas in 2009.

In general, migrant workers are hardest hit during economic downturns both because of their characteristics—they are, on average, younger and more recent entrants to the labour market, have less work experience in the host country and hold less stable contracts—and because the sectors in which they are employed—construction, manufacturing, hospitality services—suffer early and heavy job losses during recessions. Existing evidence suggests that the current downturn is no exception: between 2000 and 2007, the unemployment rate of non-EU nationals in the European Union was, on average, five percentage points above that of nationals. In the third quarter of 2008, the gap in unemployment rates had increased to eight percentage points (European Commission, 2009). In the United States, the unemployment rate rose from 4.3 per cent in the third quarter of 2007 to 6.3 per cent in the third quarter of 2008 among Mexican immigrants, and from 4.5 to 7.0 per cent among other Central American immigrants, while it increased from 4.8 to 5.3 per cent among all workers (Kochhar, 2008).

As a result, remittance flows to developing countries are likely to decline. The World Bank (2009f) projects a decline of 5-8 per cent in the volume of remittances between 2008 and 2009. According to the Bank, remittances from developing countries such as South Africa, Malaysia and India as well as from the Russian Federation are especially vulnerable to the crisis.

In many cases, the visa status of migrants ties them to a specific employer. Returning to the home country is the only alternative to performing undocumented work if they lose their job. However, few migrants return home during economic downturns, since the financial cost of returning is high and they may face bleaker economic prospects in their country of origin. In addition, there is no guarantee that they would be able to return to the host country if the economic circumstances at home were not tolerable.[6] The loss of employment is likely to have more devastating effects among less skilled foreign workers, given that many of them are not eligible for benefits. In the United States, for instance, the 1996 welfare reform law ended federal fund-

---

6 In Western Europe, migrants originating in new Eastern European member States have so far been the most responsive to the economic crisis (*New York Times*, 2009; Papademetriou, Sumption and Somerville, 2009). Eastern Europeans require no visa to work in other countries of the EU and they face no barriers to returning to the host country in the future.

ing for benefits to immigrants who had been in the country for less than five years; in most states, migrants who lose their jobs have very limited public support. Spain, the United Kingdom and other European countries do not allow access to unemployment or social security benefits to certain categories of migrants or to those coming from certain countries.[7] Unless they can rely on the support of family members or return home, they are at high risk of falling into poverty. The knowledge that many migrants cannot afford to go without employment can also make them more vulnerable to exploitation by employers.

The severity of the current economic crisis is quite unique; thus, the significance of historical comparisons might be limited. Nonetheless, historical evidence from the United States suggests that changes in the volume of legal migration flows following recessions, starting with the Great Depression of 1929, appear to be mostly the result of policy changes rather than a response to the economic conditions (Papademetriou and Terrazas, 2009). In contrast, estimates of irregular migration flows in recent years show a strong correlation with economic conditions. Such evidence also indicates that stricter enforcement of immigration laws to curb irregular migration has often forced undocumented migrants into increasingly informal and precarious employment situations and has further isolated them from the host society.

Exclusion's many other forms

Social exclusion is endemic and assumes many other forms. Four major spheres where social exclusion prevails demand special emphasis. The first encompasses the hidden world of disability. Persons with disabilities have been said to constitute approximately one tenth of the world's population, and based on more inclusive definitions, they could very well represent a significantly higher proportion. The world of disability is a socially constructed domain of exclusion and reflects persisting societal bias. A second sphere, steadily widening its contours, is that of ageing, with older persons all too often being relegated to invisibility—and with distressing consequences as age and disability begin to overlap, as they inexorably do in later life. The third sphere is that of statelessness, where communities of displaced persons, often already marked for social exclusion, are expelled from their homes and barred from the security of citizenship. The fourth sphere is that of sexuality, where cultural biases exclude and oppress. Regrettably, further reflection could extend this list.

---

7 For more specific information on access to services and other migration-related policies, see the International Labour Organization good practices on labour migration database (http://www.ilo.org/dyn/migpractice/migmain.home), and Labour migration policy index: phase II, report prepared for the Business Advisory Board to the International Organization for Migration (Oxford, Oxford Analytica, 1 October 2008).

Conclusion

The concept of social exclusion contributes to an understanding of the nature of poverty and helps identify the causes of poverty that may have been otherwise neglected. It also encourages deeper thinking on the subject of social policies for reducing poverty. When society is viewed through the lens of social exclusion, the processes imposing deprivation that form part of the fabric of that society can be isolated.

Fighting exclusion and fostering social cohesion are a prerequisite for poverty reduction and constitute a no less important priority. The value of the social exclusion approach lies in its focus on the social relations that engender deprivation. Such processes include some groups and exclude others, and have economic and political, social and cultural dimensions. Social inclusion is a question of rights—both individual and group rights.

Not only is neglecting social exclusion unethical, but the consequences of such neglect may range from petty crime to open conflict. A social exclusion perspective posits that the collective good or the needs of individuals will not be fulfilled if matters are left to private initiative alone: purposeful action is needed. Social exclusion involves issues of inequality, respect and recognition, and social policy may itself be an exclusionary mechanism. The root causes of exclusion and its consequences are varied and complex, and causative factors range from specific features of social structures to the growth of single parenthood and the break-up of traditional family structures.

Governments alone cannot eliminate exclusion, which is often the reality lived by those who experience poverty: people themselves may have to reclaim their place in society. While the responsibility for fighting exclusion lies with entities at different levels of society, including grass-roots organizations and non-governmental actors, it may be argued that the imposition of collective solutions, such as universal access to education, would eliminate the need to target those who are excluded. There is in any case an urgent need to look at processes and relations and cultural transformation of norms and expectations, which reveal that, ultimately, there are many ways to describe exclusion.

Chapter V
Macroeconomic policies and poverty reduction

Poverty, in all its complex dimensions, is a condition with a social and economic context and poverty reduction (or the lack thereof) always occurs within a macroeconomic context. History shows that high rates of economic growth sustained over a period of time are necessary for poverty reduction, while the distribution of the benefits of growth determines the impact on poverty. The macroeconomic policy framework often sets the parameters for social policies by defining the policy and fiscal space for government action. The following analysis focuses on macroeconomic policies and how they influenced poverty reduction in the past.

For two and a half decades starting from the end of the Second World War, Governments of the industrialized countries, through active reflationary macroeconomic management, achieved rapid reconstruction and prosperity underpinned by full employment and low inflation. Governments in developing countries also played a very active role in promoting economic growth and structural change after independence from colonial powers was gained. Developing countries as a group experienced impressive economic growth and structural change within their economies. Industry was the fastest-growing sector, resulting in a rapid rise in industry's share of gross domestic product (GDP) in "virtually all the developing economies" (World Bank, 1978).[1] However, there were variations among developing countries; growth and structural

---

[1] In recognition of this achievement, the General Assembly designated the 1960s as the First United Nations Development Decade (see Assembly resolution 1710 (XVI) of 19 December 1961). Reviewing the performance of the developing countries over 25 years (1950-1975), the *World Development Report 1978* (World Bank, 1978) noted:

> The developing countries have grown impressively over the past 25 years: income per person has increased by almost 3 per cent a year, with the annual growth rate accelerating from about 2 per cent in the 1950s to 3.4 per cent in the 1960s ... Moreover, it compared extremely favourably with growth rates achieved by the now developed countries over the period of their industrialization: income per person grew less than 2 per cent a year in most of the industrialized nations of the West over the 100 years of industrialization (p. 3).

The *Report* also noted:

> The Progress made by developing countries is more impressive considering that their populations have been growing at historically unprecedented rates. During 1950-1975, their total population increased at 2.4 per cent a year. This is substantially faster than the population growth rates—typically about 1 per cent a year—that the now developed countries had to contend with during the period of their industrialization (pp. 4-5).

change in most low-income countries in Africa and Asia, where the majority of the world's poor live, were slow.

Despite impressive economic growth, progress in the quality of life was slow. About 40 per cent of the population in developing countries—or nearly 800 million people—remained in absolute poverty. The situation had become difficult in the 1970s for most developing countries with the breakdown of the Bretton Woods system of fixed exchange rates and the oil price shocks. Industrialized countries faced stagflation caused mainly by those shocks. The countries that borrowed recycled petrodollars[2] from commercial banks faced debt crises in the 1980s when interest rates were raised sharply in the United States of America and the United Kingdom of Great Britain and Northern Ireland to control inflation. Only a few economies withstood the rigours of the difficult international economic environment and continued to grow rapidly.

These developments in the 1970s and 1980s served as a catalyst for an ideological shift in terms of macroeconomic policy and the role of the State, which meant the retreat of the Keynesian compact whereby Governments played a significant role in economic stabilization. The hallmark of this shift has been smaller government, its functions confined to the realm of property rights, law and order and maintenance of macroeconomic stability, identified with low inflation and balanced government budgets.

The contrasting experiences of Latin America and East Asia in the 1980s provided the context within which the dominating macroeconomic policy prescriptions evolved. Many key Latin American countries experienced high inflation, recession or slow growth, and unsustainable fiscal deficits with money creation. They suffered from the inefficient and protectionist policy of import substituting industrialization and ultimately failed to reduce poverty. In contrast, fiscally prudent East Asian countries experienced low inflation, outward-oriented industrialization, robust growth and sustained declines in poverty. This experience combined with the demise of the Soviet Union and the embracing by Eastern Europe of the market economy reinforced the ideological supremacy of neoclassical economics.

It was in this atmosphere that a series of economic policies were formulated by several Washington, D.C.–based institutions such as the World Bank, the International Monetary Fund (IMF) and the United States Department of the Treasury. This so-called Washington Consensus promoted the idea of sound monetary policy and fiscal prudence as the pillars of macroeconomic policy and argued the case for privatization and limited government, extolling as well the virtues of globalization, epitomized by free trade and unrestricted capital movements (Williamson, 1990). Achievement of low inflation and balanced budgets (and, later, opening of the capital account) became the core

---

2 Deposits in Western banks by oil exporting countries, which enjoyed revenue windfalls from the oil price hikes.

conditionalities in the IMF rescue packages as the World Bank pursued structural adjustment (trade liberalization, financial deregulation and privatization) through loan agreements.

The present chapter offers a critical evaluation of the impact of the macroeconomic policy framework of the Washington Consensus on growth and poverty reduction. The evaluation of structural adjustment programmes (economic liberalization) is the theme of chapter VI. After assessing the impacts of macroeconomic policies on economic growth, poverty and inequality, the chapter will review the underlying reasons for the outcomes and then offer an alternative framework for pro-poor macroeconomic policies aimed at achieving employment creation with price stability.

Growth performance

If growth was undermined by the high inflation generated by macroeconomic instability and the protectionism driven by statism, the elimination of these obstacles should have unleashed the energies of the private sector in full force and economic growth should have accelerated. However, that has not happened: "Economic growth rates in those countries that adopted the 'stabilize, liberalize, and privatize' agenda has turned out to be low not only in absolute terms, but also relative to other countries that were reluctant reformers and relative to the reforming countries' own historical experience" (Rodrik, 2004, pp. 1-2). The World Bank (2005, p. 95) notes:

> Macroeconomic policies improved in a majority of developing countries in the 1990s, but the expected growth benefits failed to materialize, at least to the extent that many observers had forecast. In addition, a series of financial crises severely depressed growth and worsened poverty ... [B]oth slow growth and multiple crises were symptoms of deficiencies in the design and execution of the pro-growth reform strategies that were adopted in the 1990s with macroeconomic stability as their centrepiece.

In Latin America, after radical reforms had been pursued, mostly under IMF/World Bank stabilization and structural adjustment programmes, growth performance did not even begin to match the performance achieved when Governments exerted tight control over the economy (table V.1).[3] Most of the transition economies of Eastern Europe experienced modest or negative growth rates following the Washington Consensus–inspired reforms and macroeconomic policies.

---

3 In the 1990s, Argentina pursued International Monetary Fund (IMF) and World Bank programmes strictly. However, the unemployment rate soared from 6.5 per cent in 1991 to over 17 per cent in 1995 and the number of people living in poverty increased from 22 per cent in 1993 to over 27 per cent in 1995, as the Gini coefficient (a conventional measure of inequality) rose from 0.45 in 1992 to 0.47 in 1995.

Table V.1
Decadal GDP growth performance of developing regions, 1960-2000 (*percentage*)

Region	1960-1970	1970-1980	1980-1990	1990-2000
East Asia *minus* China	6.4	7.6	7.2	5.7
South Asia	4.2	3.0	5.8	5.3
Latin America	5.5	6.0	1.1	3.3
Africa	5.2	3.6	1.7	2.3

Source: Bosworth and Collins (2003).

South Asia's performance appears respectable owing mainly to growth acceleration in India beginning in the 1980s. Despite the general belief that its growth acceleration could be attributed to the liberalization of 1991, India's take-off actually began a decade earlier, during the early 1980s and under heavy protectionism (Rodrik, 2004). The stellar performance of East Asia cannot be attributed to the conventional policies. Instead, its varied policies can best be described as reflecting market pragmatist heterodoxy (see Chang, 2006, chaps. 1-3).

Private investment has also been adversely affected by the orthodox macroeconomic policy framework of the past three decades geared, among other things, to achieving low single-digit inflation rates. This policy priority typically required a high-interest-rate regime. Furthermore, financial sector deregulation and the opening of the capital account of the balance of payments usually involved high real interest rates (see chap. VI). Hence, such macroeconomic policy and economic liberalization have constrained domestic private investment (United Nations Conference on Trade and Development, 2006).

What role did the macroeconomic policy mix play in a disappointing growth performance?

A number of growth-retarding factors which resulted from the macroeconomic policy mix can be identified, including (*a*) declines in public investment and (*b*) growth volatility.

There have been precipitous declines in public investment since the early 1980s in both Latin America and Africa, the two regions which experienced growth slowdowns. Public investments have generally declined in Latin America since the debt crisis starting from around 1982, while the collapse in sub-Saharan Africa during the early and mid-1980s was reversed slightly before the decline continued, more gradually, in the 1990s (International Monetary Fund, 2004). The declines in public investment were the direct result of excessive emphasis on the attainment of balanced budgets with little regard for the composition of government expenditure. In most cases, the budget was brought to a balance or surplus by cutting public investment rather than by raising taxes. Cuts in non-discretionary expenditure, such as public sector salaries or subsidies, were also avoided because of the political sensitivity involved.

The countries of those regions did not opt to raise taxes, as many faced significant problems with regard to tax administration. The IMF/World Bank programmes and policy advice improved the efficiency of tax administration but have done little to help raise tax revenues and have tended to result in the reduction of direct taxation in favour of indirect taxation. The removal of trade-related taxes with trade liberalization and various tax incentives to attract foreign investors have seriously eroded the fiscal space for many developing countries, as the declines in revenue were not compensated for by the expected increases in indirect consumption-based taxes, such as the value-added tax (VAT) (see chap. VI). Thus, developing countries were faced with the difficult task of improving their fiscal balances while their revenues were falling. The situation was made worse by the fact that declines in public investment were not matched by increases in private investment, as had been hoped.

Reviewing the situation, an IMF report (International Monetary Fund, 2004, p. 3), prepared in consultation with the World Bank and the Inter-American Development Bank, noted:

> The share of public investment in GDP, and especially the share of infrastructure investment, has declined during the last three decades in a number of countries, particularly in Latin America. Since the private sector has not increased infrastructure investment as hoped for, significant infrastructure gaps have emerged in several countries. These gaps may adversely affect the growth potential of the affected countries and limit targeted improvements in social indicators.

The report also acknowledges that fiscal analysis and policy, which focus on overall fiscal balance and gross public debt, may have unduly constrained the ability of countries to take advantage of increased opportunities to finance high-quality infrastructure projects. Research at the Inter-American Development Bank found that public investment in infrastructure in the period 1987-2001 was negatively affected by IMF adjustment loans, while debt increases were associated with higher public infrastructure investment (Lora, 2007).

The agricultural sector has suffered most from declines in public investment, as public spending in agriculture plummeted across developing countries in recent years (Akroyd and Smith, 2007). In Africa, public spending on agriculture fell from 6.4 per cent of total public spending in 1980 to 5 per cent in 2004; in Asia, total public spending in agriculture fell from 14.8 to 7.4 per cent, while Latin America witnessed a decline from 8 to 2.7 per cent over the same period (International Labour Organization, 2008, p. 22).

Growth volatility

A growing body of empirical research finds a robust negative cross-country relationship between growth and volatility and a significant negative correlation between growth and medium-term business cycle fluctuations (Kroft and Lloyd-Ellis, 2002; Aysan, 2007). One of the causes of increased output growth volatility has been pro-cyclical macroeconomic policy aimed at price stability and fiscal balance. It is well known that macroeconomic policies targeting price stability cause excessive fluctuations in output as the burden of adjustment falls on only one variable (output). Most developing countries are prone to supply shocks owing to their high dependence on agriculture and imported energy; and output fluctuations are greater when macroeconomic policies remain focused on price stability in the face of such shocks (Walsh, 2000).

Focusing on price stability is supposed to create favourable conditions for private investment, capital inflows and exports, which should spur growth. Thus, the decline in output and employment is supposed to be short-lived. This belief was behind the advice of IMF given to Indonesia to raise interest rates and restrain Government expenditure at the height of the 1997-1998 crisis. As was the case for many other developing countries, Indonesia remained faithful to this policy framework even after it had left the IMF programme, and has continued to pursue contractionary monetary policy to contain inflation due to recent hikes in food and energy prices in international markets.[4]

Also, many developing countries do not have the policy space within which to implement counter-cyclical macroeconomic policies in response to shocks for two reasons. First, the requirement to keep budgets in balance forces them to cut expenditure during downturns as revenue falls. Second, countries with open capital accounts are not supposed to be able to simultaneously pursue an autonomous monetary policy and control the exchange rate while maintaining an open capital account. While all three actions are potentially feasible, only two are supposed to be possible at any point in time, though in practice, many countries pursue supposedly suboptimal combinations of the three policy objectives after being encouraged or forced to open their capital accounts.

Additionally, most developing countries do not have the resources or fiscal space within which to undertake large-scale counter-cyclical measures. As noted earlier, there have been significant reductions in trade-related revenues

---

4   In contrast, Bangladesh refused to follow the advice of IMF and other multilateral financial institutions to pursue contractionary monetary policy in order to rein in food and energy price-induced inflation, exacerbated by cyclone Sidr.

following trade liberalization in many developing countries in recent decades. Various incentives including tax exemptions and cuts aimed at attracting private investment have also reduced fiscal space by reducing government revenue.

Many low-income countries, especially in Africa, found their external indebtedness rising following trade liberalization. Their imports rose at a much faster rate than their exports; as a result, they faced serious balance-of-payments problems (see chap. VI). These countries were forced to borrow, either from international capital markets at high interest rates owing to their low credit rating, or from IMF with conditionalities attached. While the rising external debt seriously constrained their ability to pursue poverty-reducing developmental activities, the conditionalities of adjustment loans forced them to continue with the very policies that had led to their predicament in the first place.

In sum, declines in public investment and excessive growth volatility, which have had adverse impacts on the overall growth performance of many developing countries, especially in Latin America and Africa, and the transition economies of Eastern Europe and the Commonwealth of Independent States, were due to macroeconomic policy reforms. They have not only reduced both policy and fiscal space for the adoption of counter-cyclical policy measures designed to reduce output volatility, but also contributed to greater volatility, thus retarding growth. The stability of nominal macroeconomic variables, such as consumer price levels and the fiscal balance, has failed to generate the much-hoped-for private investment.

Impact on poverty and inequality

The disappointing growth performance obviously slowed poverty reduction. The rise in inequality further diminished the impact of growth on poverty reduction. There is a large body of literature that attributes this rise to globalization and structural adjustment programmes (see Goldberg and Pavcnik, 2007, for a survey). Other policies have also contributed to increased inequality.

Conservative monetary policy aimed at lowering inflation is supposed to be good for the poor. Since wage adjustments typically fall behind price rises, inflation reduces the real wage. Since most of the poor are wage earners, the income share of the poor in national income declines vis-à-vis that of profit earners. If there are any savings to be had, the poor mostly hold them in cash; but inflation reduces the real value of money holdings and if inflation is unanticipated, the poor will be harmed even more disproportionately, as they have weaker bargaining power and are generally less able to hedge against inflation.

However, there are a number of counter-arguments with respect to conservative monetary policy. If inflation reduces real wages, then employment should rise, creating more income-earning opportunities for workers. Therefore, the employment effect of inflation (creating more jobs because of lower labour costs) can outweigh the real-wage effect (lower income) on poverty. This is likely to be the case, as the inflation (real wage) elasticity of poverty is found to be significantly less than the output (employment) elasticity of poverty. For example, one IMF study using pooled data from a cross section of 85 countries found the inflation (real wage) elasticity of the income of the poor to be 0.03 compared with an output (employment) elasticity of 0.94 (Ghura, Leite and Tsangarides, 2002).

Furthermore, most of the poor are net debtors and inflation reduces the real value of their debt. Finally, as highlighted above, mainstream macroeconomic policy frameworks have increased the volatility of output and employment. Output variability has a negative impact on both poverty and inequality (see box V.1); poor, unskilled workers are the first to lose jobs and it takes much longer for the job market to recover than for output to increase.[5] Reductions in public expenditure on health, education and other social programmes that

---

Box V.1
Income instability and the people living in poverty

People living in poverty are more vulnerable to income swings; there is also an asymmetry between the poor and the non-poor in responding to positive and negative shocks. Empirical studies find that the bottom two income quintiles experience disproportionately greater suffering from volatile income swings (Breen and Garcia-Penalosa, 2005; Laursen and Mahajan, 2005). People living in poverty do not have diversified income sources, are less skilled and are less mobile both between sectors and spatially. Moreover, they have less access to credit and insurance markets, and depend more on public transfers and social services (Guillaumont Jeanneney and Kpodar, 2005).

The inability of people living in poverty to cope with negative shocks can result in a loss of human capabilities, which is difficult to reverse. Thomas and others (2004) have shown that poor families remove their children from school when family incomes fall suddenly. Income instability also impacts negatively on nutritional status, as necessary consumption cutbacks are made (Dercon, 2006). For a cross-section of Asian and non-Asian countries, greater income volatility, measured as the standard deviation of the growth rate of gross domestic product (GDP) per capita, had negative effects on health outcomes (Rahman and Aradhyula, 2007).

Furthermore, in many developing countries, even when official poverty rates are low, a large number of people remain vulnerable. They are often just above the poverty line, or "in absolute terms, on the edge of the poverty line, using the World Bank standard of $2 per day" (Birdsall, 2002, p. 8). A small shock to the economy, or mishaps such as adverse weather, illness in the family or the sudden death or incapacity of earning members of the family, can therefore push a significant number of people into poverty. Various estimates show that recent food and energy price hikes pushed over 100 million people into poverty (Islam and Buckley, 2009).

---

5 It is crucial to make a distinction between "output recession" (based on quarterly declines in GDP) and "labour market recession" (based on the evolution of real wages and employment). The latter usually takes much longer to recover from than the former. Historical evidence culled by Reinhart and Rogoff (2009), based on 14 cases, suggests that it took 4.8 years on average for the unemployment rate to revert to its pre-crisis level, though GDP returned to its pre-crisis level in 1.9 years.

are carried out in order to maintain fiscal balance also disproportionately affect the poor. This is especially true during economic downturns.

What concerns the poor is not the overall price level that the conservative monetary policy aims to control, but the prices of particular commodities or services that dominate their consumption basket. Thus, stabilization of prices of food and basic services such as health care, education and public transportation has much greater impacts on poverty reduction than the stabilization of overall inflation. Monetary policy, however, is not well suited for the task of stabilizing prices of goods and services in the poor's consumption basket. Instead, fiscal measures such as subsidies are needed.

The way forward

The way forward requires a fundamental shift away from the paradigm of the Washington-based institutions, or even the so-called post–Washington Consensus, to the kind of thinking that produced full employment with price stability following the Second World War. While policies will vary depending on particular country situations, some broad guidance from the experiences based on that thinking can be useful today.

Macroeconomic policies should strive for both short-run stability and long-term development. Therefore, public investment for building up infrastructure, technological capabilities and human resources is critical for growth and productive employment generation and, hence, for poverty reduction.

Public expenditure must also give priority to primary health care, universal basic education and human security—all of which are pro-poor. There is a substantial body of research on pro-poor budgets and the poverty alleviating effects of fiscal policy (Roy and Weeks, 2004; McKinley, 2004, 2008). Such an approach does not focus on government spending per se, but on whether government expenditure reduces poverty by disproportionately benefiting the poor relative to the non-poor (Osmani, 2005), explicitly linking macroeconomic policy with poverty reduction and human development.

Focusing on inflation and fiscal deficits alone reflects too narrow a view of stabilization. Therefore, stabilization needs to be defined more broadly to include stability of the real economy, with smoothened business cycles and reduced fluctuations of output, investment, employment and incomes. Achieving such stability of the real economy may require larger fiscal deficits and higher rates of inflation than prescribed by the conventional macroeconomic policy mix, especially in the face of economic shocks or natural calamities.

Much of the importance placed on fighting inflation today stems from the hyperinflation prevailing in several Latin American countries in the wake of the debt crises of the 1980s. Yet episodes of hyperinflation are historically rare and occur only in extreme economic and political circumstances. At the same time, there is no evidence that moderate inflation in the range of 10-15 per cent harms growth. Nor is there any convincing evidence that inflation necessarily accelerates to hyperinflation even if it exceeds 20 per cent.[6] Stabilization of the prices of food and other products that weigh heavily in the poor's consumption basket has a more favourable effect on poverty reduction than the stabilization of the overall price level or the consumer price index (CPI).

Broad-based stabilization policies that focus on the real economy can boost economic growth in several ways. They can respond better to sudden contractions in investment and output due to either external shocks or natural calamity-related supply shocks, which can have negative dynamic effects on a country's growth path. For example, a prolonged output decline in an emerging manufacturing sector will deter new investment and technological change and thereby seriously erode productive capacity and future efficiency. Labour-intensive small and medium-sized enterprises are the most adversely affected by such a prolonged and deep recession, as they depend mostly on internal finance and operate on very thin cash-flow margins. Broad-based stabilization policies can thus stop unemployment from rising sharply and persisting, thereby preventing deskilling and demoralization of the labour force.

In many developing countries, a large number of (middle-income) people remain vulnerable to poverty, as they live at the edge of the poverty line. A small shock can therefore push them into poverty. This can be prevented through broad-based stabilization policies which recognize the right to decent employment of every willing and able citizen, as well as the direct link between decent jobs and poverty. We hardly need a more poignant reminder than the current global financial and economic crisis to illustrate this point. Thus, the government must assume responsibility as an "employer of last resort",[7] through, inter alia, various job guarantee schemes, ranging from those keeping more employees than necessary in State-run enterprises to such programmes as provide (as in the United States) federal funding for employment in state and local governments. Finally, by reducing the variability of income and employment, broad-based stabilization policies also prevent inequality from rising and thus enhance the poverty-reducing effect of growth.

Therefore, broad-based stabilization policies that boost economic growth and increase per capita incomes can lead to faster poverty reduction. The poverty reduction impact of growth will be enhanced if growth can be made more equitable or pro-poor through careful design of public expenditure.

---

6   Studies find inflation could accelerate if it exceeds 35-40 per cent (see Bruno and Easterly, 1998; and Dornbusch and Fischer, 1993).

7   According to Beveridge (1944, p. 18), full employment "means having always more vacant jobs than unemployed (people), not slightly fewer jobs" and "that the jobs are at fair wages, of such a kind, and so located that the unemployed (people) can reasonably be expected to take them; it means, by consequence, that the normal lag between losing a job and finding another will be very short". For an analysis of the definition's applicability in developing countries, see Wray (2007).

This means *fiscal policy* must be dominant at *all* times, not just when monetary policy loses its effectiveness.[8] Recognizing that both the level and composition of government expenditure can have significant impacts on growth, poverty and inequality[9] means abandoning the narrow concept of "sound" finance measured by the debt/gross domestic product (GDP) ratio. Instead, the concept of "functional" finance, which evaluates government finance based on its impact, should be adopted.[10] From this perspective, a better measure of fiscal sustainability is the debt-servicing ratio ([principal + interest payments]/GDP), that is to say, debt will be sustainable if government expenditure is both productivity- and growth-enhancing. In other words, Governments still need to guard against unproductive expenditures.

Fiscal space: Owing to the volatile nature of aid (see box V.2) and the increased vulnerability to shocks, there has to be a renewed commitment to domestic resource mobilization in developing countries, which should also be seriously counter-cyclical by accumulating fiscal resources during boom periods and using such resources to finance expansionary policies or targeted interventions during downturns. The goal of a "stabilization fund" is to create the necessary fiscal space within which to sustain investments in human capital and basic infrastructure across business cycles and to scale up passive and active labour-market policies (such as job guarantee schemes) as well as social protection so as to minimize the impact of external shocks on poverty.

Monetary and exchange-rate policies should play a supportive role and accommodate the Government's need for development activities and counter-cyclical measures. This means more active coordination between fiscal and monetary authorities and a limiting of central bank independence.[11] Confi-

---

8   For example, in a situation like the current global crisis or the stagnation of Japan in the 1990s, many orthodox economists, including those at IMF and the World Bank, favour fiscal stimulus as the effectiveness of monetary easing hits its limit with interest rates hovering near zero (as was also the case during the stagnation of Japan in the 1990s). However, they consider this only a short-term measure until the monetary policy regains its effectiveness.

9   See Domar (1946). Domar (1944, pp. 801 and 804) notes the following:

> That deficit financing may have some effect on income ... has received a different treatment. Opponents of deficit financing often disregard it completely, or imply, without any proof, that income will not rise as fast as the debt ... There is something inherently odd about any economy with a continuous stream of investment expenditures and a stationary national income.

10   Lerner (1943, p. 39) notes:

> The central idea is that government fiscal policy, its spending and taxing, its borrowing and repayment of loans, its issue of new money and its withdrawal of money, shall all be undertaken with an eye only to the *results* of these actions on the economy and not to any established traditional doctrine about what is sound or unsound (italics in original).

11   Leaving aside technical arguments, a broader issue of democratic governance and technocratic insulation of institutions is at stake. Milton Friedman (1962, p. 219) noted that

Box V.2
Can aid ease fiscal constraints?

One of the rationales for foreign aid has been the need to ease financial constraints on the Government. Prior to the present crisis, official development assistance (ODA) flows to developing countries had risen after 2001 and then declined after 2005. In 2008, aid flows from Development Assistance Committee (DAC) donors increased again, reaching almost $120 billion, returning to a share of 0.3 per cent of donor countries' combined gross national income (GNI). This was still far less than the 0.7 per cent share of GNI agreed to in the 1960s and reiterated many times since, for example, at the International Conference on Financing for Development, held in Monterrey, Mexico, in March 2002.

ODA can play an important counter-cyclical role, provided such flows go up when the receiving country's economy slows and revenues decline, and thereby contribute to the country's long-term development. However, aid flows have been found to be generally pro-cyclical, and this pro-cyclicality is likely to recur during the current global crisis owing to the synchronized downturns in all economies. Even if donors maintain their aid shares of national income, the absolute amount of aid will fall owing to the decline of national incomes in most Organization for Economic Cooperation and Development (OECD) economies since late 2008.

An additional problem is the uncertainty of aid disbursement and associated volatility. Even before the current global financial and economic crisis, low-income countries, especially the least developed countries, had seen large fluctuations in annual aid flows of up to 2-3 per cent of GDP for the least developed countries as a group (see United Nations, Conference on the World Financial and Economic Crisis and Its Impact on Development, 2009, para. 23). Studies show that shortfalls in aid are frequently followed by reductions in government spending and sometimes by increases in taxes—and sometimes by both. In other words, the typical aid-receiving country is unable to offset an unexpected non-disbursement of aid by borrowing, and has to resort to costly, swift and, possibly, inefficient fiscal adjustment (see Buliř and Hamann, 2003, for a good survey of the issue).

An IMF assessment prior to the current crisis noted that the volatility of aid flows is likely to increase in the years ahead. One reason for this has been identified as the switch from project to programme aid. Programme aid flows tend to be more volatile than project aid, usually committed upfront and disbursed on a multi-year basis. Thus, it warns that:

"money is too important to be left to the central bankers". Friedman (1985, p. 8) elaborated his concerns as follows:

> Is it really tolerable in a democracy to have so much power concentrated in a body free from any direct political control?... One economic defect of an independent central bank... is that it almost invariably involves dispersal of responsibility... Another defect... is the extent to which policy is... made highly dependent on personalities... A third technical defect is that an independent central bank will almost invariably give undue emphasis to the point of view bankers... The defects I have outlined constitute a strong technical argument against an independent central bank.

Stern and Stiglitz (1996, p. 18) have made the point more succinctly:

> The degree of independence of the central bank is an issue of the balance of power in a democratic society. The variables controlled by the central bank are of great importance and thus require democratic accountability. At the same time, the central bank can act as a check on government irresponsibility. The most successful economies have developed institutional arrangements that afford the central bank considerable autonomy; but in which there is a check provided by public oversight, an oversight that ensures the broader national interest is taken into account in the final decisions.

> The development community runs the risk of slipping into a low-level equilibrium—that is, countries that budget prudently over the medium term would discount pledges of assistance; donors would then see fewer funding gaps, in turn causing aid commitments to fall behind intended increases or even in absolute terms. Signs of this happening are already evident, with many low-income countries discounting aid commitments in their plans (Eifert and Gelb, 2005, p. 1).
>
> Therefore, to reduce volatility in official financing and to allow developing countries to sustain long-term investments, the predictability of such financing should be enhanced through multi-annual agreements between donors and recipient countries, in line with the 2005 Paris Declaration on Aid Effectiveness and the 2008 Accra Agenda for Action on improving aid effectiveness.[a]
>
> There is a fierce debate about the effectiveness of aid in promoting growth and poverty reduction. Recent research has found a large positive effect of "developmental" aid on economic growth, but also arrived at contrary conclusions with regard to the importance of policy environment for diminishing returns to aid. Development aid yields positive impacts only in the long run, highlighting the importance of long-term commitment of donors (Minoiu and Reddy, 2007). From this perspective, donors' preference for programme aid over project aid in recent years has been detrimental, a conclusion similar to that of the IMF study cited above. Not only is the disbursement of programme aid less predictable, but it also comes with conditionalities which undermine national ownership of the development agenda.
>
> ---
> a The Paris Declaration on Aid Effectiveness, endorsed on 2 March 2005, is an international agreement to which over 100 ministers, heads of agencies and other senior officials adhered and through which they committed their countries and organizations to continue to increase efforts in harmonization, alignment and managing aid for results with a set of monitorable actions and indicators. The Accra Agenda for Action (document A/63/539, annex) was agreed in 2008 and builds on the commitments agreed in the Paris Declaration (see www.oecd.org/dac/effectiveness/parisdeclaration).

dence of the private sector in macroeconomic policies rests more on the credibility of the Government's commitment to counter-cyclical measures and long-term development than on having a fixed low inflation target, as the former reduces uncertainty about future profit expectations. While central banks can use the traditional instrument of interest rates (or instruments such as reserve requirements) to keep inflation moderate, specialized credit regulation can be a second instrument for effecting employment creation and poverty reduction.

Fully flexible or fixed exchange-rate regimes are inherently inferior, as they simply give up major macroeconomic policy objectives. In an open developing economy, the exchange-rate regime has to be both stable and flexible. The stability of exchange rates is needed to support growth-promoting and poverty-reducing trade and structural change. A stable exchange-rate regime is also needed for domestic price stability and to avert the wealth effects of exchange-rate fluctuations in the face of currency mismatches in portfolios. The demand for flexibility comes from the need to have some degree of freedom to manage trade and capital account shocks in order to minimize their adverse impacts on income, employment and poverty.

Policy space: In addition to managing exchange rates, monetary authorities should also actively manage the capital account in order to enhance the

Government's policy space. This will allow depreciation of the exchange rate and expansionary policies in response to external shocks, and thereby mitigate adverse impacts on poverty.[12] Capital account openness should not be viewed as entailing an all-or-nothing proposition. The increased importance of equity flows has widened the effective scope for capital account management. A capital account may be open to equity flows, especially for foreign direct investment (FDI), but closed to volatile short-term flows or to excessive external borrowings by the private sector.

---

12 Even the Bretton Woods institutions do not now look at capital account restrictions so unfavourably as they used to a decade or so ago. For example, on capital account liberalization, the World Bank (2009d, pp. 47-48) notes:
> Capital restrictions might be unavoidable as a last resort to prevent or mitigate the crisis effects. A few emerging countries have introduced capital controls and other measures to better monitor and, in some cases, limit the conversion of domestic currency into foreign exchange ... capital controls might need to be imposed as a last resort to help mitigate a financial crisis and stabilize macroeconomic developments.

Chapter VI
Economic liberalization and poverty reduction

Economic liberalization encompasses the processes, including government policies, that promote free trade, deregulation, elimination of subsidies, price controls and rationing systems, and, often, the downsizing or privatization of public services (Woodward, 1992). Economic liberalization has been central to adjustment policies introduced in developing countries since the late 1970s, mostly in the context of the conditions for lending set by international financial institutions. Thus, government policies were redirected to follow a non-interventionist, or laissez-faire, approach to economic activity, relying on market forces for the allocation of resources. It was argued that market-oriented policy reforms would spur growth and accelerate poverty reduction.

From this perspective, government intervention in markets is seen as both inefficient and distortionary. It is argued that even if an interventionist State acts with good intentions, it does not have the competence to manage the economy well. By moving scarce resources into less productive economic activities, the State is thought to reduce overall economic growth, with adverse consequences for poverty reduction.

Additionally, for public choice theory, rational, self-interested individuals maximize their economic benefits and overall economic welfare. In civic life, politicians, bureaucrats and citizens are all considered to act solely out of self-interest in the political arena. Politicians and State bureaucrats, acting from self-interest, use their power and the authority of the Government to engage in rent-seeking behaviour, which distorts the allocation of resources and results in disincentives for private investment and entrepreneurship (Buchanan, 1980). Therefore, the power of the State and political actors, including the ability to intervene in the economy, should be limited.

Within this framework, the State creates enabling conditions in the form of macroeconomic stability, guaranteeing property rights, and maintaining law and order for rapid economic growth driven by private sector (both domestic and foreign) investment. As economic growth rises, poverty will fall (Dollar and Kraay, 2002). Distribution and social justice benefit from the trickle-down principle, as economic growth will eventually benefit all members of society. The free market, based on comparative advantage, will thus bring about economic expansion through labour-intensive export activities, which will create employment and hence improve the general well-being of the entire society.

The present chapter critically evaluates the growth, employment and poverty impacts of three major elements of recent economic liberalization—trade liberalization, financial liberalization and privatization.

Trade liberalization

Trade and economic growth: the theory

Proponents of trade liberalization expect that removing trade barriers will lead to short-run or static welfare gains (or higher income levels) and in turn reduce poverty.[1] The gains from trade result from the fact that different countries are endowed with different resources (natural and acquired); hence, the opportunity cost of producing products varies from country to country. Opportunity cost is measured by the sacrifice (for example, in the production of one good) to produce *one extra unit* of another good, given that resources are scarce. Under trade protection, resources are concentrated in inefficient production in economic sectors that have high trade barriers. When barriers are removed, resources shift away from those inefficient sectors in which that country has no comparative advantage to the efficient sectors in which it does have a comparative advantage.

Gains from trade may not be distributed equitably and are determined by several factors, including the international rate of exchange between two goods, what happens to the terms of trade, and whether the full employment of resources is maintained as they are reallocated when countries specialize (see box VI.1). The closer the international rate of exchange is to a country's own internal rate of exchange, the less it will benefit from specialization and the more the other country will benefit. As Bhagwati (1958) has shown, in extreme circumstances, one country may become absolutely worse off if real resource gains from trade are offset by the decline in the terms of trade, a phenomenon that he called "immiserizing growth" (Bhagwati, 1958).

The problem for many developing countries is that the type of goods in which they will specialize under a free trade regime—namely, primary commodities—is likely to cause the terms of trade to deteriorate and may lead to an underutilization of their resources. First, primary commodities generally

---

[1] Neoclassical economic theory has long contended that trade enhances welfare and growth. In his *An Inquiry into the Nature and Causes of the Wealth of Nations* (1776), Adam Smith stressed the importance of trade as a vent for surplus production and as a means of widening the market, thereby improving the division of labour and the level of productivity. Smith maintained the following:

> Between whatever places foreign trade is carried on, they all of them derive two distinct benefits from it. It carries the surplus part of the produce of their land and labour for which there is no demand among them, and brings back in return something else for which there is a demand. It gives value to their superfluities, by exchanging them for something else, which may satisfy part of their wants and increase their enjoyments. By means of it, the narrowness of the home market does not hinder the division of labour in any particular branch of art or manufacture from being carried to the highest perfection. By opening a more extensive market for whatever part of the produce of their labour may exceed the home consumption, it encourages them to improve its productive powers and to augment its annual produce to the utmost, and thereby to increase the real revenue of wealth and society.

> **Box VI.1**
> **Trade liberalization and exports in Africa**
>
> According to proponents of trade liberalization, increased exports following trade liberalization will ensure higher rates of economic growth, beneficial for the poor. However, Africa's export performance following trade liberalization does not support such claims. While greater market access may well have led to the achievement of the expected results, trade liberalization resulted in the loss of tariff revenues, eroding fiscal space, and undermined existing productive capacities and capabilities.
>
> Most African countries have liberalized their trade regimes. Trade liberalization occurred principally from the late 1980s and in the 1990s, and involved the "tariffication" of non-tariff barriers, cuts in the number and value of tariffs, exchange-rate liberalization and removal of export barriers. Overall, export performance in African countries following trade liberalization has been disappointing. Indeed, although trade liberalization has increased exports expressed as a percentage of GDP, this effect has been weak, and trade balances in African countries have deteriorated since liberalization with greatly increased imports.
>
> Analysis of values and volumes of exports from Africa show that, following liberalization, African exports continued to grow at slower rates in volume terms than in other regions. Only the rising prices of fuels, minerals and other primary commodities since 2002 have maintained African export value growth at levels comparable with that in other developing regions.
>
> Export diversification is very low in Africa, an outcome consistent with the theory of comparative advantage. African countries remain principally primary commodity exporters, as dictated by their resource endowments. Thus, the dependence of most African countries on a small number of export products has increased following liberalization. Many countries in the region are now less able than before liberalization to withstand price collapses for a few key commodities.
>
> The main destinations for African exports do not appear to have been strongly affected by African countries' efforts to liberalize trade. Although there has been some diversification in the destinations of African exports, the declining importance of European countries as export markets seems to be part of longer-term trends in growth and demand, unrelated to trade liberalization. The greater importance of Asia as a market for African exports reflects strong growth in that region requiring African primary commodities, especially minerals. Recent changes in the share of African exports going to North America, meanwhile, have been driven mainly by determined United States efforts to diversify oil supplies and corporate investment in sub-Saharan Africa.
>
> Source: United Nations Conference on Trade and Development (2008).

have low prices and the demand for them does not rise as fast as income (low income elasticity of demand). As a result, when their supply increases, prices can drop dramatically, since demand grows only slowly with income growth. Secondly, primary commodity production is land-based and subject to diminishing returns,[2] and there is a limit to employment in activities subject to diminishing returns at a reasonable living wage.

By contrast, in manufacturing, no fixed factors of production are involved, and production may be subject to increasing returns. Thus, what is often ob-

---

2   When all inputs are increased proportionately, output does not increase by the same proportion. This happens in land-based activities as the availability of better-quality land diminishes. On the other hand, when output increases more than proportionately with proportionate increases of all inputs, this is described as increasing returns to scale.

served is a secular deterioration of the terms of trade for countries producing primary commodities vis-à-vis countries specializing in manufacturing (Ocampo and Parra, 2003). Therefore, in practice, for countries specializing in activities subject to diminishing returns, the real resource gains from specialization may be offset by the real income losses from unemployment.

Empirical studies do not point to significant employment generation due to trade liberalization.[3] Furthermore, according to a World Bank study, more than 70 per cent of gains from complete trade liberalization will accrue to rich countries, and more than two thirds of static gains to developing countries from complying with the outcomes of the Doha Round will go to big countries such as Argentina, Brazil and India in the case of agriculture and to China and Viet Nam in the case of textiles and garments (Anderson and Martin, 2005).

According to proponents of trade liberalization, the major reason for the rapid growth arising from trade liberalization is the dynamic gains from trade. The dynamic gains accrue from augmenting the availability of resources for production by increasing the quantity and productivity of resources. One of the major dynamic benefits of trade is that it widens the market for a country's producers. If production is subject to increasing returns, export growth becomes a source of continued productivity growth since there is also a close connection between increasing returns and capital accumulation. For a small country with no trade, there is very little scope for large-scale investment in advanced capital equipment, and specialization is limited by the extent of the market. Other important sources of dynamic benefits from trade include: stimulus to competition, acquisition of new knowledge and ideas and dissemination of technical knowledge, more FDI, and changes in attitudes and institutions.

Trade can raise productivity, however, if increasing returns to scale are dominant in the export sectors. If, instead, scale economies are more widespread in import-competing sectors which contract after liberalization, productivity gains will be limited. Another possibility is that protection increases inefficiency by drawing too many firms into sectors shielded from foreign competition. Liberalization brings about rationalization and increased productivity. This will occur, however, only if there is ease of entry and exit into markets. In reality, firms may remain in an industry for a long while after protection is lifted, thus limiting increases in productivity. Finally, if competition for export markets is intense, uncertainty may make firms reluctant to undertake new productivity-enhancing investments.

Empirical evidence

The high-performing Asian economies have provided the main reference point for the resurgence of claims about trade liberalization. The economies of Japan;

---

3 See chapters by G. Andrea Cornia, Eddy Lee, and Bernard Hoekman and L. Alan Winters in Ocampo, Jomo and Khan, eds. (2006).

the Republic of Korea; Taiwan Province of China; Singapore; Hong Kong Special Administrative Region, China; Malaysia; Indonesia; and Thailand have recorded some of the highest GDP growth rates in the world—averaging approximately 6 per cent per annum from 1965 until 1990—and also some of the highest rates of export growth, averaging more than 10 per cent per annum. Thus, quite often, their spectacular economic success has been linked to exports or outward orientation, notwithstanding the 1997-1998 economic crises in East Asia.[4] However, this success has hardly been based on free trade or laissez-faire (see box VI.2). For example, the Governments of Japan and the Republic of Korea have been highly interventionist, pursuing export promotion on the basis of import substitution (Amsden, 1989; Chang, 2006). The World Bank (1993) has acknowledged that what is important for growth is not whether the free market rules or the Government intervenes, but rather getting the fundamentals for growth right, including government control of financial markets in order to lower the cost of capital, and policies to promote exports and protect domestic industry.

> Box VI.2
> **Did trade liberalization reduce rural poverty in China?**
>
> China's success in reducing poverty with the reforms of 1978 is undeniable. The 1980s and 1990s saw a significant fall in rural poverty. However, as Ravallion and Chen (2004) argue, this had very little to do with trade liberalization. Several other factors were at work.
>
> The specifics of the situation in China at the outset of reform should not be forgotten. The Great Leap Forward and the Cultural Revolution had not helped reduce rural poverty in the period from the 1960s to the mid-1970s. Most of the rural population, forced into collective farming, had weak incentives to work and produce productively. Hence, there were some relatively easy gains from de-collectivizing agriculture and shifting the responsibility for farming to households. This brought a huge gain to the country's poorest, but a one-time gain.
>
> In China, the Government operated an extensive food grain procurement system which effectively taxed farmers by setting quotas and fixing procurement prices below market levels. By raising the procurement prices, the Government of China brought both poverty and inequality down in the mid-1990s. When so many of a country's poor are to be found in its rural areas, it is not surprising that agricultural growth plays an important role in poverty reduction. China's experience is consistent with the view that agriculture and rural development are crucial to pro-poor growth in low-income developing countries.
>
> Why did agricultural growth have strong poverty-reducing effects in China? Relatively equitable land allocation was achieved by breaking up collective farms. Most farmers, therefore, had efficiently sized plots. Farmers who owned small plots of land and lacked incentives to invest in new technology were not common, though they were common in many other developing countries.
>
> Source: Ravallion and Chen (2004).

---

4 Brahmbhatt and Dadush (1996) found that, among 93 developing countries studied, the rapidly growing East Asian exporting countries were integrating fastest into the global economy, while low-income countries of sub-Saharan Africa and some middle-income countries in Latin America were integrating less or more slowly.

A later study by the World Bank (2002) of both economic growth and equality in developing countries from 1977 to 1997 found that the more globalized countries (as measured by trade relative to GDP) enjoyed faster economic growth, but did not experience significant changes in income inequality. However, as Rodrik (2001, p. 1) points out, "the countries that integrated into the world economy most rapidly were not necessarily those that adopted the most pro-trade policies". According to Rodrik, "the Bank is acknowledging that trade liberalization may not be an effective instrument, not just for stimulating growth, but even for integration in world markets". Rodrik concludes that "rapid integration into global markets is a consequence, not of trade liberalization or adherence to World Trade Organization strictures per se, but of successful growth strategies with often highly idiosyncratic characteristics".[5]

Thus, both the 1993 and 2002 studies of the World Bank recognize that high growth was not necessarily due to trade liberalization or export orientation. What matters most is the successful growth strategies based on countries' own historical and socio-economic circumstances. The empirical work claiming a positive causal relationship between trade liberalization and growth suffers from serious methodological flaws. After careful evaluation of the major cross-country empirical work, one study states that "[w]hen we ask whether the results are informative for the practice of trade policy, we conclude that the answer is 'no' " (Hallak and Levinsohn, 2004, p. 3).[6] A later study (Andersen and Babula, 2008) which addresses some flaws of earlier ones finds likely positive links between trade and economic growth, but doubts the ability of developing countries to achieve productivity growth through trade liberalization. To do so, it may well be necessary to invest enough in appropriate education and training facilities. However, by removing an important source of revenue through tariff reductions—which is not compensated for by other sources of revenue—trade liberalization further restricts Governments' fiscal space for such productivity-enhancing investment (see box VI.3).

Summarizing lessons from a decade of reforms in the 1990s, the World Bank (2005, p. 134) notes:

> The distributive effects of trade liberalization are diverse, and not always pro-poor. ... evidence from the 1990s suggests that even in instances where trade policy has reduced poverty, there are still distributive issues ... Global markets are the most hostile to the products produced by the world's poor—such as agricultural products and textiles and apparel.

---

5   The admission in question comes when the report describes its sample of "more globalized" countries: "We label the top third 'more globalized' without in any sense implying that they adopted pro-trade policies. The rise in trade may have been due to other policies or even to pure chance" (World Bank, 2002, p. 34).
6   For a similar conclusion, see Rodríguez (2007).

> **Box VI.3**
> **Fiscal impact of trade liberalization**
>
> Although there are large differences among countries, income from trade taxes represents, on average, one third of total tax revenues in developing countries. In some very open and small least developed economies, import-related taxes constitute as much as 65 per cent of total revenue (see Gupta, 2007). Laird and de Córdoba (2006) show that developing countries obtain about $156 billion in tariff revenues annually, but this base would fall by 41 per cent under the ambitious "Swiss formula" proposal of tariff cuts for non-agricultural products. The study also shows tariff losses of at least $63 billion for developing countries due to non-agricultural market access (NAMA) alone, against projected welfare gains of less than $16 billion (0.2 per cent of developing-country national income) from the Doha Round.
>
> With promises of $4 billion against such high fiscal losses due to trade liberalization, Aid for Trade may not be of much help for developing-country Governments. For some countries, the fiscal loss from trade liberalization could be as high as 10 per cent of GDP, which is more than their public expenditure on health, education and other social priorities combined.
>
> Between 1970 and 1998, 84 low- and middle-income countries surveyed experienced lower fiscal revenue as a result of falling trade-related tariffs (see International Monetary Fund, 2002). IMF recommends replacing the trade-related revenues with value-added and sales taxes. However, the proposed substitution raises questions of feasibility and equity. In terms of feasibility, the capacity of low-income countries to recover income losses is limited. Implementing indirect taxes (value-added and sales taxes) demands increased administrative capacity which many countries do not have; and for every dollar lost in tariffs, poor and middle-income countries have been able to recover, at best, 30 cents from other sources (see Baunsgaard and Keen, 2005). Thus, while the consumption-based indirect taxes fail to compensate for the lost tariff revenues, they are also found to be regressive, and disproportionately affect low- and middle-income households.
>
> The IMF Trade Integration Mechanism (TIM) did not contemplate the loss of fiscal revenues from the outset. This was only explicitly added in a recent reformulation of the mechanism in the context of the Aid for Trade discussion. As the Fund facilities are not concessional, this means that a rate similar, or very close, to the market interest rate must be paid on the borrowed funds. Hence, the Mechanism basically increases debt in order to compensate for an ostensibly temporary adjustment of the balance of payments.

Financial liberalization

The arguments for financial liberalization also rest on the supposed link between financial development and economic growth, and hence poverty reduction. There are two dimensions of financial liberalization: (*a*) domestic financial sector deregulation and (*b*) opening of the capital account.

The rationale for financial deregulation, including international financial liberalization, was provided back in the early 1970s by McKinnon (1973) and Shaw (1973). They claimed that one of the reasons for the poor growth performance of many developing countries had been administratively determined very low (in some cases, negative) real interest rates which discouraged savings and encouraged inefficient use of capital. Thus, financial liberalization—primarily involving deregulation of interest rates—would lead to higher levels of savings. Liberalization would also channel funds to finance more productive projects. Therefore, an increase in real interest rates following liberalization should encourage saving and expand the supply of credit available to domestic investors, thereby enabling the economy to grow more quickly. This growth-promoting effect of domestic financial sector deregulation should be enhanced by opening the capital account of the balance of payments, which would allow more foreign capital to flow into the country, attracted by higher domestic real interest rates.

While increases in real interest rates have often been the outcome of liberalization episodes, their impact on domestic saving and investment has been mixed (Reinhart and Ioannis, 2008; Galbis, 1993). McKinnon himself has acknowledged that financial liberalization may lead to episodes of "over-borrowing". This over-borrowing syndrome may be magnified when domestic liberalization is coupled with capital account liberalization (McKinnon and Pill, 1999). Additionally, if the rising levels of debt are denominated in a foreign currency, this will increase a country's vulnerability to exchange-rate fluctuations. Banking crises are often preceded by financial liberalization; indeed, liberalization often leads to crisis (Kaminsky and Reinhart, 1999). A World Bank study of 53 countries for the period 1980-1995 found that banking crises were more likely to occur in liberalized financial systems (Demirgüç-Kunt and Detragiache, 1999; see also box VI.4). One reason why China, India and Viet Nam remained relatively unaffected by the contagion from the Asian financial crisis was their tight controls on short-term capital flows.

Box VI.4
Financial crises and poverty

Financial liberalization has increased the frequency and intensity of financial and banking crises, especially in emerging economies. Liberalization of the capital account increases the inflow of foreign capital but also threatens the stability of financial institutions by increasing exchange-rate and domestic lending risks.

A conspicuous feature of capital account liberalization in developing countries is so-called liability dollarization. This occurs when the private sector acquires liabilities in foreign currency, although assets are denominated in local currency. This makes the balance sheet of the private sector highly sensitive to shifts in the exchange rate. Significant exchange-rate depreciations can lead to large and negative wealth effects as liabilities increase in value relative to assets. Such wealth effects often cannot offset the positive impact on competitiveness engendered by exchange-rate depreciations.

Developing countries often experience sharp changes in capital flows. The most damaging in terms of impact on real output, employment and wages are so-called sudden stops, when there is an unanticipated cessation of capital flows that is not linked to any systematic policy errors committed by developing-country Governments. These sudden stops reflect failures and shortcomings in international capital markets. Under normal circumstances, Governments would seek to mitigate the impact of a capital account crisis on the real economy by engaging in counter-cyclical policies.

Unfortunately, the presence of liability dollarization—as well as the lack of preparedness—acts as a binding constraint on policy space. Monetary authorities develop a "fear of floating" and thus are reluctant to allow the depreciation of the exchange rate and engage in expansionary policies because of the rather large negative wealth effect stemming from liability dollarization.

Cline (2002) has tracked the path of per capita income growth before, during and after the year of a financial crisis triggered by sudden large outflows of foreign capital for each of eight major cases. In every case, there was a decline in per capita growth in the crisis year, most dramatically a decline by 15 per cent in the case of Indonesia. The financial crises between 1994 and 2002 impoverished at least 40 million–60 million people, and possibly almost as many as 100 million, out of a total of 800 million people in the economies concerned. By far the largest adverse impact occurred in Indonesia, owing to the country's large income decline and large share of population in poverty.

Thus, by the end of the last decade, financial liberalization had become the single most controversial policy prescription. After the currency crises in East Asia and the Russian Federation, the focus of the debate shifted from when to liberalize the capital account to whether to liberalize it at all. Rodrik (1998), for example, argues that there is no evidence in the data that countries without capital controls have grown faster, invested more or experienced lower inflation.

Significantly, Aizenman (2005) found no evidence of a "growth bonus" associated with increasing the foreign financing share. In fact, the evidence suggests just the opposite: throughout the 1990s, countries and regions with higher self-financing ratios grew significantly faster than countries and regions with lower self-financing ratios (see box VI.5). The positive and economically significant effect of self-financing ratios on real per capita GDP growth has been confirmed for 1970-2000.

Box VI.5
Financial liberalization and growth

There exists a large body of empirical research on financial liberalization and growth, but the results have been largely inconclusive. Nevertheless, support for the claim that financial liberalization inevitably boosts growth is slim. Kose, Prasad and Terrones (2006) have shown that capital account openness did not increase access to international finance for domestic investments. The same authors (2003) showed that capital account liberalization increased consumption volatility relative to output volatility in emerging economies. Prasad, Rajan and Subramanian (2007) also show no positive link between foreign capital and economic growth; instead, fast-growing developing countries relied less on foreign capital.

Rodrik and Subramanian (2008) argue that the case for financial globalization and capital account liberalization is based on the misguided premise that developing countries are savings-constrained and that the inflow of foreign capital eases this constraint. In their view, the unavailability of foreign capital is not a binding constraint on growth in these countries. They are much more likely to be investment-constrained, with low levels of investment resulting from low expectations of profitability and returns. Consequently, increasing access to foreign capital flows would have little positive effect on raising growth-promoting investments.

For the vast majority of countries surveyed, their investment rates fell when United States interest rates were low and external liquidity was plentiful. This should not have happened with countries that were savings-constrained. Low interest rates should raise borrowing and, with it, investment. Among the countries surveyed, the only two exceptions were China and India, which had shielded themselves from financial globalization (see Rodrik and Subramanian, 2008).

In contrast, capital account openness has seen capital flowing out of developing countries to the rich countries, especially the United States, funding its unsustainable consumption boom and asset price bubbles in recent years. Capital account liberalization has also not resulted in any significant decline in the cost of finance. Instead, the cost of finance has behaved "perversely", rising sharply during economic downturns (forcing real interest rates to rise) and falling during booms (yielding low real interest rates). Regarding the current crisis, even the World Bank (2009d, pp. 47-48) recently noted:

> Capital restrictions might be unavoidable as a last resort to prevent or mitigate the crisis effects. A few emerging countries have introduced capital controls and other measures to better monitor and, in some cases, limit the conversion of domestic currency into foreign exchange ... capital controls might need to be imposed as a last resort to help mitigate a financial crisis and stabilize macroeconomic developments.

As a result, macroeconomic policies have become pro-cyclical. For example, during the current global economic and financial crisis, private capital flows to developing countries have dropped sharply, and risk premiums for external financing have surged. Net private capital inflows to developing economies declined by more than 50 per cent during 2008, dropping from the peak of more than $1 trillion registered in 2007 to less than $500 billion. Another significant decline of 50 per cent is expected for 2009. The risk premium on lending to emerging and developing countries soared, on average, from 250 to about 800 basis points within the space of a few weeks in the third quarter of 2008.

In light of the disappointing experience, authorities should institute mechanisms to restrict large and sudden flows of short-term capital or "hot money" (Epstein, Grabel and Jomo, 2003). By employing diverse capital management techniques during the 1990s, Chile, Colombia, Taiwan Province of China, India, China, Singapore and Malaysia were able to achieve critical macroeconomic objectives. These techniques included the prevention of maturity and locational mismatches; attraction of desired foreign investments; reduction of overall financial fragility, currency risk, and speculative pressures; insulation from the contagion effects of financial crises; and enhancement of the autonomy of economic and social policy.

Finally, financial sector deregulation led to the privatization of State-owned financial institutions and, in most cases, the abandonment of specialized financial institutions established to subsidize and direct credit to small and medium-sized enterprises, agriculture and other development priorities. As a result, in many developing countries, financial deregulation has adversely affected rural banking. Unprofitable rural branches of commercial banks have closed, making access to credit more difficult for farmers and other people living in rural areas (Deraniyagala, 2003; Chowdhury, 2002; see also box VI.6). Privatization has also reduced the developmental role of Governments, result-

> **Box VI.6**
> **Financial deregulation, inequality and poverty**
>
> Developing countries need to invest in both agriculture and manufacturing in order to diversify their economies as well as to reduce poverty through employment creation and food price stabilization. However, despite much higher social returns to agricultural and manufacturing investment, following financial sector deregulation, banks and financial institutions have increasingly financed collateralized stock market and real estate investments. Private commercial banks discriminate against employment-intensive sectors such as agriculture and small-scale enterprises owing to the higher transaction costs of lending to a larger number of small borrowers and the lack of collateralizable assets of small farmers and owners of small and medium-sized enterprises. Ghosh (2008b) maintains that "[t]he agrarian crisis in most parts of the developing world is at least partly, and often substantially, related to the decline in the access of peasant farmers to institutional finance, which is the direct result of financial liberalization".
>
> The situation has been made worse by the closing of Government-run specialized financial institutions for agriculture and small and medium-sized enterprises as part of financial deregulation. Furthermore, previously Government-owned privatized banks have closed rural branches deemed not to be profitable, as there is no longer any requirement to ensure rural banking services. These measures have reduced credit availability for farmers and small producers, and have contributed to the rising costs of needed working capital, thereby exacerbating rural distress. In rural India, for example, there is strong evidence that the deep crisis in farming communities—resulting in farmer suicides, mass migration and even deaths from hunger—has been related to the decline of institutional credit, forcing farmers to turn to usurious private moneylenders. A study by the Inter-American Development Bank (2007) of 17 Latin American countries for the period 1977-2000 found that financial liberalization has had a significant effect on increasing inequality and poverty.
>
> In sum, financial deregulation has undermined important social functions of finance by making it less inclusive. It has also destroyed an important industrial policy instrument historically utilized by most successful late industrializers. Most late industrializing countries, at least since the twentieth century, have created well-regulated financial markets and often State-controlled financial institutions designed to mobilize savings to support priority investments. They used directed credit policies and differential interest rates to support nascent industries with the potential to expand into export markets. They also created development banks with the mandate to provide long-term credit on attractive terms. These financial sector policies contributed significantly to rapid economic transformation and poverty declines in those countries.

ing in the poor performance of small and medium-sized enterprises and agriculture as well as deindustrialization, with adverse impacts for employment and poverty reduction.

Privatization

The privatization of State-owned enterprises, including utilities, is another central component of adjustment policies for developing countries. Privatization is often a crucial requirement for securing aid funding, and is a key policy of the Poverty Reduction Strategy Papers (PRSPs), with the World Bank continuing to link privatization to poverty reduction.

How can privatization reduce poverty?

The rationale for privatization is rooted in public choice theory which predicts that privatization will spur development of the private sector. Privatization is supposed to improve the efficiency of enterprises by focusing on financial performance. Through better resource allocation and improved efficiency (due to the absence of rent-seeking), privatization is expected to spur economic growth and hence reduce poverty. Proponents of privatization also project fiscal benefits, occurring from the one-time revenue gains for the government that "sells" presumably failing State-owned enterprises and is relieved of the burden of financing investment (Campbell-White and Bhatia, 1998). This phenomenon is expected to allow Governments to spend more on services for the poor.

But how does privatization actually help develop the private sector? This remains unclear. It could increase private investment in a sector, but whether this leads to output and welfare benefits will depend on competition, among other factors. It could signal government support for the private sector. However, for many developing countries (for example, countries in sub-Saharan Africa), lack of investor interest has been a common feature of privatization, with Governments offering increasing concessions to entice investors to acquire their assets—often to meet the requirements of donors and creditors (Bayliss, 2003). Privatization can also create an environment where the private sector attempts to stifle competition and flout regulations in order to enhance profits. In the absence of effective regulation, where Governments have recourse to valid sanctions against private firms, the State will be powerless to prevent market abuses. In such a situation, it is not privatization that will develop the private sector, but rather effective Government regulation.

Private firms will invest only when and where they expect to make a profitable return. Therefore, they will want to invest only in profitable activities and will not buy losing enterprises. Thus, the Government will not only be left with losing enterprises, but also lose a regular source of revenue from enterprises sold to the private sector. For example, in their study of privatization in Africa, Campbell-White and Bhatia (1998) found that the enterprises sold had not been financially draining government resources. In the case of profit-making units, the fiscal effect of privatization is almost invariably negative. If the Government sells an asset that provides an income flow (profits, etc.) equal to or greater than that based on the prevailing interest rate on Government securities, then the Government would lose a future income stream by selling it.

Additionally, if revenue from privatized enterprises becomes uncertain, firms may back out of investment projects. In Zimbabwe in 1999, the United Kingdom firm Biwater withdrew from a proposed private water project because the project's intended beneficiaries (consumers) were too poor to pay a tariff to ensure the profit margin that Biwater was seeking (Bayliss, 2002). They may also seek guarantees from Governments to ensure revenue flows rather than take the risks. In infrastructure, private companies will ensure that their investments are recouped with profit. In power generation projects, private investors often will not invest without a power purchase agreement (PPA) in place under which the publicly owned utilities agree to purchase the output of the plant at a fixed price often cited in foreign exchange for a period of 20-30 years. Such agreements can be crippling for Governments. In the case of the Enron-owned Dabhol power project in India, the terms of the power purchase agreement became so onerous for the government of Maharashtra State—owing to currency devaluation and the high cost of fuel—that it defaulted on payments (Bayliss and Hall, 2000).

There is also no clear evidence that the private sector performs better than the public sector. While private ownership may bring better management skills and incentives, this is by no means inevitable.

There are numerous examples of utility privatization failures. For example, in Puerto Rico, four years after a subsidiary of the French multinational Vivendi took over management of the water authority, its financial situation deteriorated to such a degree that the State had to provide subsidies (Bayliss, 2002). Private investment in infrastructure, for example, in a water supply programme in a developing country, is not normally a very attractive proposition because it involves a large upfront investment and a long-term pay-off. For this reason, privatization projects are often designed in such a way as to enable private firms acquiring interests in service delivery to make quick profits, leaving the longer-term, more expensive investments to the Government. For example, in Guinea and Côte d'Ivoire, private operators were given responsibility for billing consumers for water, while the Governments committed to invest in infrastructure. The fact that the private firm made a profit while the State-owned enterprise continued to accumulate losses was due not so much to the difference in ownership as to the type of business each party engaged in. Further, given the private firm's interest in increasing revenue, the focus was on installing water meters, increasing billing and bill collection, rather than on improving access to water (Brook Cowen, 1996). This can impact negatively on the poor, who have limited access to basic infrastructure.

Private firms are also sometimes guaranteed rates of return which allow for price or user charge increases. In the Plurinational State of Bolivia, the privatized water company raised prices sharply in the late 1990s to enable it to earn such rates of return, provoking widespread popular protests (Lobina, 2000). Case studies of African countries have also shown that water prices rose substantially after privatization—to the point where water became inaccessible to the poor (Magdahl and others, 2006). In addition, developing-country Governments often have weak regulatory capacity to monitor price increases by privatized firms. Whether privatization-related price hikes increase poverty will depend on the extent to which the poor are consumers in these sectors, the extent of the price increases and their ability to cope. Extensive privatization in Mongolia since the early 1990s has led to sharp price hikes in essential utilities, with negative effects on the real incomes of the poor (box VI.7; see also Nixson and Walters, 2006).

One common immediate effect of most privatizations is reduced employment. This occurs not only because there tends to be substantial overstaffing in public enterprises, but also because the new owners typically prefer to begin with fewer employees than they need in order to allow for greater flexibility. In addition, there are the linkage and multiplier effects of privatization-related changes. Employment conditions can be adversely affected in upstream and downstream activities, as well as in the local community through the indirect-demand effects of workers' incomes. A study by Van der Hoeven and Sziráczki (1998) showed that utility privatization in developing countries has significant employment-reducing effects, sometimes impacting up to 50 per cent of the workforce.

A study by Macarov (2003) on the effects on the poor of cutbacks in government spending in areas such as medical services, education and social welfare found that they often resulted in the formation of a system with two tiers, one for the rich and the other for the poor. After reviewing the distributional impact of privatization activities involving utilities in a wide range of developing economies, principally in Africa and Latin America, Bayliss (2002) con-

---

Box VI.7

Privatization in Mongolia

Privatization has been a major part of Mongolia's transition to capitalism. Its move to a market economy has been accompanied by increases in poverty and income inequality. More than 10 years after it began its transition, Mongolia remains one of the poorest countries in the world.

Privatization continues to be a central part of economic reform in Mongolia, as in other transition economies. The goal has been to increase private sector participation in the economy, to which successive Governments have remained committed. Previously, Mongolia's economy had been narrowly based on the export of copper, cashmere wool and gold, as well as on a large amount of donor aid from the former Soviet Union. In 1991, after the collapse of the Soviet Union and the demise of its trading arrangements, privatization in Mongolia exemplified a "shock therapy" approach to transition. The overall effect was a significant decline in standards of living, with dramatic rises, in the early period of transition, in levels of poverty and inequality, which have remained at very high levels.

The Government, which owned 75 per cent of all property, adopted a voucher system of privatization. In the first phase, each person was issued three red vouchers which could be used to buy shares in small State and cooperative businesses. Shortly afterwards, each person was issued one blue voucher, with which he or she could bid for ownership of the larger State enterprises. Mongolia's Stock Exchange was also established to allow trading in shares.

Privatization was undertaken without any analysis or consideration of the impact on poverty and income distribution. In an evaluation of this experience, Nixson and Walters (2006) found that privatization had affected poverty adversely in Mongolia by 2000. They also concluded that, among other consequences, the Government had ignored the role of agencies that provided poor people with collective goods and services; reduced available livelihood options, making poorer families more vulnerable to economic shocks; and allowed utility prices and service charges to be increased after privatization.

cluded that privatization had demonstrably harmed the poor, either through loss of employment and income, or through exclusion from, or reduced access to, basic services, as the result of private firms' principal concern with profits, prices and costs. At the same time, weak governance and regulatory capacity in many developing countries led to poor control of market abuses by private utility companies.

The way forward

The empirical evidence derived from the outcomes of economic liberalization indicates that excessive reliance on markets and the private sector carries high risks. The World Bank (2005, p. 133) has noted:

> There are many possible ways to open an economy. The challenge for policymakers is to identify which best suits their country's political economy, institutional constraints, and initial conditions. As these vary from country to country, it is not surprising that there is a striking heterogeneity in country experiences regarding the timing and pace of reforms.

A much more nuanced approach, based on lessons from history, is needed. Clearly, economic growth and structural change are necessary for sustained poverty reduction. Wholesale trade liberalization, however, is not the best strategy for this. To enhance the poverty-reducing effects of growth and structural change, the economic transformation process must challenge inequality and the exclusion of poor and disadvantaged groups. For sustained reductions in poverty, the focus should also extend to productivity growth and employment creation. Developing countries should therefore consider, selectively, the formulation of trade and industry policies to augment the development of new potentially viable production capacities and capabilities.

Not only should financial policy in developing countries be concerned with ensuring financial stability, but it must also be counter-cyclical, developmental and inclusive. In many developing countries, this will require explicitly addressing the needs of food agriculture through rural banking and other inclusive finance initiatives. Governments should consider reintroducing specialized development banks, especially to promote employment-intensive small and medium-sized enterprises and agriculture. This may involve directed and subsidized credit as well as other proactive financial policy initiatives. Undoubtedly, directed credit programmes create "distortions" in the financial market and may be vulnerable to rent-seeking. However, the possible cost of such distortions must be weighed against the "cost" of financial market imperfections that discriminate against small borrowers.[7]

---

[7] Beginning in 1984, Ecuador had eliminated or scaled down directed credit programmes and removed administrative controls on interest rates as part of financial sector liberalization programmes. Since then, the supply of credit has declined drastically, with the contraction of Government-provided loanable funds, and reached a figure as low as 9 per cent

Private commercial banks can be compelled to comply with requirements to serve rural and other disadvantaged regions, agriculture and small and medium-sized enterprises as well as disadvantaged social groups. Governments can consider a range of policy options and instruments needed to achieve such objectives. For example, in India, all banks (public and private) are required to lend at least 40 per cent of net credit to "priority sectors". If banks fail to meet this requirement, they are instead obligated to lend money to specified Government agencies at very low interest rates.[8]

Alternatively, the central banks can combine India's type of penalties for failure with incentives, such as asset-based reserve requirements, support for pooling and underwriting small loans, and support of employment-generating investments through use of the discount window. Asset-based reserve requirements can be an effective tool for creating incentives for banks to invest in socially productive assets (see Pollin, 1998; Epstein, 2002). Also, based on known employment elasticities, the central banks could list a set of employment-generating investments; lower reserve requirements would then apply for loans for such investments than for speculation or for buying stocks and shares.

Central banks can also take steps to create liquidity and risk-sharing institutions for loans to small businesses that show promise for generating employment but that do not have adequate access to the credit market. For example, central banks can provide financial and administrative support for asset-backed securities, through which loans would be made to small businesses and other employment-intensive activities, bundle these investments, and then sell them as securities on the open market. Finally, central banks can open a special discount window facility to offer credit, guarantee or discount facilities to institutions that on-lend to firms and cooperatives engaged in employment-intensive activities.

After the uncritical and often blind embrace of privatization during the 1980s and 1990s, a more cautious, if not critical, approach has emerged in recent years for at least two reasons (Bayliss and Fine, 2007). First, the revenue flows from State-owned enterprises are essential for maintaining and enhanc-

---

of GDP in 1990. The firm-level debt structure data show that, together with the decline in total credit, the share of long-term loans as a share of total debt fell from 12 per cent in the early 1980s to 8 per cent in 1992. The growth rate of real long-term credit was negative for most years. The firm-level data also show that the percentage of directed credit was much higher for longer-term maturities prior to liberalization reforms. This proportion of directed long-term credit relative to total long-term credit declined from 59.3 per cent in 1985 to 35.9 per cent in 1990. The proportion of directed short-term credit relative to total short-term credit declined from 31.1 per cent in 1985 to 3.3 per cent in 1992. The decline in the access to long-term credit negatively affected firms' performance, especially in terms of productivity. In particular, the lack of access to long-term credit adversely affected firms' ability to acquire improved technology (see Schiantarelli and Jaramillo (1996)).

8 Studies by Banerjee and Duflo (2004) found that most banks complied with the regulation and the programme contributed significantly to the expansion of agriculture and small-scale industries.

ing Governments' fiscal space. Second, State-owned enterprises can be important instruments for poverty reduction efforts.

The performance of State-owned enterprises should not be evaluated solely based on bookkeeping "bottom lines", as they often have other objectives, such as employment creation or social protection. Employment in State-owned enterprises may represent a better way of providing social security than social security payments themselves from the point of view of self-esteem, learning by doing and reciprocal obligations. Privatization must not ignore employment conditions and likely job losses, as they affect poverty, especially of the working poor. There should be adequate protection of employment conditions as well as active labour-market programmes in place. Similarly, provision of utilities must remain inclusive regardless of ownership. Public utilities, if privatized, must stipulate mandatory adequate service provisions to disadvantaged groups and areas.

Chapter VII
Labour-market and social policies and poverty reduction

The present chapter provides a critical assessment of labour-market and social policies since the 1980s and their impact on poverty, the working poor and vulnerable groups in society. During these three decades of structural adjustment and macroeconomic conservatism, the emphasis has been on labour-market flexibility, and social policy has been reduced to a limited series of measures intended to compensate for the negative effects of structural adjustment among certain sectors of the population.

Since the publication of the groundbreaking 1987 report *Adjustment with a Human Face* (United Nations Children's Fund, 1987), the negative impact of structural adjustment programmes on social indicators, especially for health and education, is now widely recognized. Later, the World Bank and the International Monetary Fund (IMF) were forced to abandon the various failed generations of structural adjustment programmes in favour of Poverty Reduction Strategy Papers (PRSPs) for countries seeking assistance. The Poverty Reduction Strategy Papers have also been heavily criticized, not least for being structural adjustment programmes in disguise and for neglecting employment generation, generally deemed to be necessary for sustainable poverty reduction. Nevertheless, the operational guidelines of the World Bank now require analysis of the impact of adjustment programmes on people living in poverty, and in many countries compensatory measures have been introduced. Critics argue that its "social safety net approach" generally involves temporary institutions responding to market failure with costly targeting methods which tend to miss many of those in need.

Labour-market policies: counting the cost for the working poor

The promotion of full and productive employment was proclaimed as one of the three pillars of social development by the Copenhagen World Summit for Social Development in 1995. The centrality to poverty reduction of productive employment and decent work for all is widely recognized and accepted, as evidenced by the inclusion of target 2, "Achieve full and productive employment and decent work for all, including women and young people", under Millennium Development Goal 1 of halving poverty by 2015.[1]

---

[1] At the World Summit for Social Development, held in Copenhagen in 1995, world leaders acknowledged the link between the creation of productive employment and poverty reduction and committed to taking national and international actions to promote full and productive employment. The 2005 World Summit revived this commitment with a

However, the creation of productive and decent jobs has failed, in the past three decades, to receive the prominence it deserves in the development agenda. Hence, full employment has not been among the targets of macroeconomic policies. As discussed in chapter V, international organizations that dominate macroeconomic policymaking have focused their efforts on helping countries achieve and maintain low inflation and balanced budgets on the assumption that stability of nominal macroeconomic variables would generate rapid growth. Economic liberalization has been promoted on the assumption that it would improve efficiency in resource allocation and enhance international competitiveness which, in turn, would spur growth. Employment creation was supposed to follow economic growth, as long as the labour market remained flexible, unhindered by measures that increased hiring and firing costs. Thus, the structural adjustment programmes typically included programmes for labour-market flexibility.

As highlighted in chapters V and VI, the implications of this logic were not borne out by economic reality. Rapid economic growth, not to mention job growth, did not necessarily materialize in many developing countries after the achievement of low inflation, low budget deficits or surplus, and structural reforms. Even during the period of prolonged economic expansion prior to the onset of the current global financial and economic crisis, the pace of job creation was very slow. This gave rise to the term "jobless growth", which captures the disappointing performance on the employment front in a period of reasonably high economic growth.

A growing body of research shows that a major reason for jobless growth has been the lack of structural change owing to market-oriented policies based on the theory of "comparative advantage" (see chap. VI). Yet, the response to the phenomenon remained guided by the development paradigm of the Washington Consensus, and the priority was to increase national labour-market flexibility. Labour-market policies—such as provision of a minimum wage and employment protection—are seen as barriers to employment growth, especially in the formal sector. The wisdom of the Washington Consensus with regard to labour-market policy was summarized in the *World Development Report 1990* (World Bank, 1990, p. 63):

> Labour-market policies—minimum wages, job security regulations, and social security—are usually intended to raise welfare or reduce exploitation. But they actually work to raise the cost of labour in the formal sector and reduce labour demand... increase the supply of labour to the rural and urban informal sectors, and thus depress labour incomes where most of the poor are found.

Furthermore, economists at the international financial institutions worried that labour institutions would undermine structural adjustment programmes

---

renewed sense of urgency. In 2008, a new employment target was added under Millennium Development Goal 1 on poverty reduction.

designed to cure balance-of-payments deficits or other economic problems. In their analysis, elimination of a balance-of-payments deficit required that a country shift resources from non-traded goods and services to traded goods sectors. In advocating against selective trade and industry policies as instruments for structural change, they argued that the least costly way to achieve this was to devalue the currency, which raises the price of tradable goods and services relative to non-tradable goods and services and thus attracts resources into the traded sectors. Since devaluation is likely to cause inflation due to high import prices, organized unions were expected to resist devaluation in an attempt to protect real wages from falling, which would then offset the impact of devaluation in moving resources in desired directions. Resistance to reforms was also feared as a result of the job losses arising from adjustment.

It was claimed that the removal of regulations would enhance labour-market efficiency as well as international competitiveness, leading to employment growth. In short, the creation of "flexible" labour markets was seen as a requirement for boosting domestic and foreign private sector investment. Thus, the World Bank, in its most influential flagship publication, *Doing Business*, included the Employing Workers Indicator (EWI), withdrawn on 27 April 2009, which ranked countries on the basis of information pertaining to such issues as minimum wage levels, maximum hours per workweek, requirements for advanced notice for layoffs, and severance pay. This ranking of countries created a strong incentive among Governments in developing countries to compete in dismantling labour regulations, even if they had acceded to the various conventions of the International Labour Organization (ILO) on labour standards and decent work. Another outcome was a growth of export processing zones (EPZs) which attempted to entice foreign investors through a scaling back of regulations and exemptions from national labour laws. The recent financial and economic crises notwithstanding, the dilution of labour standards and regulations has been a contributing factor to the increase in the working poor and growing earnings inequality, particularly in developed countries.[2]

There have been, however, several challenges mounted against the orthodox view of labour-market regulations. For example, "efficiency wage" theory argues that higher-than-equilibrium (or average) real wages can reduce worker shirking (Shapiro and Stiglitz, 1984), reduce labour turnover (Salop, 1979) and increase labour productivity. An influential study showed that the introduction of minimum wages had no negative effect on employment levels in the United States of America (Card and Krueger, 1995). A rigorous review of previous cross-country studies claiming a strong relationship between unemployment and institutions found that their results were not robust (Baker and others, 2002). It also did not find any strong evidence that further erosion of social and

---

2 See Levy and Temin (2007) and Mishel, Bernstein and Shierholz (2009). In developing countries, owing to a high degree of informality, labour regulations and protection do not apply to informal economy workers. Thus, deregulation of the labour market had little impact on them, if any.

collective protections for workers—such as unemployment insurance, minimum wage and employee rights in cases of dismissal—would have significant positive impacts on employment prospects.

An extensive recent survey of the literature on the impact of government regulations and collective bargaining on labour outcomes in developing countries revealed that, although most studies found modest adverse effects of a minimum wage on employment, it also raised the total income of low-paid workers (Freeman, 2009). Other mandated benefits had similar effects on employment and workers' incomes. There was not much difference in the adjustment responses of countries to economic shocks—such as balance-of-payments problems—attributable to the strength of labour institutions. On the other hand, labour-market institutions were found to be critical at those times when countries experienced great change, as during China's growth and Argentina's economic collapse in 2001-2002. In the 1980s and 1990s, the labour share fell or remained stagnant in most developed and developing countries (Giovannoni, 2008). Weakened labour-market, social security and economic liberalization policies since the 1980s explain most of the international patterns observed.

Such theoretical challenges and empirical findings did not, however, stop the policy drive to increase labour-market flexibility. In many countries, increased labour-market flexibility has resulted in insecure work status, employment and income (Standing, 2007). This trend has been accompanied by increasing informalization of work, especially in developing countries. Offshoring and outsourcing have also created a heightened sense of fear and insecurity among workers in industrialized countries. Economic insecurity—and hence vulnerability to poverty—increased for workers over this period, even during the boom years (see *The Employment Imperative: Report on the World Social Situation 2007* (United Nations, 2007) for more details). Now, given the economic and financial crises, worker insecurity has risen dramatically, with global unemployment projected to increase by 50 million from 2007 to the end of 2009, and an estimated 200 million workers could be pushed back into extreme poverty (International Labour Organization, 2009c).

The informal economy has always been significant in developing countries, particularly in Latin America and sub-Saharan Africa. Owing to the failure of labour-market deregulation to accelerate job creation in the formal sector, the informal economy accounts for the dominant share of employment in most developing countries. For example, in Indonesia, the informal economy's share in total employment is about 70 per cent. This creates an enormous challenge for those countries in their efforts to reduce poverty. Jobs in the informal economy usually entail low skill and low productivity, often pay below-subsistence wages (wages are 44 per cent lower, on average, than in the formal economy), have poor working conditions and typically offer no legal or social protection (see box VII.1). Although not everyone in the informal economy is poor, there is a high likelihood that the working poor are concentrated in the informal economy in very low productivity activities.

> Box VII.1
> **Urban waste pickers**
>
> A significant number of men, women and children in developing countries make a living collecting, sorting, recycling and selling materials recovered from waste dumps, kerbsides and dumpsters. In some of the world's larger cities, thousands of people live and work in municipal dumps—an estimated 20,000 in Calcutta, 12,000 in Manila and 15,000 in Mexico City.
>
> According to the World Bank, 1 per cent of the urban population—many of these being women and children—earn a living from waste collection and/or recycling. In the least developed countries, up to 2 per cent of the urban population make their living in this manner.
>
> Waste pickers are often treated, at best, as a nuisance by public authorities and at times as if they were criminals. Moreover, they tend to have low social status and face public scorn, harassment and sometimes violence. Waste pickers are also vulnerable to exploitation by the middlemen who buy their recovered material. It has been noted that in some cities of Colombia, India and Mexico, waste pickers can receive as little as 5 per cent of the prices that industry pays for the recyclables, with the rest going to middlemen (Medina, 2005).
>
> On account of their low earnings, waste pickers tend to live in deplorable conditions, lacking water, sanitation and other basic infrastructure. Their poor working and living conditions also make them vulnerable to health and safety risks, including exposure to dangerous waste, and various illnesses and disease.
>
> Not surprisingly, life expectancy rates are low in waste-picking communities. In Mexico City, for example, dumpsite waste collectors live an average of 39 years, compared with an average of 69 years for the general population.
>
> Source: www.wiego.org.

Social policies

Several elements of social policies are discussed briefly below in connection with the developments in social policy over the past three decades.

Social protection[3]

Social protection refers to a group of policy measures and programmes that reduce poverty and vulnerability and seek to protect society's more vulnerable members against livelihood shocks and risks, enhance the social status and rights of the marginalized, protect workers and diminish people's exposure to risks associated with ill health, disability, old age and unemployment.

Social pensions and insurance

Social insurance and pension schemes seek to enable the working-age population and older persons to smooth consumption over their lifetimes. Social insurance programmes can be either employment-based or universal. In devel-

---

[3] A more detailed discussion of social protection can be found in the *Report on the World Social Situation 2007* (United Nations, 2007), chap. V.

oping countries, the proportion of poor households covered by employment-based social insurance is usually small, reflecting the dominance of informal labour markets. These programmes usually require that beneficiaries make at least partial contributions and involve risk-pooling.

Non-employment-based old-age pension schemes are increasingly common in developing countries, existing in countries such as South Africa, Namibia, Nepal and Mauritius, where the amount paid rises with the age of the pensioner (Johnson and Williamson, 2006). Advocates point out that social pensions reduce old-age poverty and are affordable, and typically account for a small percentage of gross domestic product (GDP). For example, in 1999, State pensions accounted for 0.3 per cent of GDP in Costa Rica and for 0.1 per cent of GDP in Zimbabwe (Coady, Grosh and Hoddinott, 2004).

Social assistance and transfers

These include support programmes for vulnerable groups, such as the unemployed and persons with disabilities. They are redistributive measures, mainly funded through progressive taxation. In this regard, the pattern of poverty has been closely related to inequality, and countries with larger redistributive systems have tended to be more equal, with lower poverty rates (Giovannoni, 2008).

Social protection in a time of crisis

The world economy has witnessed a series of economic crises over the past four decades, including the two oil price shocks in the 1970s, the Latin American debt crisis in the 1980s, and the financial crisis in East Asia and the Russian Federation during 1997-1998. These crises had enormous impacts on poverty. For example, in Indonesia, the poverty rate had shot up from about 11 per cent prior to the crisis to over 30 per cent in 1998. The recent food and energy price hikes pushed over 100 million people into poverty. Millions of people have already lost their jobs owing to the current global financial and economic crisis.

To minimize the impact of the crisis on the poor and vulnerable, countries adopt different strategies that offer immediate relief to those in distress. However, most of these programmes are time-bound, being designed to provide emergency support until the economy recovers. They are also, in most cases, donor-funded.

The emphasis, however, should be on the need to provide economic security to all citizens, regardless of where they work and live, and of the state of the business cycle (see box VII.2 and Islam, 2009). The objective should be to achieve a holistic approach to social protection which uses complementary instruments to cater to the particular needs of different groups in the formal economy, the informal economy and rural areas. Studies by ILO and other organizations show that incentive-compatible unemployment compensation

> **Box VII.2**
>
> **Are unemployment compensation programmes feasible in developing and emerging economies?**
>
> Critics usually contend that unemployment compensation or unemployment insurance programmes are not suitable for emerging market economies, as they are not fiscally affordable, lead to an increase in the incidence and duration of job searches and can be abused by recipients.
>
> These concerns are exaggerated. In the wake of the Asian crisis, most middle-income Asian economies would have been able to operate an unemployment insurance programme of "average Organization for Economic Cooperation and Development (OECD) generosity" using effective payroll tax rates of 1.0-2.0 per cent, with the former tax rate applicable to unemployment rates of about 4 per cent and the latter to those of about 8 per cent (Vroman, 1999; Lee, 1998).
>
> Thus, the key issue regarding unemployment compensation programmes in middle-income developing and emerging economies is not really fiscal affordability but rather disincentive effects, expressed most notably in the view that unemployment compensation programmes induce more and longer unemployment.
>
> The debate over unemployment insurance has overlooked the consumption smoothing channels by which this particular instrument of social protection motivates job searches and overemphasizes the disincentive effects (Chetty, 2008). Unemployed workers are often short of money (cash) and are likely to become even more so during recessions. Thus, unemployment insurance prevents the consumption level of unemployed workers from falling below a certain minimum or floor and enhances the net welfare of unemployed workers, if the positive consumption smoothing effect outweighs the negative disincentive effect, which seems to be the case.
>
> Policymakers in developing economies have tried to respond to the disincentive effects through the enactment of restrictive statutory provisions and measures, such as social investment funds (SIFs) and severance payments (SPs), as substitutes. Both these types of provisions have been ineffective. In the Plurinational State of Bolivia, for example, the benefits of social investment funds barely reached 1 per cent of total employment in the crisis years and 0.1 per cent of employment in normal years. The evidence from Latin America and the Caribbean shows that severance payments are ubiquitous. Yet, they only cover about 20 per cent of the formal sector workforce and are likely to be paid mainly to those least likely to experience unemployment. In Indonesia, severance payments are now among the most generous in the developing world.
>
> This has led to a good deal of debate about the likely deleterious consequences of such labour-market regulations. One fallacy is to regard severance payments as a substitute for unemployment compensation programmes. The unemployment compensation programmes respond to a particular type of labour-market risk for particular groups in society that cannot be met by other measures. Hence, unemployment compensation and other forms of social protection should be seen as complements; when creatively combined, they enable workers in developing economies to have access to a range of risk-mitigating provisions.
>
> Finally, the recent policy emphasis seems to be on targeted social protection programmes—such as conditional cash transfer programmes, public works employment and subsidization of the consumption of inferior goods—that focus on "bailing out the poorest" households.
>
> Source: Islam (2009).

programmes for formal sector workers are technically feasible and fiscally affordable (financed with 1-2 per cent of payroll taxes) for developing economies (Lee, 1998; Vroman, 1999; Vroman and Brusentev, 2005).

A basic social security package for all is also technically feasible and fiscally affordable for developing economies, and in many cases requires investment of about 4 per cent of GDP.[4] Greater effort directed towards domestic resource mobilization, in conjunction with transitional assistance from the donor community, can make such a basic social security package attainable in all developing countries. Once a social security protection system is in place, it is much easier to pursue enterprise-level flexibility and to cope with global economic downturns.

Active labour-market policies

Given that job losses disproportionately affect the poor and those at risk of slipping into poverty, active labour-market policies that focus on training programmes and employment services for displaced workers must be integral to a comprehensive social protection system. The World Bank (2009d) argues that well-designed training programmes in more than 90 countries have had a significant impact on the livelihoods of displaced workers. In the long term, active labour-market policies should aim to develop an education and training system that enhances the productive potential and employability of the workforce.

Education and poverty reduction

Education can play a key role in poverty reduction. Research shows that education and human resource investments promote economic growth. Workers with higher levels of education boost productivity, both directly and by enabling efficiency-enhancing technological change (Hanushek and Woessmann, 2008). Thus, education can have a positive impact on poverty reduction owing to its growth-promoting effects. However, there can be instances where the relationship between education, growth and productivity is weak, as observed in the Arab region where increases in the supply of skilled labour have been largely independent of output and productivity growth. In Egypt, for example, adults with secondary education account for 42 per cent of the population, but 80 per cent of the unemployed (World Bank, 2008c). Complementary demand-side policies are needed to ensure employment creation in order that the productivity-enhancing potential of education may be realized.

Research shows that individual rates of return to education are generally high. Learning benefits individuals by facilitating their entry into higher-earning occupations leading to a rise in earnings. Returns to education are found to be higher in low-income countries for lower levels of schooling and for

---

4　An ILO (2009d) simulation exercise for Nepal, for example, shows that nearly 100 per cent of the basic social security package can be financed from domestic resources, provided that the Government of Nepal can partly reallocate social expenditure, increase the goods and services tax rate marginally, improve income tax collection and introduce modest health insurance contributions.

women (Psacharopoulos and Patrinos, 2004; Heckman, Lochner and Todd, 2006). In rural areas, education can enable farmers to improve technology, with schooling strongly associated with higher wages, agricultural productivity and incomes (Appleton and Balihuta, 1996).

Education also impacts poverty through its effects on health. Improved education, especially of a mother, is associated with lower levels of child and maternal mortality as well as better nutrition and health, as emphasized by the United Nations Educational, Scientific and Cultural Organization's (UNESCO) Education for All (EFA) movement and the Millennium Development Goals.[5]

Progress by developing countries in the last decade on many education indicators has been impressive. Sub-Saharan Africa raised its average net primary enrolment ratio from 54 to 70 per cent between 1999 and 2006—representing an annual increase six times greater than that during the previous decade. In South and West Asia, the net primary enrolment ratio rose from 75 to 86 per cent over the same period. In developing countries, the total number of primary school staff employed rose by 5 per cent between 1999 and 2006 (United Nations Educational, Scientific and Cultural Organization, 2008). Between 2001 and 2006, South Asia almost halved the number of out-of-school children (World Bank, 2008a).

Despite these gains, however, serious gaps in progress remain. In 2006, some 75 million children (55 per cent of them girls), almost half in sub-Saharan Africa, were not in school, suggesting that millions of children will still be out of school in 2015—the Millennium Development Goal target date for ensuring universal primary education. Quality of education is extremely important and often overlooked because it is not easily measured. It is not enough for children to be enrolled and to attend school: they must also gain basic literacy and numeracy skills and complete primary education in a timely manner. In developing regions, 19 per cent of children of secondary school age are still enrolled in primary education compared with 4 per cent in developed regions: clearly students are not progressing as well as they should. The fact that a large number of children of secondary school age are in primary school also adds stress to the primary school system and strains resources that should be allocated to new students.

These gaps often indicate insufficient resources available and the failure of Governments to deal with persistent inequalities based on income, gender, ethnicity and other markers for social exclusion. With Governments under pressure to reduce budget deficits, social expenditure—on, inter alia, education and health—suffered the most during the past three decades of structural adjustment. Thus, these sectors have become increasingly dependent on donor fund-

---

5 The Education for All initiative grew out of the World Conference on Education for All, held in Somtien, Thailand, in 1990, and was given greater specificity at the World Education Forum, held in Dakar in 2000.

ing. Unfortunately, total aid commitments to basic education have also declined in the past few years. Although the period from 1999 to 2004 was marked by a significant increase in aid to education, rising from $7.3 billion to $11.0 billion (United Nations Educational, Scientific and Cultural Organization, 2008), total aid, including that to basic education, has stagnated since then.

Income-based inequalities

Table VII.1 reveals stark differences in educational attainment between the rich and the poor. Income disparities are mirrored by differences in the average years of education attained by persons aged 17-22. Moreover, across the developing world, educational attainment also differs by gender, ethnicity and location, with these disadvantages intersecting with income-based differences.

Gender-based inequalities

Improving the educational attainment of girls—and women—can reduce poverty in many ways. Higher levels of education for girls typically increase their labour-force participation rates and earnings (Psacharopoulos and Patrinos, 2004). Female education lowers infant and child mortality, as well as

Table VII.1
Average years of education for the poorest and richest quintiles in age group 17-22, selected countries, 1999-2005

	Poorest 20 per cent	Richest 20 per cent	Gap
Bangladesh, 2004	3.7	8.1	−4.4
Burkina Faso, 2003	0.8	5.6	−4.8
Ethiopia, 2005	1.6	7.4	−5.8
Ghana, 2003	3.2	9.2	−6.0
Guatemala, 1999	1.9	8.3	−6.4
India, 2005	4.4	11.1	−6.7
Mali, 2001	0.4	4.8	−4.4
Mozambique, 2003	1.9	5.0	−3.1
Nicaragua, 2001	2.5	9.2	−6.7
Nigeria, 2003	3.9	9.9	−6.0
Peru, 2000	6.5	11.1	−4.6
Philippines, 2003	6.3	11.0	−4.7
United Republic of Tanzania, 2004	3.9	8.1	−4.2
Zambia, 2001	4.0	9.0	−5.0

Source: United Nations Educational, Scientific and Cultural Organization (2008).

maternal mortality rates. It is estimated that an additional year of female schooling reduces the probability of child mortality by 5-10 percentage points (Schultz, 1993). Women's education also confers intergenerational education benefits, with each additional year of formal education completed by a mother seeming to correlate with her children's remaining in school for from an additional third to one half of a year (Filmer, 2000). Female education also reduces fertility rates, which in turn can increase labour-force participation and earnings.

The positive relationship between female education and earnings is, of course, contingent on labour-market opportunities. In both developed and developing countries, labour-market discrimination means that better education does not always translate into higher earnings for women. For female education to impact positively upon poverty, economic as well as social discrimination must be tackled.

Although there has been considerable narrowing of the gender gap in education over the past decades, significant barriers to female education still remain. For example, girls still constituted 55 per cent of all out-of-school children in 2006, down from 59 per cent in 1999. Worldwide, for every 100 boys out of school, there are 122 girls. In some countries, the gender gap is much wider. For example, for every 100 boys out of school, there are 270 girls in Yemen, 316 girls in Iraq and 426 girls in India (United Nations Educational, Scientific and Cultural Organization, 2006).

Health and poverty in developing countries

The current high-level focus on health by the international community recognizes the strong relationship between poverty and health. Three of the eight Millennium Development Goals call for specific health improvements by 2015: reducing child deaths, reducing maternal mortality and slowing the spread of HIV/AIDS, malaria and tuberculosis. The Commission on Macroeconomics and Health demonstrated the link between health and economic development, resulting in the coming together of Governments and the private sector to establish the Global Fund to Fight AIDS, Tuberculosis and Malaria in 2002.

Table VII.2 presents Government spending on health and education and defence. Government expenditures for defence in low- and lower middle income countries are generally much higher than for health.

Government spending on health care has risen moderately since the late 1990s, mainly making up for cuts in previous years (Goldsbrough, 2007). Given the low incomes and therefore small tax base in developing countries, even increasing budgetary allocations will not be sufficient to address pressing health concerns.

Table VII.2
Government expenditure priorities, country groups by income and selected regions, 2005 and 2006 (*percentage of total*)

	Health (2005)	Education (2006)	Defence (2006)
Low-income	6.9	..	18.3
Lower middle income	5.9	..	15.7
Upper middle income	..	14.1	..
High-income	10.9	12.5	10.6
East Asia and the Pacific	2.1	..	17.2
Latin America and the Caribbean	..	..	..
Middle East and Northern Africa	8.2	..	16.2
South Asia	3.5	..	18.4

Source: World Bank (2008c).

Note: Military expenditure is shown as a percentage of central Government expenditure, while health and education are shown as a percentage of total government expenditure. Central Government expenditures include the expenditures of all bodies that are agencies or instruments of a central Government authority. In countries with strong subnational authorities, these figures can substantially understate total government expenditures; thus, care should be taken in making national comparisons.

Pro-poor health policies

Increasing fiscal allocations for health is not sufficient to help the poor achieve improved health and to meet the internationally agreed health goals. Most health spending disproportionately benefits the better off in society. This is evident from the increasing inequality in respect of health. As can be seen in figure VII.1, the ratio of the under-five mortality rates for the bottom quintile to that for the top quintile increased in many developing countries. In both developing and developed countries, poor women are more likely to die in childbirth than rich women (Graham and others, 2004; Mayor, 2001). Clearly, therefore, achievement of the international development targets, including reducing infant and child mortality rates and improving access to reproductive health care, requires focusing on the health issues of the poor.

However, given the problems associated with targeting, making improvements in the health of the poor will also benefit others. Public expenditure on primary health care and public health is more pro-poor than spending on hospital-based curative care. Water and sanitation-related diseases are a major cause of ill health, particularly among children. In Ghana, Brazil and the Philippines, it was found that public investments in sanitation benefited households with the least education more than the well educated (Alderman

Figure VII.1
Ratio of under-five mortality rate for the bottom quintile to that for the top quintile, selected developing countries, late 1980s and mid to late 1990s

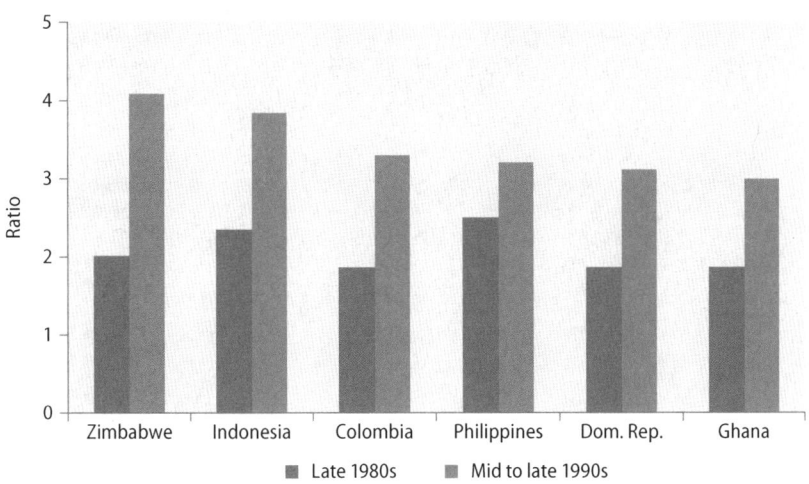

Source: World Health Organization, Regional Office for the Western Pacific (2002).

and Lavy, 1996). Therefore, public-health services are a key dimension of government services addressing the health of the poor. The critical issue will be how best to ensure that those services actually reach the poor (see box VII.3).

Social integration policies

Various social groups, including women, older persons, persons with disabilities and indigenous people, suffer multiple disadvantages and are generally more likely to suffer exclusion and live in poverty. Long-term exclusion may lead to chronic poverty. Hence, policies aiming at counteracting and preventing exclusion should be pursued in earnest at the normative, institutional and instrumental levels. The normative level encompasses legal provisions that ensure equal treatment of all citizens regardless of their personal attributes; that framework should ensure both individual and collective (group-based) rights. The institutional framework for inclusion promotes institutions that develop and execute inclusive policies for broad-based participation. At the instrumental level, specific policies are designed to promote integration. When such policies are being designed, concurrent changes and reforms may be required at all three levels, affecting laws, institutions and instruments, inasmuch as they are interdependent (Inter-American Development Bank, 2007).

Social integration policies should address physical security, including health and food security; investment in human resources, such as education and health; and social protection measures, social sector investments and spe-

> **Box VII.3**
> **User fees: health and poverty effects**
>
> User fees were introduced in the 1980s and 1990s as part of structural adjustment programmes throughout the developing world. During the early to mid-1980s, a considerable amount of effort went into justifying user fees as an appropriate policy tool in view of limited government resources. User fees were considered necessary for cost recovery, mobilizing revenues and promoting efficiency.
>
> In the past five years or so, however, there has been a policy shift regarding user fees, with the World Bank conceding through its research—though this has not necessarily been reflected in its operations—that there is no one approach to user fees in poor countries, and that alternative mechanisms for publicly funding health care need to be explored (see World Bank, 2003). Most key players in the health arena now recognize that user fees constitute a significant barrier to access to health services.
>
> Even set at relatively low levels, user fees reduce access to health care. Even when user fee systems include waivers for the poor, in practice they are often difficult to access or tend to be abused by the relatively better off. It has been estimated that abolition of user fees could prevent between 153,000 and 305,000 child deaths annually—between 4 and 8 per cent of the total—in African countries (Gilson and McIntyre, 2005). Removing user fees has proved to be an effective strategy for increasing access to health care. In Uganda, fee removal combined with other health policy reforms has dramatically improved health service utilization (Yates, 2009). These reforms helped poor people, in particular, to gain access to health services, and contributed to better health equity.
>
> Nor has the cost-recovery goal of user fees been achieved. It is estimated that user fees contribute, on average, to no more than 5 per cent of total health sector revenue (ibid.). At the same time, removing fees will entail additional resource requirements. It is therefore important to ensure that additional funding is available for countries that want to remove fees. To support the permanent removal of user fees and to ensure that the poor benefit from such actions, fee removal needs to be part of a broader package of reforms that includes increased budgets to offset lost fee revenue.

cific policies aiming at the equalization of opportunities for all. Ultimately, socially transformative policies are needed so that the socially excluded and marginalized can become part of the society they live in and intergenerational poverty and exclusion can be eradicated.

Different types of exclusion may require distinct forms of intervention. Thus, the promotion of economic inclusion requires broad support for the decent work agenda, while social inclusion efforts include, but are not limited to, fighting discrimination and inequality, redistributive measures and the promotion of participation.

Anti-discrimination policies

Discrimination, often firmly embedded in social structures and cultural norms, lies at the core of deprivation. Thus, anti-discrimination policies and anti-poverty efforts are essential for successful social integration. It is crucial to promote policies that explicitly prohibit discrimination based on race, colour, sex, language, religion, political or other opinion, national or social origin, property, birth or other status. There are several universal human rights instruments including the Universal Declaration of Human Rights,[6] the International Covenant on Civil and Political Rights[7] and the International Covenant on Economic, Social and Cultural Rights,[8] and the International Convention on the Elimination of All Forms of Racial Discrimination.[9] Many address the rights of particular groups and minorities, such as the Convention on the Rights of the Child,[10] the Convention on the Elimination of All Forms of Discrimination against Women,[11] the Convention on the Rights of Persons with Disabilities,[12] the International Convention on the Protection of the Rights of All Migrant Workers and Members of Their Families,[13] the United Nations Declaration on the Rights of Indigenous Peoples[14] and others.

They all address discrimination relating to different personal and group attributes. Since the Conventions are legally binding once ratified, they oblige Governments not only to remove any discriminatory provisions from national legal frameworks, but also to actively promote the rights of groups that face the worst forms of discrimination, including women, indigenous people, migrants and others.

The international community has developed comprehensive frameworks and action plans to advance the social integration of vulnerable groups, among them the World Programme of Action for Youth[15] and the Madrid International Plan of Action on Ageing (United Nations, 2002a, chap. I, resolution 1, annex II). National action plans have been developed to advance such frameworks. Nevertheless, their implementation poses a significant challenge, as they usually do not mandate the allocation of adequate public budgets for implementation.

Policies designed to reduce inequality in access to opportunities

Legal recognition of rights does not necessarily lead to a reduction in inequalities in respect of access to services, let alone in respect of social outcomes. The promotion of equality of rights and opportunities for disadvantaged groups requires redistribution of resources so as to reduce the disparities and advance both social inclusion and poverty reduction efforts.

Carefully designed redistribution approaches, promoting equal access to opportunities and improving income distribution are important for socially

---

6 General Assembly resolution 217 A (III).
7 See General Assembly resolution 2200 A (XXI), annex.
8 Ibid.
9 United Nations, *Treaty Series*, vol. 660, No. 9464.
10 Ibid., vol. 1577, No. 27531.
11 Ibid., vol. 1249, No. 20378.
12 General Assembly resolution 61/106, annex I.
13 United Nations, *Treaty Series,* vol. 2220, No. 39481.
14 General Assembly resolution 61/295, annex.
15 General Assembly resolution 50/81, annex.

inclusive policies. Progressive taxation and increased social spending also address inequality. However, more efforts should be made to bridge the yawning gap between wages and property income. Labour-market institutions (such as tripartite wage-setting systems involving workers, employers and the Government, and minimum wage and severance pay legislation) can play an important role in this regard. However, as noted earlier, labour-market reforms in the past three decades have significantly weakened these institutions and hence have contributed to income inequality.

Neoliberal economists claimed that low taxation and low social spending support growth and that income disparity offers incentives for effort and risk-taking and increases efficiency. Such claims are being increasingly challenged, with evidence showing that higher levels of taxation and public spending do not necessarily lead to lower growth (Social Watch, 2007). In OECD countries, high spending on well-designed social protection systems has not been negatively correlated with growth levels or GDP per capita. Similarly, in new member countries of the European Union (EU), higher social spending has not hurt growth. With one of the highest levels of public pension spending of the new EU members, Poland has had one of the strongest growth performances since 1989 (Jorgensen and Serrano-Berthet, 2009).

Ensuring access to productive assets (land and capital) for excluded groups may help to both combat poverty and promote inclusion. For instance, land reforms and land titling, particularly in agrarian societies, can benefit women, indigenous peoples and other minority groups. In addition, as shown by the experience of the Republic of Korea and Taiwan Province of China, radical land reforms in the early phase of development can contribute significantly to the reduction of inequality as well as to the promotion of growth, thus ensuring "shared" growth (Birdsall, Ross and Sabot, 1995).

Policies promoting participation

The promotion of participation, encompassing involvement in social, cultural, economic and political life for all members of society based on equality of rights and opportunities, is a basic element of many development efforts. The importance of participation for poverty reduction and social integration policies is based on the basic premise that people should be able to influence decisions that impact on their lives. Poverty itself is a tremendous barrier to participation, yet without promoting participation and inclusion, poverty reduction policies may simply never be well implemented. Hence, it is important to both remove barriers to participation and promote active participation. Social inclusion is impossible to achieve without a high degree of political inclusion, which entails democratic participation and a role for all in society.

The right to participation and representation of all groups can be ensured with affirmative action policies, such as proportionate representation in the political process, and through quota systems. For instance, gender quota systems have proved to be the most effective way of ensuring women's political representation. In 2006, countries with quotas nearly doubled the number of women elected, compared with countries without any gender quotas, which did not do so.

Many Governments have used affirmative action policies to promote greater access to public institutions. For instance, in India, certain numbers of parliamentary seats are reserved for Dalits (the lowest caste); there are also quotas for admission into secondary schools, colleges, and medical and engineering schools and for employment in government services (Kabeer, 2006a). In Chile, persons with disabilities get 10 extra points when applying for public subsidies or housing programmes, while Brazil has quotas for entry into university for black and indigenous people, and at least 11 countries in Latin America guarantee political representation by offering a number of seats in the national legislature on the basis of gender, race or ethnicity (Dani and de Haan, 2008, p. 134).

However, the affirmative action policies are not without problems. They can alienate other groups, and hence run the risk of generating conflict. This can happen especially when redistributive affirmative actions are implemented in the context of a stagnant economy or threaten the powerful and entrenched interests. Additionally, opposition can be acute if affirmative action policies are designed in an autocratic manner without broad consultation.

Effective social integration requires a broad vision

Combating social exclusion successfully depends not only on the commitment of government, but also on the attitudes of society as a whole towards those it excludes. In many societies, the very existence of the excluded is often denied or concealed. Before policies are formulated, the existence of exclusion and those who are excluded should be recognized.

The implementation of socially integrative policies is not the sole responsibility of Governments but should be shared by all sectors of the economy and society at large, together with the private sector and civil society organizations. It is vital to promote and encourage partnerships between the public sector, the private sector, and civil society in its broadest sense, including, among others, faith-based organizations, grass-roots movements and trade unions to implement social inclusion policies in the interest of the excluded. It is still the Governments, however, that must establish mechanisms that facilitate the involvement of all other important actors at the national and local levels.

Social policy and poverty reduction: from universalism to targeting and back

Over the last three decades, under the influence of the "trickle down" perspective, the concept of social protection—implying universalism—has given way to that of social safety nets, implying targeting. Universalism in social policy emphasizes the basic right of each and every citizen to the provisioning of social services; thus, the entire population is the beneficiary. Targeting, on the other hand, focuses on eligibility and hence involves means-testing to determine the "truly deserving". However, policy regimes are rarely based on purely universal or purely targeting principles. They normally operate somewhere on a continuum between these two extremes, "but where they lie on this continuum can be decisive in spelling out individuals' life chances and in characterizing the social order" (Mkandawire, 2007, p. 305).

With the rise of new economic and social philosophies in the late 1970s and early 1980s, the balance in social policy radically tilted towards targeting in both developed and developing countries. In the developed countries, the focus shifted from welfare to workfare; hence, there have been dramatic erosions of labour-market institutions aimed at increasing labour-market flexibility. At the same time, there have been cuts in welfare payments with higher eligibility criteria to force welfare recipients to join the workforce. It is claimed that, while higher welfare payments and easy access are disincentives to work, minimum wages and other employment benefits are deterrents for job creation. Thus, the two-pronged attacks on both labour-market interventions and welfare benefits are seen as solutions to unemployment and hence poverty. However, there is now mounting evidence linking these policy shifts to the rise in inequality and the prevalence of the working poor.

The rise in neoliberalism in developing countries has been associated with the structural adjustment programmes (SAPs) of the Bretton Woods institutions. Thus, the agenda of labour-market flexibility became part of the microeconomic reforms required by structural adjustment programmes, and social policy has been reduced to a set of temporary safety net programmes. After an initially painful phase, structural adjustment is expected to re-establish basic macroeconomic equilibrium and promote economic growth without inflation. It is argued that a strong economy will make permanent social policies unnecessary.

When Governments are required to operate within strict budgetary constraints and to improve the efficiency of resource allocation under structural adjustment programmes, social issues are considered a government expense, not an investment. This has led to massive declines in public expenditure on education, health, worker training and low-income housing and implementation of other social policies in both developed and developing countries. Low-income countries in sub-Saharan Africa, and South and West Asia, where some 80 per cent of the population are out of school, tend to invest very little in education. In sub-Saharan Africa, 11 of the 21 low-income countries with data spend less than 4 per cent of gross national product (GNP) on education. In South Asia, Bangladesh devotes only 2.6 per cent of its national income to education, India 3.3 per cent and Pakistan 2.7 per cent. For 40 out of the 105 countries with data, the share of national income devoted to education decreased between 1999 and 2006 (United Nations Educational, Scientific and Cultural Organization, 2008).

Furthermore, in many countries, social services were privatized to alleviate the fiscal crisis. It was argued that privatization would make service delivery more efficient and avoid the micro- and macroeconomic distortions that arise from the provision of free public services.

As part of balancing the government budget, user fees were introduced for public services previously provided free, particularly in former socialist transition economies. In many other economies, particularly in Latin America, user fees were increased; and everywhere, new operating principles—based on business and commercial profit criteria—were introduced. User fees were also expected to reduce the strain on overburdened public services, as they would discourage those who did not really need them and thereby eliminate wastage.

These changes in the provision of public services and the orientation of social policies have had significant repercussions with respect to the quality and breadth of coverage. Access to social services is no longer considered one's right as a citizen, but is based on one's ability to pay. Thus, these changes generated new social inequalities. At the same time, there is a slew of empirical evidence showing that targeting is not effective in addressing the issue of poverty (see box VII.4).

Further, contrary to the theoretical claims regarding its efficiency and cost savings, targeting is found to be extremely costly and to demand levels of administrative sophistication or capacity that do not exist in most developing countries. Ironically, the trimming of the government under the structural adjustment programmes itself contributed, to a large extent, to the erosion of State capacity, as there is a limit to what the State can do with so few resources. It is a contradiction in terms for the internationally agreed social development goals—"education for all", "primary health care for all", etc.—to be conceived in universalistic terms, while the means to achieve them remain highly selective and targeted (Mkandawire, 2007).

Lessons learned from the past three decades call for social policy to return towards universalism. This is necessary based not only on the principle of social justice rather than administrative procedures but also on pragmatic grounds: limited resources must be used to benefit people. Moreover, when the other, non-income dimensions of poverty are taken into consideration, poverty is much more widespread in developing countries than the poverty-line measurement would suggest. Targeting the majority of the population loses meaning. Social policy needs to take on a developmental perspective to promote economic and social development so as to ensure that growth will benefit all members of society.

Box VII.4
Impact of structural adjustment programmes on health and poverty in Africa

Structural adjustment programme–related reforms in Africa have deepened poverty, undermined food security and self-reliance and led to resource exploitation, environmental destruction and population displacement. The health sector particularly was adversely affected, and few steps were taken to protect vulnerable populations and basic services.

Prior to the 1980s, district hospitals, community health centres and other health outreach posts provided medical services and essential drugs free of charge. With the reforms, user fees and other cost-recovery measures were introduced, and the commercial sale of drugs was liberalized. Dispensation of essential drugs through the public distribution system declined. With complete deregulation of the pharmaceutical industry and liberalization of drug prices, imported branded drugs soon displaced domestically produced drugs. By 1990, domestic production of pharmaceuticals had virtually ceased.

Many donor Governments discontinued budget support for the health sector, which paralysed the public-health system. There was no money for medical equipment and maintenance; salaries and working conditions declined. In one African country, a public sector doctor earned US$ 49 monthly. With the growth of private medicine, tens of thousands of doctors and health workers fled the public sector, in some cases emigrating.

By the end of the 1990s, the health systems in most sub-Saharan countries had virtually collapsed. Fewer people could afford medicines or user fees at hospitals, let alone annual check-ups. One result was the resurgence of infectious diseases such as malaria, tuberculosis and cholera. A World Health Organization (WHO) study revealed that in some developing countries, malaria deaths tripled in the first four years of the reforms, owing partially to the collapse of curative health services and the soaring prices of antimalarial drugs.

Reduced resource allocations to health, education and other social sectors following the adoption of the structural adjustment programmes saw many slide back into poverty. Many families in sub-Saharan Africa have been unable to meet their most basic needs. Such conditions have been blamed on the debt burden and economic policies imposed by the World Bank.

Sources: Samba (2004); and Mkandawire (2007).

Chapter VIII
Poverty reduction programmes

As poverty levels remained stagnant or increased despite economic growth, it became clear that growth by itself does not reduce poverty, and macroeconomic recovery does not necessarily translate into significant social improvement. This has forced Governments and multilateral lending institutions to create or support programmes for combating poverty.

A menu of poverty reduction programmes can now be found in most developing countries. They include such instruments as conditional cash transfers, microfinance and rural employment guarantee schemes catering to workers outside the formal economy. The present chapter assesses some currently popular programmes aimed ostensibly at poverty reduction.

Microfinance

Developing countries are generally marked by low levels of financial intermediation. The fact that, as a rule, commercial banks find it unprofitable to operate in remote rural areas has resulted in absence of a formal market for lending and borrowing. Even where there are commercial banks, people living in poverty are disadvantaged owing to their lack of assets needed for collateral and good credit histories. Therefore, the poor and those living in remote areas are forced to borrow from moneylenders who charge usurious interest rates. The microcredit movement has sought to address the credit needs of people living in poverty.[1]

The 2006 Global Microcredit Summit (Halifax, Nova Scotia) pledged to provide microfinance to 175 million poor households by 2015. Governments and development agencies support the expansion of microfinance institutions which often specifically target women, who account for the vast majority of clients. Traditional networks and peer reviews ensure creditworthiness and loans are secured through joint liability. There are a range of models for microfinance institutions including non-governmental organizations, credit unions, cooperatives, banks and non-bank financial institutions and Government organizations. In some cases, the institutional forms are hard to distinguish from government banks operating microfinance services in collaboration with non-governmental organizations or credit cooperatives.

There is a growing body of literature on microfinance and its impact on poverty (see Chowdhury, 2009, for a brief survey). However, there are con-

---

1   The terms "microfinance" and "microcredit" are used interchangeably here. However, in the literature, the term "microfinance" is employed in a broader sense to cover other financial services such as microsavings services and micro-insurance.

siderable difficulties in generalizing from the findings of these studies owing to the different methodologies used, problems in disentangling the effects of microfinance from other effects on incomes, and the variety of institutional structures involved. A recent survey (Center for Global Development, 2007) summarized these difficulties as follows:

> There are many stories of the transformative effect of microfinance on individual borrowers but until *recently*, there has been surprisingly little *rigorous* research that attempts to isolate the impact of microfinance from other factors, or to identify how different approaches to microfinance change outcomes (italics added).

In terms of poverty reduction, two key questions have been raised: first, to what extent has microfinance made a lasting difference in bringing households out of poverty on a permanent basis? second, to what extent do microfinance programmes reach the "core poor" and not just the better off among the poor?

The most cited sources on the impact of microfinance on poverty are the studies edited by Hulme and Mosley (1996). They found that poor households do not benefit from microfinance: it is only non-poor borrowers who do well with microfinance and enjoy significant positive impacts. More troubling is the finding that a vast majority of those with starting incomes below the poverty line actually ended up with less incremental income after getting microloans, compared with a control group whose members did not obtain such loans. Another study (Khandker, 2005)—sponsored by the World Bank—involving 1,800 households in Bangladesh, found only very marginal improvements for microcredit borrowers. For example, the incomes of women who had received microcredit increased by only 8 taka for each 100 borrowed. Commenting on this finding, Roodman and Qureshi (2006, p. 38) noted: "Thus a $250 one-year loan would raise a borrower's income by $12.50-per-year, or about $0.03-per-day. For someone living on $2-per-day, that is a 1.5 per cent increase. This does not live up to the microfinance hype."[2]

Credit is only one factor involved in opening and operating a business. Other complementary factors—most importantly a recipient's entrepreneurial skills—are crucial for making credit more productive. Most poor people do not have the basic education or experience to understand and conduct even low-level business activities. They are mostly risk-averse, often fearful of losing what little they have.[3]

Critics note as well that for microenterprises to be successful they also need other complementary services, such as access to decent roads and affordable means for moving their products to markets as well as marketing support in order to reach customers (see Pollin, 2007). Finally, there is the nagging

---

2 Roughly 81 per cent of the population of Bangladesh live below the $2-a-day poverty line. The corresponding shares in Pakistan and Sri Lanka are about 70 and 40 per cent.

3 This does not mean, however, that they do not want to better themselves.

issue of very high interest rates charged by most microcredit institutions; for example, it was found that 350 leading microfinance institutions charged between 20 and 40 per cent per year, after taking inflation into account (Morduch, 2008).

Seasoned advocates of microfinance agree that microfinance alone cannot eradicate poverty. For example, the Director of the Microcredit Summit Campaign has written:

> Microfinance is not the solution to global poverty, but neither is health, or education, or economic growth. There is no one single solution to global poverty. The solution must include a broad array of empowering interventions and microfinance, when targeted to the very poor and effectively run, is one powerful tool (Daley-Harris, Pollin and Montgomery, 2007, p. 1).

In the words of microcredit pioneer and Nobel Laureate Professor Mohammed Yunus (2003, p. 171):

> Microcredit is not a miracle cure that can eliminate poverty in one fell swoop. But it can end poverty for many and reduce its severity for others. *Combined with other innovative programmes* that unleash people's potential, microcredit is an essential tool in our search for a poverty-free world (italics added).

Thus, there is broad agreement about the need to complement microfinance in order to reduce poverty. Some microfinance institutions and non-governmental organizations are therefore also offering training designed to build management and entrepreneurial skills. Non-governmental organizations such as BRAC in Bangladesh provide basic education in rural areas using innovative methods. These are all potentially positive developments for poverty reduction efforts.

Finally, microcredit-financed enterprises can best prosper in an expanding economy. The potential for increased productivity will remain mostly unrealized in the absence of demand-side factors. In other words, without a supportive macroeconomic, trade and industry policy framework, microenterprises will remain very small, with few backward or forward linkages or employment-creation possibilities.

There is, however, a growing consensus that microfinance can help people living in poverty maintain their consumption level over periods of cyclical downturns or unexpected crises. This positive role of microfinance should not be dismissed altogether. If consumption or expenditure smoothing means that parents can send their children to school, or buy essential medications, and maintain the nutritional intake of their children, then microfinance is likely to have positive long-term impacts on productivity and hence on poverty.

Microfinance thus fulfils an important safety-net task, especially in countries where there is no State-sponsored social security system. During an economy-wide crisis, people living in poverty are often forced to borrow from moneylenders or the employer/landlord for whom they work. If microfinance institutions extend lending to the very poor in these circumstances then they can help break the power and hold of moneylenders and landlords. Unfortunately, however, most microfinance institutions have been found wanting when it comes to lending to the very poor. Nonetheless, it seems that microfinance has made a significant dent in the informal usurious credit markets by undermining usury and debt bondage in some agrarian societies. Thus, microfinance is having a modernizing impact, even if that impact is inadvertent, unacknowledged and unsung.

There is also the learning-by-doing effect. The borrowers learn some basic principles of business, and with luck—and perhaps some help—may be able to become more viable and even expand. Microfinance also gives the unemployed and people living in poverty some opportunities, hope and self-esteem.

In promoting microfinance, policymakers must not ignore the needs of microenterprises in the informal economy. The owner-operators of these microenterprises have already proved their entrepreneurial acumen, but face numerous constraints ranging from inability to access the formal credit market to difficulties in marketing their products. These enterprises should be supported with easy access to credit and other financial services (for example, insurance).

Recognizing this, the United Nations (2006, p. 6) has advanced the idea of "inclusive" finance as an integral part of financial sector development:

> There needs to be a continuum of financial services available to households as they increase their standards of living and for enterprises as they grow into the business mainstream. This is a critical issue for the development of financial sectors. It involves adequate financial services for small and medium-sized enterprises (SMEs) often called the "missing middle", as well as the smallest microentrepreneurs.

Small and medium-sized enterprises have been disadvantaged by financial sector reforms during the past three decades, which have promoted profitable financial institutions by eliminating specialized State-run financial institutions, which catered to the needs of small and medium-sized enterprises and the agricultural sector. As the United Nations (ibid., p. 7) notes: "Mainstream for-profit financial institutions have largely ignored the lower segment of the market. This includes SMEs, microentrepreneurs... Instead, these mainstream institutions have sought mainly high-value clients." These high-value clients usually reside in urban areas, while the majority of poor people live in rural areas in developing countries.

Conditional cash transfers

Conditional cash transfers (CCTs) have recently become a widely used means of addressing aspects of poverty in developing countries. Conditional cash transfers are cash grants provided to poor and disadvantaged people on condition that they make specific commitments, such as sending their children to school and having regular health check-ups. These transfers are therefore often designed as a mix of cash transfers and service provision, emphasizing strong linkages with the labour market and intra-household responsibilities.

In the developing world, conditional cash transfers were first introduced in a few countries in Latin America and South Asia but are now becoming increasingly widespread. An early, iconic conditional cash transfer scheme, Progresa, in Mexico, began in 1997 with 300,000 households and its successor, Oportunidades, now reaches 5 million households. In Brazil, the Bolsa Familia programme began in the mid-1990s as an experiment in two municipalities and currently covers 11 million families. In Colombia, the initial target of the Familias programme had been 400,000 families, but it had expanded to cover 1.5 million households by 2007. Smaller programmes in poorer countries such as Kenya and Bangladesh cover a few thousand families (World Bank, 2009a).

Conditional cash transfers account for varying proportions of mean household consumption, ranging from 20 per cent in Mexico to 4 per cent in Honduras (World Bank, 2009a). Evaluations also show that conditional cash transfers improve outcomes related to health, nutrition and education. The impact of Progresa on education enrolment in Mexico has been significant (de Brauw and Hoddinott, 2008). Even the short-lived Red de Protección Social (RPS) in Nicaragua, in operation between 2000 and 2006, directed funds to female household heads, significantly improving school enrolment and other education indicators, and reduced stunting by an impressive five percentage points in programme communities (Maluccio and Flores, 2005). Evaluations of the cash-for-relief programme in Ethiopia, used to address crop failures, found cash grants were used to pay off debts, restore land productivity and help regenerate livelihoods (Standing, 2007).

As many evaluations have shown that conditional cash transfers increase school enrolment, the issue of whether they also reduce child labour is highly pertinent. This would be expected and, indeed, the experience of several programmes supports such an assumption. For example, Brazil's Child Labour Eradication Programme (PETI), which targets working children and insists that a child stop working in order for the household to receive benefits, has successfully achieved its objectives. In contrast, the incentive provided by a cash transfer from Paraguay's Tekoporã programme was not sufficient to reduce child labour and could even have stimulated it indirectly (Vera Soares, Perez Ribas and Hirata, 2008). A possible reason for this seemingly paradoxical result is that when household income (in this case, the mother's income) increases, children may opt out of school to take on paid work. Household utility may be further enhanced by the fact that children take on paid work.[4]

---

4 Some recent evaluations of conditional cash transfers (for example, that of Teixera (2008) on Brazil's conditional cash transfer programme Bolsa Familia) have examined their

Should cash transfers be conditional?

A contentious issue relating to conditional cash transfers is that of the desirability of imposing conditions. Conditioning transfers is supposed to induce desirable changes in behaviour. Conditioning can also work to overcome information asymmetries. For instance, Governments may need to better understand the benefits of immunization, and a conditional cash transfer programme that conditions immunization can overcome this information asymmetry. Besides enhancing the public interest, conditionalities may also strengthen the bargaining position of women, whose preferences may be better aligned with the Government's, but who may lack bargaining power within the household. Conditions also help make the transfers more acceptable to the average taxpayer (de Brauw and Hoddinott, 2008).

However, there is a significant cost in monitoring behaviour and many developing countries lack the administrative capacity to monitor adequately. Conditionality can also create opportunities for corruption, as individuals responsible for certifying that conditions have been met could demand bribes for doing so. Furthermore, some poor families may find it difficult to meet conditions owing to the lack of easily accessible health services or schools and may suffer serious consumption losses if excluded from conditional cash transfer programmes. Conditional cash transfers generally target only households with school-age children, which means that all impoverished households without school-age children will be excluded.

Progresa in Mexico was apparently quite effective in reaching very poor households in very poor areas, but less effective in reaching the "moderately poor" (Skoufias, 2001). In both Nicaragua and Mexico, about 20 per cent of beneficiaries were not poor (Coady, Grosh and Hoddinott, 2004). In Bangladesh, where targeting has been much weaker, about 40 per cent of beneficiaries were found to be not poor (Standing, 2008b). Another study found that covering all rural children, rather than targeting all identifiably poor children, would have had a greater poverty reduction impact with only a marginal increase in expenditure (Kakwani, Soares and Son, 2005).

More importantly, conditioning transfers is often based on the assumption that illiteracy, child labour or poor health outcomes are the result of irrational behaviour engaged in by the poor or of their incapacity to understand their

incentive effects on labour supply, and found that cash transfers induced a reduction in labour hours supplied. One problem with this kind of study is that it ignores the price effects of transfers. Cash transfers essentially reduce the cost of obtaining services, and thus should lead to higher demand (for example, for children's education) or usage of social services (for example, health-care centres). Therefore, the net effect of cash transfers should depend on the relative size of the price and income effects. More importantly, such findings of adverse incentive effects (or negative income effects) on labour supply imply that the poor are poor either because they are "lazy" (in other words, they prefer more leisure), or because their expectations are "low" (in other words, they work for a low minimum target income).

own best interests—a moot assumption which can be challenged on many grounds. This becomes tantamount to blaming the victims for their condition, is demeaning to the poor, and hence is likely to be resented (Standing, 2007).

In the context of the ideology on which such an assumption is based, poverty becomes rooted in individual pathologies, rather than posited as having structural causes. The responsibility for poverty is thus placed squarely on the shoulders of the person who is poor (Handa and Davis, 2006; Schubert and Slater, 2006). Blaming the victim allows the potential role of the State in poverty alleviation to be reduced. Within this ideology, social assistance schemes should be well targeted in order to reduce social security expenditure (Quinn and Magill, 1994). In contrast, universal social protection programs seek to support individuals positively with significant State financial commitments (Organization for Economic Cooperation and Development, 2003).

Conditional cash transfers or job creation?

Would resources allocated to conditional cash transfers have a greater impact on poverty if used for job creation programmes? While there is insufficient empirical evidence to conclusively settle this question, several points are noteworthy. First, the effects of job creation programmes and conditional cash transfers often vary with location. In rural areas, where families tend to have a larger number of children, conditional cash transfers could be more effective in increasing household incomes. By contrast, in urban areas, where vulnerable groups such as new migrants cannot find secure employment, job creation projects may have sustained effects on poverty reduction. A simulation study for Kenya (Zepeda, 2007)—which compared the potential poverty reducing effects of conditional cash transfers with those of job creation programmes—found that the latter would have a greater impact on the poorest income deciles in urban areas. Second, rural work is also often seasonal and unstable, and stable job creation programmes could be important in poverty reduction. In India, under the National Rural Employment Guarantee Act, the Government guarantees at least 100 days of employment per year to poor rural workers. Finally, in both rural and urban areas, if job creation programmes are tied to improving economic and social infrastructure such as building schools and hospitals, they could have strong multiplier effects on poverty reduction.[5]

Unconditional and universal transfers

Given some of the problems associated with conditionality and targeting, the question whether direct cash grants to people living in poverty should be universal and/or unconditional has been raised. Unconditional cash grants

---

5 For a comprehensive evaluation of various job guarantee schemes in developing countries, see Wray (2007).

are increasingly being offered to limit acute poverty and hardship in emergency situations. These programmes are typically implemented together with material-based (in kind) aid, such as food aid, but go beyond the immediate consumption goals of commodity transfers to aim at enhancing livelihoods and longer-term incomes. The cash-for-relief programme in Ethiopia, in response to insufficient rainfall in 2002 and 2003, provided small cash grants over a period of three to six months directly to the most vulnerable households. Evaluations of this project found that the cash grants were successful in regenerating the livelihoods of people living in affected communities; the grants had been used not only for consumption, but also for reducing debts and improving land productivity. The programme also restored basic infrastructure, thereby ensuring the sustainability of the affected communities (Brandstetter, 2004). Similarly, the emergency cash relief programme implemented in north-eastern Somalia in 2003-2004 ensured rapid economic recovery for vulnerable households (Standing, 2007). Another successful example is the pilot Kalomo social cash transfer scheme initiated in two districts by the Government of Zambia. The programme provided an unconditional and regular cash transfer, enabling beneficiaries to develop a sense of autonomy in respect of how to spend the money.

In case of emergency, it is possible to institute universal cash transfer schemes such as a basic income grant with no conditions. Critics of such programmes argue that a basic income grant reduces total employment in an economy by reducing labour supply and the willingness to work by raising the acceptable wage floor. However, in developing countries, the availability of basic income grants may increase productivity and help smooth consumption. For example, income grants reduce the need for workers to send remittances to their families, thus increasing the wage available for their own consumption, or for skills upgrading. This, in turn, could increase productivity through better health and human resources outcomes. Higher productivity will increase overall output and labour demand. If a basic income grant is successful in boosting long-term growth, the fiscal burden of the transfer would be reduced. The issue of whether a basic income grant can serve as a key intervention for poverty reduction has been debated in the case of South Africa.

Supporters of targeted anti-poverty policies criticize calls for universal programmes, which they view as expensive and politically unrealistic. According to them, taxpayers will oppose financing universal programmes. They also argue that universal programmes provide the most benefits or services to the middle class or those with low incomes who are best prepared to improve themselves.

However, if the taxpayers are not willing to pay for universal social security programmes, then why should people just above the poverty line, struggling without benefit of health coverage, childcare or adequate unemployment insurance, pay for programmes that go exclusively to people below the poverty line? As a matter of fact, in developing countries, a large number of people—either on or just above the poverty line—remain highly vulnerable to shocks to the economy or to changes in personal circumstances. Some estimates identify as much as 80 per cent of the population as being vulnerable.

Within the framework of universal programmes, less privileged people can receive extra benefits without stigma—as "targeting within universalism". While targeted programmes can generate forces that undo their aims, social policies that deliver benefits across different social groups and income classes can generate broad political coalitions that sustain and protect those social policies.

Employment guarantee schemes

Public works programmes have developed into major policy instruments for employment creation in situations of high or chronic unemployment or in times of crises. These programmes aim to help people living in poverty by providing them with paid employment in rebuilding affected areas after a disaster or in creating needed infrastructure, which, in turn, enhances their welfare. The majority of these programmes are temporary, but a few offer employment guarantee schemes that secure some minimum employment on an ongoing basis. Some developing countries, including Argentina, China, Indonesia and the Republic of Korea, are devising public works programmes in response to the current crisis.[6]

These programmes have enhanced the incomes of participants, while maintaining, improving or creating valuable infrastructure. For instance, a study of the most famous scheme, the Maharashtra Employment Guarantee Scheme in India, found that participants earned four times their forgone income (Datt and Ravallion, 1994). However, few of the programmes provide sustainable employment opportunities. They often treat unemployment as a transient problem and are merely effective for the short term, following an emergency or an economic shock, but rarely stimulate job creation in the private sector or offer long-term solutions to unemployment or underemployment.

There is also little evidence of targeting the poorest. Often, the programmes are not located in regions with the highest rates of poverty or unemployment. An assessment of seven public works programmes in South Africa, for instance, found that some districts with very high poverty and unemployment had no labour-intensive public works projects, while other districts with low poverty rates had four or more projects (Adato and Haddad, 2001). This was not the result of political capture by powerful districts: in the example of South Africa, the allocation of projects was determined using presumably objective criteria; however, local authorities in richer communities had better means of, and more assistance in, preparing their applications.

Even the much talked about Maharashtra Scheme failed to attract those most in need (United Nations, 2007a). Some argue that these programmes

---

6 According to the World Bank (2009g), only one quarter of vulnerable developing countries are in a position to undertake significant counter-cyclical spending.

should set wages below the market wage rate, or even below the minimum wage, to ensure self-selection by the poorest (Subbarao, 2003). In practice, recruiting workers for programmes offering remuneration below the market wage has been challenging. In many cases, wages are raised during implementation of the programme through workers' collective bargaining (Adato and Haddad, 2001; Subbarao, 2003). Moreover, paying less than the minimum wage does not solve the problem of poverty, but simply swells the ranks of the working poor.

However, research at the International Labour Organization (ILO) (Wray, 2007) has shown that more universal and permanent employment guarantee schemes can be so designed as to sidestep the problems that beset existing temporary and targeted programmes. For example, a universal employment guarantee scheme can provide full-time work (and part-time work if desired) with no time limits and pay a uniform wage to all workers.[7] A minimum wage becomes effective only in combination with a job guarantee. Therefore, the wage paid by employment guarantee schemes can become the effective minimum or social wage. Further, the package of benefits offered sets a standard, which would normally be matched by other employers; this could include health care, childcare, sick leave, vacations and social security contributions.

Finally, such programmes could be added to existing social protection provisions to give workers who have lost their jobs more choices. Since formal sector white-collar workers are unlikely to benefit from employment guarantee schemes targeted for people living in poverty, especially in rural areas, State-owned enterprises can offer them temporary employment at a socially acceptable minimum wage. By joining the programme, these workers can maintain their self-esteem and skills, and avoid joining the ranks of the long-term unemployed. Thus, when the economy recovers, their access to better jobs becomes easier and the private sector has a pool of skilled workers ready for employment, without having to pay for retraining. The public sector benefits too, as workers bring in skills and experience from their earlier private sector jobs. This kind of programme for formal sector workers can be funded by levies (like unemployment insurance contributions) payable during boom times.[8]

Poverty reduction through property rights

There are strong links between poverty and lack of property, as people living in poverty not only lack income, but are also without the assets needed to generate income. Land is a critical asset, particularly for the rural poor, as it provides a means of livelihood, and the landless are often among the world's poorest.

---

7 According to the World Bank (2009g), only one quarter of vulnerable developing countries are in a position to undertake significant counter-cyclical spending.

8 Hyman Minsky (1965; 1966; 1986) articulated such a proposal in the mid-1960s and the mid-1980s.

In India, for example, over 30 per cent of the landless and near landless live in poverty, while in Bangladesh, they make up two thirds of people living in poverty (Meinzen-Dick, Kameri-Mbote and Markelova, 2007). There are also indications that landownership increases investment in the education of children and hence can help reduce intergenerational poverty.

In rural communities, landownership and land rights are associated with social standing in the community. The intra-household distribution of property rights is also important, as it typically discriminates against women. In many cases, women gain access to land only through the male members of the household, and they are vulnerable to eviction or loss of land in case of the man's death, divorce or disinheritance. Landownership by women, on the other hand, has contributed to their empowerment and to a decline in domestic violence (Panda and Agarwal, 2005; Bhatla, Chakraborty and Duvvury, 2006).

The links between poverty and lack of property often prompt calls for land reforms, with transfers from large landlords to the landless. Such land reform, however, requires commitment by the State to withstand resistance from powerful landed owners.

Land can also be used as collateral for loans for investment, or sold to raise capital for investment in an income generating activity. This has led to campaigns—popularized by Hernando de Soto—to grant a title to land to urban slum-dwellers who live on land not owned by them. According to de Soto, the world's poor are sitting on a huge amount of potential capital, but are hindered by bureaucracies. For example, in Haiti, individuals must take 176 bureaucratic steps over an average of 19 years to own land legally. Thus, de Soto (2000) has argued that assigning property rights would give people living in poverty access to credit, thereby ending the "capitalist apartheid" allegedly so prevalent in the developing world. A number of countries in Latin America and Africa have attempted, strongly aided by donors, to formalize land titles following de Soto's argument, despite the fact that de Soto has offered little real evidence that formalizing property titles actually leads to greater credit access and thus to poverty reduction in the developing world.

In Peru, where the Government and the Commission for Formalizing Informal Property, which de Soto helped create in 1996, formalized the property of millions of rural and urban people, poverty levels have actually increased over the past few years (Bourbeau, 2001). According to legal advocate Murtaza Jaffer (quoted in Bourbeau, 2001, pp. 78-79): "Efforts to convey individual titles to the poor in planned settlements have overestimated the ability of these 'owners' to find economic livelihood in the absence of additional support beyond allocation of land. The poor soon sell their interests, returning once more to unplanned settlements and despair."

In short, formalizing land titles suffers from impediments similar to those experienced along the microfinance route to poverty reduction. In the absence of an expanding economy, new landowners will not be able to expand their capabilities. They often lack the education and entrepreneurial skills needed to undertake business activities with borrowed money. They are risk-averse and more worried about failing and hence losing their asset (land) used as collateral. Poverty itself is a barrier to risk-taking and enterprise.

Furthermore, the campaign for formalizing land titles ignores the role of culture and tradition, and assumes that with the same rights to property, everyone will behave similarly in order to maximize utility or profit. However, not everyone shares the same belief system, as has now become clear from findings in the new field of behavioural economics. Many traditional societies regard savings as a virtue, and borrowing as a manifestation of distress to be avoided. In many Muslim countries, interest-based financing is being replaced by financing based on profit-loss sharing. In such a system, there is no need for collateral, as the financier becomes a co-owner of the business.

In many societies, there are other means of conferring property rights on people living in poverty involving a mixture of legal systems, including statutory law and customary mechanisms. In Africa, for example, over 90 per cent of the rural population access land through customary mechanisms. In addition to customary law, property rights are influenced by a range of other legal, cultural and normative frameworks, including religious laws and practices, international treaties, and development project regulations. Which of these frameworks are accepted and enforced depends on power and social relations among different claimants. These complexities have not always been recognized in programmes aimed at legally empowering the poor with land titles.

Statutory legal reforms should also take into account the secondary property rights held by various claimants, such as the right to collect water, firewood, fish or medicinal plants or grazing rights for their livestock. Loss of these rights could seriously erode livelihoods, especially those of the poorest (Frias, 2005; Wily, 2006). Many formal systems focus only on landownership, thus excluding these secondary claims. Accordingly, the poor and marginalized often depend more on customary or religious justifications for claiming their rights to resources. Well-intentioned programmes designed to formally clarify land rights for poor people may hurt their overall interests and thereby fail to reduce poverty.

Governance reforms and poverty reduction

Since the late 1990s, attention has also been given to governance reforms as a precondition for poverty reduction (see Van Arkadie, 2005, for a review thereof). This followed some influential research, especially in the World Bank, on the alleged link between corruption and economic performance. The governance reform agenda received added impetus following the Asian financial crisis, in whose creation, it was claimed, especially in the West, that "cronyism" had played a major role. The governance reform agenda has also promoted ostensibly "good"—understood mainly as market-friendly—policies to achieve its goal of ensuring aid effectiveness. Thus, the dominant "good governance" paradigm identifies a series of capabilities necessary for a market-friendly State. These include capabilities to protect stable property rights, enforce the rule of law, effectively implement anti-corruption policies and achieve government accountability. Many of these capabilities are clearly desirable as ends in themselves; but in the good governance framework, these capabilities are identified as preconditions for sustained growth, as they are supposed to ensure that markets will be efficient and less subject to market failures. It is therefore argued that good governance is a precondition for poverty reduction by ensuring sustained growth. Additionally, "pro-poor" good governance reforms are supposed to enhance the scale and efficiency of service delivery to people living in poverty.

However, neither theory nor evidence strongly supports the plausibility of the view that governance reform significantly reduces poverty (Khan, 2009). The stabilization of property rights, the rule of law and the significant reduction of corruption—that is, the achievement of good governance goals—require fiscal capabilities not available in most developing countries. As structural and fiscal constraints prevent significant improvements in governance capabilities, market failures are likely to remain significant, and are unlikely to be significantly reduced by governance reforms. Developing countries therefore need to focus on alternative governance capabilities, which can enable them to directly address key market failures. Khan describes this as a growth-enhancing governance agenda which focuses on developing governance capabilities appropriate for directly addressing a few key market failures.

Van Arkadie (2005) observes that the governance discourse is also concerned with political agendas/objectives, entailing the incorporation of visions of desirable political models. Good governance practice is sometimes justified for the economic benefits it will generate, and at other times as a political end. This creates no problems when arguments drawing on either of these perspectives work in the same direction to generate sustained growth and poverty reduction. However, the discussion becomes problematic when the evidence suggests that politically desirable concepts of good governance are not a necessary condition for fast economic growth or poverty reduction and may even be inconsistent with them. In such cases, a choice may have to be made among governance, growth and poverty reduction objectives. As pointed out by Van Arkadie (2005, p. 222): "The fundamental difficulty... is to come to terms with political and social realities as they exist, and to judge what is appropriate and what is possible given those realities, rather than promoting images of society largely based on an idealized interpretation (typically not very deep) of OECD experience".

Concluding remarks

Microfinance acts as an important safety net instrument and the microfinance movement seems to have reduced the influence of informal moneylenders. Microfinance has also had wider social impacts, ranging from the empowerment of women to the improvement in self-esteem of the poor and unemployed. However, its overall poverty reduction effects remain doubtful in the absence of other complementary factors, such as entrepreneurial skills and the growth of overall demand in the economy.

The programme of formalizing land titles for urban slum-dwellers is a simplistic poverty reduction tool for whose significant and lasting poverty reduction effect there is little evidence. As with microcredit programmes, the overall effects of slum land titling on poverty reduction remain dubious without the inclusion of appropriate complementary factors. If appropriate land titling programmes are part of redistributive land reforms aimed at reducing inequality, especially in rural areas, they may be far more effective in poverty reduction, as was the case for the agrarian reforms of East Asia in the 1950s.

Both microfinance and land titling focus on capital market imperfections, while ignoring other market imperfections. They assume that people living in poverty are all potential entrepreneurs, constrained only by their inability to access credit. However, if most people are potentially entrepreneurial risk-takers, when and where property rights are well guaranteed, then they will not be constrained by lack of access to credit; one would then expect to find a lack of people willing to work, as most people would want to start their own businesses. In reality, close to 75 per cent of the working-age population in developed countries are employees, not employers (entrepreneurs). The creation of stable and decent jobs through appropriate policies and institutional support is far more likely to contribute to poverty reduction, as recognized by the Millennium Development Goals.

Policymakers in the colonial past attributed poverty in part to behavioural problems and cultural deficiencies that they hoped would be corrected by special training and community action programmes for people living in poverty. The welfare reform consensus of the mid-1980s converged on the notion that mandated work and job training could best alleviate poverty. Neoliberals are keen on making welfare contingent on work, and want to discipline welfare clients, while liberal welfare reformers want to deliver more training, health care and childcare to the underprivileged. However, almost everyone seems to think that the best way to proceed is with programmes targeted at the poor. Thus, there has been a proliferation of conditional cash transfer programmes aimed at improving the education and health of the poor as well as temporary employment guarantee schemes, especially for the rural poor.

Research, on the other hand, shows that universal social protection systems are much more effective in reducing vulnerability, and it is possible to implement such systems in most developing countries with a modest increase of budgetary resources. Within the universal social protection framework, employment guarantee schemes can be extended to cover other vulnerable people in society, not just the poor and unemployed in rural areas. This is consistent with the objective of full employment and decent work for all. By acting as a buffer and as part of an active labour-market programme, State-owned enterprises can help maintain full employment at a decent social wage.

While good governance can be an end in itself, the link between good governance and poverty reduction is much more complex, and can be obscured by the intrusion of political agendas. Furthermore, many developing countries may not have fiscal and administrative capacity needed to achieve the onerous governance reform agenda imposed by aid conditions. Thus, developing countries need to be selective and aim for growth-enhancing and poverty-reducing governance reforms.

Chapter IX
Rethinking poverty reduction interventions

Revisiting recent poverty trends

Although the world as a whole has made some reasonable progress in reducing levels of absolute poverty, many countries are not on track to meet the Millennium Development Goals of halving levels of extreme poverty by 2015. Countries such as China and, to some extent, India, and regions such as East and South-East Asia, that have experienced strong growth during the last few decades have managed to significantly reduce poverty levels, particularly in urban areas. The success enjoyed by these countries has driven global poverty down; but not every region or country has recorded such remarkable progress, and there has generally been less poverty reduction in countries experiencing little or no growth. In fact, the absolute number of poor people has gone up in several countries in sub-Saharan Africa, Latin America, the Middle East and Northern Africa, as well as in Central Asia. Economic growth in many developing countries, particularly the least developed countries, has not translated into poverty reduction. This has been especially the case when growth has been concentrated in extractive industries, which has not resulted in much job growth and structural change. High or rising inequality has also blunted the poverty-reducing effects of growth.

If the impact of the triple crises (food, energy and financial) is factored in, the outlook is not encouraging. Poverty eradication efforts are sagging under the weight of these multiple crises. The worst economic and financial crisis since the Great Depression of the 1930s has not only impacted the poor and the near-poor in the developing world, but also hurt a much larger proportion of the lower and middle classes in developed economies. Millions of jobs have been lost, as well as millions of dollars in individual savings and pensions. Consequently, many households now face a wide array of everyday basic concerns—ranging from the lack of adequate income to meet basic household consumption needs such as food and shelter to the inability to pay for children's schooling. In countries like the United States of America, many of these households are also close to financial ruin owing to health costs incurred after the loss of employer-provided health insurance. If left unattended, crises of this nature are likely to lock poor people and their families into long-term intergenerational poverty traps while increasing the vulnerability of non-poor families to poverty, as they exhaust household assets to pay for catastrophic expenditures. They also undermine prospects for future growth by weakening the human resource base of countries through underinvestments in children's schooling, nutrition and health care (Ravallion, 2008; Birdsall, 2002).

The fact that the financial crisis is coming on the heels of the sharp spikes in food and energy prices that occurred in 2007-2008 has made the fallout much worse for most developing countries. The World Bank (2009b) estimated that in 2008 the food and energy crises alone pushed between 130 million and 155 million people into poverty. The World Food Programme (WFP) has estimated that the number of chronically hungry people in the world surpassed the billion mark in 2009.[1] Most of them lack access to social safety nets and credit markets, and hence are the least able to smooth consumption effectively when faced with shocks of this magnitude (Lustig, 2000).

These developments will likely slow down or even reverse the pace of decline of poverty levels, which had been uneven in the first place. In some cases, gains made in respect of achieving the other Millennium Development Goals may also be reversed. To compound the situation, the flow of official development assistance (ODA) and remittances from developed to developing countries will likely also slacken. Debt-relief efforts are also likely to slow down despite the pledges made by leaders of the Group of Twenty (G-20) in London in April 2009 to restore growth and jobs in all countries, including the poorest countries and emerging markets.

Therefore, despite recognized success in some countries, there has been insufficient progress globally towards the elimination of poverty and deprivation. Wide-ranging deficits in terms of the human condition are endemic and ubiquitous not only in most poor countries but also, to a disturbing extent, in many rich countries among specific vulnerable sections and groups in society. What is particularly disturbing is that the relatively disappointing outcomes in many crucial dimensions have been found to persist in an era where there was rapid and sustained growth at the global level and in several large countries as well; that these deficits have remained despite all the affirmations and aspirations driving the professed commitments of the global community to achieving the goals set out in the United Nations Millennium Declaration;[2] that such a situation prevails when there are but a few years left to the end date for realizing the promises made in the Millennium Declaration; and that such a scenario had been unfolding even before the impact of the ongoing multiple global crises was factored in.

Critical reflections

Several messages come through loud and clear from the discussion and analysis conducted thus far. First, the mainstream perspectives on poverty and depriva-

---

1 See Lustig (2009) for various estimates of the poverty impacts of the 2007-2008 food crisis.
2 See General Assembly resolution 55/2.

tion as embodied in, for example, both the dollar-a-day poverty estimates and the human development index have limitations. Second, there are strong ethical and strategic reasons for moving towards a universal approach, rooted in the recognition of both human and social development deficits and the modes of intervention needed for addressing them. Third, more research and reflection are needed in order to develop a wider analytical framework that incorporates the social exclusion approach to poverty reduction efforts. Fourth, setting targets for various human development indicators has to be accompanied by an analysis of the causal mechanisms that account for the deficits in the first place and by policy interventions directed at achieving the targets.

Framing policy: some correctives

As poverty levels have not declined in several countries despite economic growth, it has become clear that growth, while often a necessary condition for poverty reduction, is not a sufficient one. Addressing inequality and promoting social inclusion are also prerequisites. Reductions in inequality need to be considered in designing economic development processes. Hence, the relationship between economic and social policy cannot be one where growth is given primacy over distribution, and where social policy comes to be understood merely as a corrective for the undesirable consequences of growth processes. Social policy has to be viewed as an essential part of a transformative process that contributes to both growth and equity, not just through responding with corrections, but also by influencing the nature of growth.

There is also a need to reconsider the effectiveness and legitimacy of means-tested targeting. Lessons learned from the past three decades call for social policy to return towards universalism. This is necessary based not only on the principle of social justice rather than administrative procedures, but also on pragmatic grounds. Limited resources must be used to benefit people. This having been said, consideration must be given to addressing the needs of the most vulnerable within a policy framework grounded in universalism. As the social exclusion approach makes clear, certain segments of the population face greater challenges than the rest of society in overcoming deficits within many dimensions. Compared with poor people, the better off are typically also better able to benefit disproportionately from public social services even if they are universally provided. For example, even with universal access to education, facilities in better-off areas are often superior to those in poor areas, which contributes to the intergenerational transfer of poverty. Thus, universal programmes need to include special efforts, backed by resource commitments, to ensure that benefits reach marginalized populations.

The line separating poor and non-poor people is becoming less clear-cut and less significant. Poverty is not the condition of a fixed group of individuals but rather one that everyone is at risk of experiencing at some point in their lives. Therefore, it would be wise to formulate policies and allocate resources to ensure the basic well-being of all individuals—those experiencing poverty and those at risk of experiencing it. This would constitute a strategy designed to stimulate recovery. Ensuring that the world's people are healthy, educated and well housed and well fed is essential if they are to be productive and contribute to making the economic recovery a reality. Therefore, approaches to poverty reduction should be developmental and holistic, integrating economic and social policies devised to ensure the achievement of people-centred development outcomes.

Anti-poverty expenditures are usually considered part of social consumption. However, the object of policy should also be to create the conditions that transform such social consumption into a productive form of social investment. A good starting point would entail changing the perspective adopted to consider the problem, followed by evidence-based assessment of current policies and practices from which to draw constructive lessons for guiding future actions.

Policy imperatives

Certain policy implications can be extracted from a broad perspective on deprivation. First, poverty reduction strategies should be developmentally oriented so as to promote structural transformations that will generate decent work opportunities for all. There is more to poverty than just insufficient income. In fact, a higher proportion of the populations of most countries would be perceived as living in poverty if other aspects of deprivation were taken into account. This calls into serious question the usefulness of approaches to poverty reduction that focus on "poor people" identified by the dollar-a-day measurement. A more encompassing approach should be adopted towards provision of essential social services such as basic health care and primary education, safe water and sanitation, and basic social protection.

Second, a high premium must be placed on interventions that correct inequalities in the initial distributions of assets, including human resources, in an egalitarian manner in order to foster more inclusive growth. Analysis shows that initial conditions are very important. On the one hand, a high degree of initial inequality in property and asset ownership is a crucial indicator of the social and economic exclusion inherent in the socio-economic system; on the other, such high initial inequality would limit the possibilities of pro-poor growth within such a system. The greater the initial degree of inequality and exclusion, the weaker the beneficial impact of any increased rate of economic growth on poor people; and the less is done in correcting initial inequalities, the more will have to be accomplished via the growth process in order to reduce poverty—but the less likely the possibility this could be achieved. This aspect of policy has been seriously underemphasized and corrections are long overdue.

Higher initial inequalities, and less inclusive growth processes, could lead to correspondingly larger deficits in the ability of vulnerable households to satisfy their basic needs. Therefore, progressive redistributive policies would become more difficult to implement. Increasingly, there seems to be acceptance of the notion that neither the initial structural inequalities nor inequalities in the growth process can be adequately addressed. Unequal growth has come to be accepted because it leads to fiscal surpluses which can subsequently be used for secondary redistribution through various tax-and-transfer processes of poverty reduction. However, there are several difficulties with such a strategy. For one, it is based on the premise of a trade-off between curbing inequality (and social exclusion) and accelerating growth. For another, a system biased against correcting inequalities is also likely to resist redistributive transfers in favour of poor people. Under such circumstances, focusing on social exclusion would be ineffective.

Third, even progress in improving asset distribution and opportunities to participate in the economic process might not have the desired outcomes in respect of eliminating bias and discrimination against individuals, and especially social groups, based on identity. All too often, differences among individuals and groups have led to the implementation of policies demanding that the excluded groups display conformity with the mainstream, while leaving the underlying discrimination unaddressed. Some social integration policies currently much in vogue seem to foster this syndrome. This is a crucial area of policy formulation that tends to be overlooked, but that should be addressed.

The crisis: exit strategies

The global economic crisis has shown that the premises of the prevailing economic policies, in particular the belief in the primacy of the market mechanism to optimize resource allocation and maximize welfare, were faulty. This failure, however, had been evident long before the crisis hit. It had been demonstrated by the inability of the prevailing approach to economic policymaking to deliver a significant and sustained reduction in global poverty and deprivation. The analysis in chapters V to VIII has shown that macroeconomic policies, focused on keeping inflation and fiscal deficits under control, and economic liberalization ostensibly to enhance the efficiency of markets and national comparative advantage, have not reduced poverty. Instead, they have often reduced growth and increased inequality. Thus, inclusive economic development, which brings dividends to poor people and the marginalized, has been elusive.

So far, the current economic crisis has not altered the dominant policy paradigm in respect of its prescriptions for development, although there is some concern with ensuring social safety nets for those most adversely affected. However, the gravity of this crisis should lead to a serious rethinking of policy approaches that have dominated the discourse on growth and poverty up to now. Alternative analyses—prioritizing the need for structural transformation that brings about sustained growth of real output, employment and incomes and promotes inclusive development which benefits poor people—must be undertaken and their findings elaborated appropriately.

If the damage inflicted by the multiple crises on the lives of poor people is to be contained, there must arise a greater willingness to change. Credible and workable alternatives do exist and, indeed, have been proposed for decades. "The difficulty lies", as John Maynard Keynes noted, "not in the new ideas, but in escaping from the old ones, which ramify, for those brought up as most of us have been, into every corner of our minds" (Keynes, 1936, p. viii). According to Keynes (ibid., p. 383): "Practical men, who believe themselves to be quite exempt from any intellectual influence, are usually the slaves of some defunct economist."

This is the moment not just for a renewal of the commitment to creating a just and sustainable development, but also, and above all, for rethinking the means to that end.

The way forward

It is time to open up a discourse on poverty reduction that centres on inclusive development and the ending of social exclusion. This requires focusing on the development process as one of structural change and transformation. Structural change should no longer be based on the assumption that prioritizing private goals is compatible with realization of public goals, nor should it be focused on encouraging international "comparative advantage" based on low levels of skills and technology. Instead, structural change should involve a transformation that shifts economies from low-productivity, low-technology paths of development to technologically dynamic, skills-intensive paths towards the generation of equitable growth and development that benefits all. In most low-income developing countries, the charting of such dynamic growth paths must be based on speeding up agricultural productivity growth and boosting non-farm economic activity in rural areas in such a way as to provide incomes and livelihoods for the rural poor and other excluded people.

It is important to recognize, however, that there is no single policy approach to achieving this type of transformation. The process will differ from country to country and will depend on initial conditions, social structures, patterns of asset ownership and institutional frameworks.

In the dominant policy discourse, State activity in the economy is seen as distorting the market mechanism, as crowding out private investment and as being misguided or based on inaccurate information. Such a conceptualization needs to be re-examined. The experience of countries and regions that have achieved rapid growth and relative success in poverty reduction has shown that the State can deliberately intervene in the economy and even distort market-based incentives in such a way as to promote inclusive growth and development.

It is necessary, therefore, to consider the role of a "developmental State" which can promote sustained economic growth and structural transformation, including inclusive development. A reversal in the thinking on the roles of the State and the market is now under way. However, such thinking needs to go beyond tweaking the circuits of the prevailing orthodoxy with its conceptualization of State activity as being limited to correcting for market failures and imperfections.

Cohesion in policymaking is also crucial for achieving sustained inclusive development. Macroeconomic and microeconomic initiatives and social policies need to converge around the goal of poverty reduction so that they do not have opposing effects on poor people. For instance, poverty-reducing effects of programmes designed to minimize risks faced by poor people, such as those entailing cash transfers or the provision of microfinance, will have limited positive effects on poverty if rapid trade liberalization leads to the collapse of nascent manufacturing sectors and the loss of employment and incomes, as has been the case in many sub-Saharan African countries in the past two decades. To avoid these types of countervailing effects, a unified policy approach that clearly targets structural transformation and inclusive development is required.

The discussion in the present report points to several policy areas where rethinking is required in order to generate transformations and growth that bring sustainable benefits to poor people.

1. **It is important that macroeconomic stabilization not be seen as restricted to controlling inflation and trade and fiscal deficits. It should focus on the stability of real output, incomes and employment.** To reach this outcome, it is necessary to relax unnecessarily stringent fiscal and monetary restrictions and enable countries to use counter-cyclical fiscal and monetary policy to boost incomes and reduce poverty. This is an urgent need in the current crisis. Devising stabilization policies that promote inclusive growth should entail looking beyond the current crisis, however, and considering the challenges of promoting longer-term growth in real output and income. In this regard, it is important that lending to poor countries not continue to overly emphasize inflation control and fiscal stringency as a form of policy conditionality.

2. **It should be recognized that the trade policy effects on poverty reduction and structural transformation are contingent on a host of other factors which are country-specific,** such as pre-trade employment patterns, social sector policies, levels of social development, landownership patterns and rural power relations, export supply capacities, technological skills and the existence of well-developed markets.

The present World Trade Organization agenda allows little room for selective protection. Yet this type of protection was used very effectively by countries and territories to gain competitiveness in export markets and to enable them to undergo structural transformation. Most developing countries today lack the skills bases, technologies and capabilities needed to compete successfully in international trade. Developing these assets is essential for structural transformation and the possibility that this requires both time-limited infant industry protection and interventionist industrial policy should be acknowledged and explored. Devising an agenda for inclusive development requires a serious rethink of the dogma of free trade. A pragmatic approach which allows countries to devise trade policy so as to develop comparative advantage in new areas in order to move up the ladder of competitiveness is required for broad-based development.

3. **Structural transformation in low-income developing countries that raises growth rates and productivity in agriculture is needed to reduce poverty and exclusion.** A developmental State that recognizes the need to invest in key inputs such as irrigation and is able to engineer long-lasting institutional change to counter problems such as inefficient landholding size and weak or non-existent markets for inputs such as credit can be central to agricultural transformation. Strategies for inclusive rural development need to take account of how climate change affects the rural poor and incorporate measures to counter negative effects in such a way as to both be sustainable and promote dynamic output and income growth.

4. **Policy should focus on stimulating investment through the creation of conditions that ease credit constraints and make investor expectations buoyant.** Financial liberalization often falls short of achieving such conditions. Increasing the availability of agricultural finance should be a priority if financial sector reform is to be directed at promoting inclusive growth.

Conventional economic thinking has proclaimed the virtues of privatization in promoting growth and development. The results of waves of privatization in developing countries challenge this view on several fronts. Privatization does not always bring fiscal gains and can sometimes even drain the Government purse. The privatization of utilities such as water and sanitation can be harmful to the poor. The same argument applies to other key liberalization policies such as financial liberalization and financial globalization. The present financial crisis makes it strikingly evident that the developing countries that are the least financially globalized, in particular India and China, have been shielded to a significant extent from negative shocks of capital outflows. This highlights the need to time financial liberalization carefully and institute necessary regulations to safeguard financial stability. Both economic theory and empirical evidence point to a weak link between financial liberalization and economic growth. Policies aimed at structural transformation should recognize that financial liberalization could depress investment and technological change. More fundamentally, the usefulness of this type of liberalization in countries with weak or non-existent credit markets must be reconsidered. Along the same lines, **Governments should rethink privatization policies. In deciding the fate of a State-owned enterprise, policymakers should take into account a range of considerations, including its "social" role as an employer, and service provision–related obligations towards the socially disadvantaged.**

5. **Social policy must be seen as integral to the development process and to structural transformation.** In the present development discourse, social policy covers a broad range of provisions such as education, health, social insurance, cash transfers and credit. The discussion in this report has shown that progress in providing accessible education and health services to the poor has been hindered by inadequate financing and regressive policies such as the introduction of user fees. While income and cash transfers for poor people and microfinance have reduced absolute poverty in specific project contexts, the reach and impact of these programmes are limited. All of this points to a need to adopt a cohesive approach to social policy, taking into account the interactions among its component areas (such as education and health) and devising strategies that take these interactions into account.

   Social policy should not be seen as a set of ameliorative measures designed to correct for market and institutional failures and to temporarily manage household risk of the poor, but rather as involving the provision of basic needs and public goods which remains primarily the responsibility of the State. State provision for the welfare of the poor is a part of structural transformation. Inclusive development cannot be achieved when such provision is inadequate, uncoordinated and piecemeal.

6. Experiences from many countries show that decent work is central to the inclusive growth that leads to poverty reduction. **The promotion of full and productive employment and decent work for all should be an objective of macroeconomic policy.** This will help ensure the consistency and coherence of economic and social policies. It will also lead to a more equitable distribution of the benefits of economic growth, and thus to a reduction of both inequality and poverty.

7. **Basic social protection for all is a must in an era of increased economic insecurity due to globalization and accompanying informalization and casualization trends in the labour market.** The current global crises and the impact on workers in developed and developing countries alike further underscore the importance of providing a social protection floor for poor people as well as for the non-poor. For people living in poverty, the extension of some form of basic social protection will help avert their falling

deeper into poverty; for the non-poor, such protection will reduce their vulnerability to poverty.

Extending basic social protection to all should be a component of all stimulus packages. In the short term, benefits will allow the people who need assistance the most to support their consumption, generating much-needed demand during economic recession; in the long run, social investment in human capital (nutrition, health and education) will strengthen future growth.

8. **Public social expenditures should be safeguarded, and even increased, in this current time of crises so as to protect investment in human capital.** They should also be incorporated in stimulus packages and international support to low-income developing countries.

The challenges ahead for poverty reduction are numerous and difficult and are made more intense by the global economic crisis. It is imperative that the gravity of this crisis lead to a serious rethinking of the policy approaches that have dominated the discourse on growth and poverty up to now. The findings of alternative analyses in support of prioritizing the need for the kind of structural transformation that brings about the sustained growth of real output and incomes, and promotes inclusive development so as to benefit the poor, must be brought to the forefront and built upon at this historic juncture.

Bibliography

Acosta, Pablo, and others (2007). What is the impact of international remittances on poverty and inequality in Latin America? World Bank Policy Research Working Paper, No. 4249 (June). Washington, D.C.: World Bank.

Adams, Richard H., Alfredo Cuecuecha and John M. Page (2008). The impact of remittances on poverty and inequality in Ghana. World Bank Policy Research Working Paper, No. 4732 (September). Washington, D.C.: World Bank.

Adato, Michelle, and Lawrence Haddad (2001). Targeting poverty through community-based public works programs: a cross-disciplinary assessment of recent experience in South Africa. Food Consumption and Nutrition Division Discussion Paper, No. 121. Washington, D.C.: International Food Policy Research Institute.

Addison, Tony (2009). Chronic poverty in the global economy. *European Journal of Development Research*, vol. 21, No. 2, pp. 174-178.

Aizenman, Joshua (2005). Financial liberalization: how well has it worked for developing countries? FRBSF Economic Letter (Federal Reserve Bank of San Francisco), No. 2005-06 (8 April), pp. 1-3.

Akroyd, Stephen, and Lawrence Smith (2007). Review of public spending to agriculture: a joint DFID/World Bank study. London: United Kingdom Department for International Development; Washington, D.C.: World Bank.

Alam, Asad, and others (2005). *Growth, Poverty, and Inequality: Eastern Europe and the Former Soviet Union*. Washington, D.C.: World Bank.

Alderman, Harold, and Victor Lavy (1996). Household responses to public health services: cost and quality trade-offs. *World Bank Research Observer*, vol. 11, No. 1, pp. 3-22.

Amsden, Alice H. (1989). *Asia's Next Giant: South Korea and Late Industrialization*. New York: Oxford University Press.

Andersen, Lill, and Ronald Babula (2008). The link between openness and long-run economic growth. Journal of International Commerce and Economics (Washington, D.C.).

Anderson, Kathryn, and Richard William Thomas Pomfret (2004). *Spatial Inequality and Development in Central Asia*. WIDER Research Paper, No. 2004/36. Helsinki: United Nations University, World Institute for Development Economics Research (UNU-WIDER).

Anderson, Kym, and Will Martin (2005). *Agricultural Trade Reform and the Doha Development Agenda*. Washington, D.C.: Palgrave Macmillan.

Appleton, Simon, and Arsene Balihuta (1996). Education and agricultural productivity: evidence from Uganda. *Journal of International Development*, vol. 8, No. 3.

Arango, Joaquín, and Maia Jachimowicz (2005). Regularizing immigrants in Spain: a new approach. Migration Information Source (1 September). Washington, D.C.: Migration Policy Institute. Available from http://www.migrationinformation.org/Feature/display.cfm?ID=331

Asian Development Bank (2002). Poverty profile (chap. II). In *Poverty in Pakistan: Issues, Causes, and Institutional Responses*. Islamabad.

Australian Bureau of Statistics (2004). *Experimental Estimates and Projections, Aboriginal and Torres Strait Islander Australians, 1991 to 2009*. Document No. 3238.0. Available from http://www.abs.gov.au/ausstats/abs@.nsf/mf/3238.0 (accessed 12 May 2009).

Aysan, Ahmet Faruk (2007). *The Effects of Volatility on Growth and Financial Development Through Capital Market Imperfections*. Munich Personal RePEc Archive (MPRA) Paper, No. 5486 (7 November).

Baker, Dean, and others (2002). Labor market institutions and unemployment: a critical analysis of the cross-country evidence. CEPA Working Paper 2002-17 (18 November). New York: New School University: Center for Economic and Policy Research.

Bandara, Amarakoon, Muhammad Hussain Malik and Eugene Gherman (2004). Poverty in countries of Central Asia. In Economic and Social Commission for Asia and the Pacific, *Bulletin on Asia-Pacific Perspectives, 2004/05: Asia-Pacific Economies: Living with High Oil Prices?* United Nations publication, Sales No. E.04.II.F.47.

Banerjee, Abhijit V., and Esther Duflo (2004). Do firms want to borrow more? testing credit constraints using a directed lending program. *CEPR Discussion Paper*, No. 4681 (October). London: Centre for Economic Policy Research.

Barker, Eileen (2007). What would Ghandi do? Available from http://www.mediate.com/articles/ebarker4.cfm (accessed 15 December 2008). Originally published in ACResolution Magazine (spring 2007).

Baulch, Bob, and John Hoddinott (2000). Economic mobility and poverty dynamics in developing countries. In *Economic Mobility and Poverty Dynamics in Developing Countries*, Bob Baulch and John Hoddinott, eds. Portland, Oregon: Frank Cass.

Baunsgaard, Thomas, and Michael Keen (2005). Tax revenue and (or?) trade liberalization. IMF Working Paper, No. 05/112. Washington, D.C.: International Monetary Fund.

Bayliss, Kate (2002). Privatization and poverty: the distributional impact of utility privatization. *Annals of Public and Cooperative Economics*, vol. 73, No. 4, pp. 603-625.

_____ (2003). Utility privatisation in sub-saharan Africa: a case study of water. *Journal of Modern African Studies*, vol. 41, No. 4, pp. 507-532.

_____, and Ben Fine (2007). Introduction and overview. In *Privatization and Alternative Public Sector Reform in Sub-Saharan Africa: Delivering on Electricity and Water*, Kate Bayliss and Ben Fine, eds. Basingstoke, United Kingdom: Palgrave Macmillan.

Bayliss, Kate, and David Hall (2000). Privatisation of water and energy in Africa, report for the Public Services International Research Unit, University of Greenwich, London.

Beveridge, William (1944). *Full Employment in a Free Society*. London: George Allen and Unwin.

Bhagwati, Jagdish N. (1958). Immiserizing growth: a geometrical note. *The Review of Economic Studies*, vol. 25 (June) pp. 201-205.

Bhalla, Surijit (2002). *Imagine There's No Country: Poverty, Inequality and Growth in the Era of Globalization*. Washington, D.C.: Peterson Institute for International Economics.

Bhatla, Nandita, Sawti Chakraborty and Nata Duvvury (2006). Property ownership and inheritance rights of women as social protection from domestic violence: cross-site analysis. In Property ownership and inheritance rights of women for social protection: the South Asia experience, synthesis report of three studies. Washington, D.C.: International Center for Research on Women.

Birdsall, Nancy (2002). From social policy to an open-economy social contract in Latin America. Working Paper, No. 21 (December). Washington, D.C.: Center for Global Development.

_____, David Ross and Richard Sabot (1995). Inequality and growth reconsidered: lessons from East Asia. *The World Bank Economic Review*, vol. 9, No. 3, pp. 477-508.

Black, Richard, Claudia Natali and Jessica Skinner (2006). Migration and inequality. Background paper for World Bank, *World Development Report, 2006: Equity and Development* (Washington, D.C., World Bank, and New York, Oxford University Press, 2006).

Bloom, David E., and Jeffrey D. Sachs (1998). Geography, demography, and economic growth in Africa. *Brookings Papers on Economic Activity*, vol. 29, No. 2, pp. 207-296.

Bosworth, Barry, and Susan Collins (2003). The empirics of growth: an update. *Brookings Papers on Economic Activity* (Washington, D.C.), vol. 34, No. 2003-2, pp. 113-206.

Bouche, Nathalie, and others (2004). The macroeconomics of poverty reduction: the case of China. Beijing: United Nations Development Programme.

Bourbeau, Heather (2001). Property wrongs: how weak ideas gain strong appeal in the world of development economics. *Foreign Policy* (November-December), pp. 78-79.

Bourguignon, François (2004). The poverty-growth-inequality triangle. Paper presented at the Indian Council for Research on International Economic Relations. New Delhi, 4 February.

Brahmbhatt, Milan, and Uri Dadush (1996). Disparities in global integration. *Finance and Development* (Washington), vol. 33, No. 3, pp. 47.

Brandstetter, Robert H. (2004). Evaluation of OFDA Cash-for-Relief intervention in Ethiopia. Final report prepared for the United States Agency for International Development/Office of U.S. Foreign Disaster Assistance (USAID/OFDA). November.

Breen, Richard, and Cecilia Garcia-Penalosa (2005). Income inequality and macroeconomic volatility: an empirical investigation. *Review of Development Economics*, vol. 9, No. 3, pp. 380-398.

Brook Cowen, Penelope J. (1996). The Guinea water lease: five years on, lessons in private sector participation. Viewpoint note, No. 78 (31 May). Washington, D.C.: World Bank. Available from http://go.worldbank.org/0W3QJRD8O0.

Brown, Graham, Frances Stewart and Arnim Langer (2007). *The Implications of Horizontal Inequality for Aid*. WIDER Research Paper, No. 2007/51. Helsinki: United Nations University, World Institute for Development Economics Research (UNU-WIDER).

Bruno, Michael, and William Easterly (1998). Inflation crises and long-run growth. *Journal of Monetary Economics* (Amsterdam), vol. 41, No. 1, pp. 3-26.

Buchanan, James M. (1980). Rent seeking and profit seeking. In *Toward a Theory of the Rent-Seeking Society*, James M. Buchanan, Gordon Tullock and Robert D. Tollison, eds. College Station, Texas: Texas A & M Press.

Bulíř, Aleš, and Javier Hamann (2003). Aid volatility: an empirical assessment. *IMF Staff Papers*, vol. 50, No. 1 (April), pp. 64.

Buvinic, Mayra, Jacqueline Mazza and Ruthane Deutsch (2004). *Social Inclusion and Economic Development in Latin America*. Washington, D.C.: Inter-American Development Bank.

Caizhen, Lu (2009). Who is poor in China? comparison of alternative approaches to poverty assessment in rural Yunnan. PhD dissertation. The Hague: Institute for Social Studies.

Campbell-White, Oliver, and Anita Bhatia (1998). *Privatization in Africa*. Washington, D.C.: World Bank.

Card, David, and Alan B. Krueger (1995). *Myth and Measurement: The New Economics of the Minimum Wage*. Princeton, New Jersey: Princeton University Press.

Center for Global Development (2007). Evaluating the impact of microfinance. Available from http://www.cgdev.org/content/article/detail/12338/ (accessed 4 December 2008).

Chambers, Robert (1997). *Whose Reality Counts? Putting the Last First*. London: Intermediate Technology Publications.

Chang, Ha-Joon (2006). *The East Asian Development Experience: The Miracle, the Crisis and the Future*. London: Zed Books.

Chen, Shaohua, and Martin Ravallion (2007). Absolute poverty measures for the developing world, 1981-2004. World Bank Policy Research Working Paper, No. 4211 (April). Washington, D.C.: World Bank.

_____ (2008). The developing world is poorer than we thought, but no less successful in the fight against poverty. World Bank Policy Research Working Paper, No. 4703 (August). Washington, D.C.: World Bank.

Chetty, Raj (2008). Moral hazard versus liquidity and optimal unemployment insurance. *NBER Working Paper,* No. 13967 (April). Cambridge, Massachusetts: National Bureau of Economic Research.

Chhachhi, Amrita (2008). Ensuring democratic citizenship: a gender perspective on contending pathways for socio-economic security in South Asia. *Indian Journal of Human Development*, vol. 2, No. 1 (January-June), pp. 133-164.

Chowdhury, Anis (2002). Politics, society and financial sector reform in Bangladesh. *International Journal of Social Economics*, vol. 29, No. 12, pp. 963-988.

_____ (2009). How effective is microfinance as a poverty reduction tool?: a note. Background paper prepared for the *Report on the World Social Situation 2010*. New York: Department of Economic and Social Affairs of the United Nations Secretariat.

Chronic Poverty Research Centre (2004). The chronic poverty report 2004-05. Manchester, United Kingdom: Institute for Development Policy and Management, University of Manchester.

Cline, William (2002). Financial crises and poverty in emerging market economies. Center for Global Development Working Paper, No. 8 (1 June). Washington, D.C.: Center for Global Development.

Coady, David P., Margaret Grosh and John Hoddinott (2004a). Targeting outcomes redux. *World Bank Research Observer*, vol. 19, No. 1 (spring), pp. 61-85.

_____ (2004b). *Targeting of Transfers in Developing Countries: Review of Lessons Learned and Experience*. Washington, D.C.: World Bank and International Food Policy Research Institute.

Collier, Paul (2007). *The Bottom Billion: Why the Poorest Countries Are Failing and What Can Be Done About It*. Oxford: Oxford University Press.

Commission of the European Communities (2007). Modernising social protection for greater social justice and economic cohesion: taking forward the active inclusion of people furthest from the labour market. Document No. COM (2007) 620. Communication from the Commission to the Council, the European Parliament, the European Economic and Social Committee and the Committee of the Regions. Brussels, 17 October.

Commission on Social Determinants of Health (2008). *Closing the Gap in a Generation: Health Equity Through Action on the Social Determinants of Health*. Final Report of the Commission on Social Determinants of Health. Geneva: World Health Organization.

Crul, Maurice, and Hans Vermeulen (2003). Introduction: the second generation in Europe. *International Migration Review (special issue)*, vol. 37, No. 4 (winter), pp. 965-986.

Cukrowski, Jacek (2006). Central Asia: spatial disparities in poverty. *Development & Transition*, No. 5/2006 (December). London: United Nations Development Programme and London School of Economics and Political Science.

Daley-Harris, Sam, Robert Pollin and Felicia Montgomery (2007). Debate on microcredit. Washington, D.C.: Foreign Policy in Focus, 21 June. Available from http://www.fpif.org/fpifttxt/4324 (accessed 21 June 2007).

Dani, Anis A., and Arjan de Haan (2008). Social policy in a development context: structural inequalities and inclusive institutions. In *Inclusive States: Social Policy and Structural Inequalities*, Anis A. Dani and Arjan de Haan, eds. Washington, D.C.: World Bank.

Datt, Gaurav, and Martin Ravallion (1994). Transfer benefits from public work employment. *The Economic Journal*, vol. 104 No. 427 (November), pp. 1346-1369.

de Brauw, Alan, and John Hoddinott (2008). Must conditional cash transfers be conditioned to be effective? The impact of conditioning transfers on school enrolment in Mexico. IFPRI Discussion Paper, No. 757 (March). Washington, D.C.: International Food Policy Research Institute.

de Haan, Arjan (2007). *Reclaiming Social Policy: Globalization, Social Exclusion and New Poverty Reduction Strategies*. Basingstoke, United Kingdom: Palgrave Macmillan.

de Soto, Hernando (2000). *The Mystery of Capital: Why Capitalism Triumphs in the West and Fails Everywhere Else*. New York: Basic Books.

Deaton, Angus S., and Jean Drèze (2009). Food and nutrition in India: facts and interpretations. *Economic and Political Weekly*, vol. 44, No. 7 (14 February), pp. 42-65.

Demirgüç-Kunt, Asli, and Enrica Detragiache (1999). Financial liberalization and financial fragility. World Bank Policy Research Working Paper,

No. 1917 (May). Washington, D.C.: World Bank Development Research Group and International Monetary Fund Research Department.

Deraniyagala, Sonali (2003). Macroeconomic reform and poverty reduction in Nepal: a synthesis. In "The macroeconomics of poverty reduction in Nepal". Kathmandu: United Nations Development Programme. Mimeo.

Dercon, Stefan (2005). Risk, poverty and vulnerability in Africa. *Journal of African Economies*, vol. 14, No. 4, pp. 483-488.

_____ (2006). Vulnerability: a micro perspective. In *Securing Development in an Unstable World*. Francois Bourguignon, Boris Pleskovič and Jacques van der Gaag, eds. Washington, D.C.: World Bank, pp. 117-146.

Dev, S. Mahendra (2001). Social security issues in India: performance, issues and policies. In *Social and Economic Security in India*. S. Mahendra Dev and others, eds. New Delhi: Institute for Human Development.

Dollar, David, and Aart Kraay (2002). Growth is good for the poor. *Journal of Economic Growth*, vol. 7, No. 3, pp. 195-225.

Domar, Evsey (1944). The burden of the debt and the national income. *American Economic Review*, vol. 34, No. 4, pp. 798-827.

_____ (1946). Capital expansion, rate of growth and employment. *Econometrica*, vol. 14, pp. 137-147.

Donadio, Rachel, and Nelson D. Schwartz (2009). As jobs die, Europe's migrants head home. *New York Times* (Global edition, Europe), 24 April. Available from http://www.nytimes.com/2009/04/25/world/europe/25migrants.html.

Dornbusch, Rudiger, and Stanley Fischer (1993). Moderate inflation. *NBER Working Paper*, No. W3896 (March). Cambridge, Massachusetts: National Bureau of Economic Research.

Eifert, Benn, and Alan Gelb (2005). Coping with aid volatility. *Finance and Development*, vol. 42, No. 3 (September).

Epstein, Gerald (2002). Employment oriented central bank policy in an integrated world economy: a reform proposal for South Africa. PERI Working Paper, No. 39 (June). Amherst, Massachusetts: University of Massachusetts, Amherst, Political Economy Research Institute.

_____, Ilene Grabel and Jomo K. S. (2003). Capital management techniques in developing countries: An assessment of experiences from the 1990s and lessons for the future. PERI Working Paper, No. 56. Amherst, Massachusetts: University of Massachusetts, Amherst, Political Economy Research Institute.

European Commission (2009). EU employment situation and social outlook. Monthly monitor (June).

_____, Directorate-General for Employment and Social Affairs (2004). *The Situation of Roma in an Enlarged European Union*. Luxembourg: Office for Official Publications of the European Communities.

European Commission, Directorate-General for Employment, Social Affairs and Equal Opportunities (2008). *Joint Report on Social Protection and Social Inclusion 2008: Social Inclusion, Pension, Healthcare and Long-term Care*. Luxembourg: Office for Official Publications of the European Communities.

Figueiredo, Jose B., and Arjan de Haan (1998). *Social Exclusion: An ILO Perspective*. Geneva: International Labour Organization.

Filmer, Deon (2000). The structure of social disparities in education: gender and wealth. World Bank Policy Research Working Paper, No. 2268. Washington D.C.: World Bank.

Food and Agriculture Organization of the United Nations (2008). *The State of Food Insecurity in the World 2008: High Food Prices and Food Security—Threats and Opportunities*. Rome.

_____ (2009). *The State of Agricultural Commodity Markets 2009: High Food Prices and the Food Crisis—Experiences and Lessons Learned*. Rome.

Förster, Michael F. (2004). Longer-term trends in income poverty in the OECD area. *Sociologický casopis (Czech Sociological Review)* (Prague), vol. 40, No. 6, pp. 785-805.

Freeman, Richard B. (2009). Labor regulations, unions, and social protection in developing countries: market distortions or efficient institutions? *NBER Working Paper*, No. 14789. Cambridge, Massachusetts: National Bureau of Economic Research.

Frías, Zoraida García (2005). Introduction: gender and land rights. In Gender and land compendium of country studies. Rome: Food and Agriculture Organization of the United Nations, pp. ix-xv.

Friedman, Milton (1962). Should there be an independent monetary authority? In *In Search of a Monetary Constitution*, Leland B. Yeager, ed. Cambridge, Massachusetts: Harvard University Press, pp. 219-243.

_____ (1985). The case for overhauling the Federal Reserve. *Challenge*, vol. 28, No. 3 (July-August), pp. 4-12.

Gaiha, Raghav (1989). Are the chronically poor also the poorest in rural India? *Development and Change*, vol. 20, No. 2 (April).

Galbis, Vicente (1993). High real interest rates under financial liberalization: is there a problem? IMF Working Paper, No. 93/7. Washington, D.C.: International Monetary Fund.

Gallup, John Luke, Jeffrey Sachs and Andrew D. Mellinger (1998). Geography and economic development. *NBER Working Paper*, No. 6849 (December). Cambridge, Massachusetts: National Bureau of Economic Research.

Ghosh, Bimal (2006). *Migrants' Remittances and Development: Myths, Rhetoric and Realities*. Geneva: International Organization for Migration and The Hague Process on Refugees and Migration.

Ghosh, Jayati (2008a). The financial crisis and the developing world. *South-North Development Monitor*, No. 6578 (29 October).

_____ (2008b). The loss of development finance. Macroscan. Available from http://www.macroscan.com/cur/oct08/cur23102008Finance.htm (accessed 14 September 2009).

Ghura, Dhaneshwar, Carlos A. Leite and Charalambos Tsangarides (2002). Is growth enough? macroeconomic policy and poverty reduction. IMF Working Paper, No. 02/118. Washington, D.C.: International Monetary Fund.

Gilson, Lucy, and Di McIntyre (2005). Removing user fees for primary care in Africa: the need for careful action. *British Journal of Medicine*, vol. 331 (10 October), pp. 762-765.

Giovannoni, Olivier (2008). Functional distribution of income, inequality, and the incidence of poverty: stylized facts and the role of macroeconomic policy. United Nations Research Institute for Social Development working paper.

Goldberg, Pinelopi Koujianou, and Nina Pavcnik (2007). Distributional effects of globalization in developing countries. *NBER Working Paper*, No. 12885 (February). Cambridge, Massachusetts: National Bureau of Economic Research.

Goldsbrough, David (2007). Does the IMF constrain health spending in poor countries? evidence and an agenda for action. Report of the Working Group on IMF Programs and Health Spending. Washington, D.C.: Center for Global Development, 20 June.

Graham, Wendy J., and others (2004). The familial technique for linking maternal death with poverty. *The Lancet*, vol. 363, No. 9402, pp. 23-27.

Grigoriou, Cristopher, Patrick Guillaumont and Wenyan Yang (2005). Child mortality under Chinese reforms. *China Economic Review*, vol. 16, No. 4, pp. 441-464.

Guillaumont Jeanneney, Sylviane, and Kangni Kpodar (2005). Financial development, financial instability, and poverty. CSAE Working Paper, No. 2005-09. Oxford: University of Oxford, Centre for the Study of African Economies.

Gupta, Abhijit Sen (2007). Determinants of tax revenue efforts in developing countries. IMF Working Paper, No. 07/184. Washington, D.C.: International Monetary Fund.

Guruswamy, Mohan, and Ronald Joseph Abraham (2006). Redefining poverty: a new poverty line for a new India. New Delhi: Centre for Policy Alternatives.

Hallak, Juan Carlos, and James Alan Levinsohn (2004). Fooling ourselves: evaluating the globalization and growth debate. *NBER Working Paper*,

No. 10244. Cambridge, Massachusetts: National Bureau of Economic Research.

Handa, Sudhanshu, and Benjamin Davis (2006). The experience of conditional cash transfers in Latin America and the Caribbean. *Development Policy Review*, vol. 24, No. 5, pp. 513-536.

Hanushek, Eric A., and Ludger Woessmann (2008). The role of cognitive skills in economic development. *Journal of Economic Literature*, vol. 46, No. 3, pp. 607-668.

Heckman, James J., Lance J. Lochner and Petra E. Todd (2006). Earnings equations, rates of return and treatment effects: the Mincer equation and beyond. In *Handbook of the Economics of Education*, vol. 1, Eric A. Hanushek and F. Welch, eds. Amsterdam: North Holland, pp. 307-458.

Hernández-Catá, Ernesto (2000). Raising growth and investment in sub-Saharan Africa: what can be done? IMF Policy Discussion Paper, No. PDP/00/4. Washington, D.C.: International Monetary Fund.

Himanshu (2008). What are these new poverty estimates and what do they imply? *Economic and Political Weekly* (Mumbai), vol. 43, No. 43 (25 October), pp. 38-43.

Holzman, Robert, and Steen Jorgensen (2004). Social risk management: a new conceptual framework for social protection, and beyond. In *Reforms, Labour Markets and Social Security in India*, Ramgopal Agarwala, Nagesh Kumar and Michelle Riboud, eds. New Delhi: Oxford University Press.

Hopenhayn, Martin (2008). Recognition and distribution: equity and justice policies for disadvantaged groups in Latin America. In *Inclusive States: Social Policy and Structural Inequalities*, Anis A. Dani and Arian de Haan, eds. Washington, D.C.: World Bank.

Hu, Angang, Linlin Hu and Zhixiao Chang (2003). China's economic growth and poverty reduction (1978-2002). Article prepared for the Conference "A Tale of Two Giants: India's and China's Experience with Reform and Growth", co-organized by the International Monetary Fund and the National Council of Applied Economic Research (India), New Delhi, 14-16 November 2003. Available from http://imf.org/external/np/apd/seminars/2003/newdelhi/angang.pdf.

Hulme, David, and Paul Mosley (1996). *Finance Against Poverty: Effective Institutions for Lending to Small Farmers and Microenterprises in Developing Countries*. New York: Routledge Press.

Hussain, Akmal (2003). *Pakistan National Human Development Report, 2003: Poverty, Growth and Governance*. Karachi: United Nations Development Programme.

India, Press Information Bureau (2007). *Poverty Estimates for 2004-05* (March). New Delhi: Press Information Bureau. Available from http://planningcommission.nic.in/news/prmar07.pdf.

Inter-American Development Bank (2007). *Outsiders? The Changing Patterns of Exclusion in Latin America and the Caribbean*. Washington, D.C.: IADB, and Cambridge, Massachusetts: David Rockefeller Center for Latin American Studies, Harvard University.

Intergovernmental Panel on Climate Change (2001). *Climate Change 2001: Synthesis Report—A Contribution to Working Groups I, II and III to the Third Assessment Report of the Intergovenmental Panel on Climate Change*, R. T. Watson and the Core Writing Team, eds. Cambridge, United Kingdom: Cambridge University Press.

International Labour Organization (2009a). *Global Employment Trends: January 2009*. Geneva: International Labour Office.

_____ (2009b) International Migration Programme (MIGRANT) good practices database: Labour policies and programmes. 9 September. Available from http://www.ilo.org/dyn/migpractice/migmain.home.

_____ (2009c). *Tackling the Global Jobs Crisis: Recovery through Decent Work Policies. Report (1(A)) of the Directorate-General*, submitted to the International Labour Conference, 98th session. Geneva: International Labour Office.

_____ (2009d). *Social Security for All: Investing in Social Justice and Economic Development. Social Security Policy Briefings*, No. 7. Geneva: International Labour Office.

_____, International Institute for Labour Studies (2008). *World of Work Report 2008: Income Inequalities in the Age of Financial Globalization*. Geneva: International Labour Office.

International Monetary Fund (2002). Improving market access: toward greater coherence between aid and trade. Washington, D.C., 21 March.

_____ (2004). Public investment and fiscal policy. March 12. Paper prepared by the Fiscal Affairs Department and Policy Development and Review Department in consultation with other departments and in cooperation with the World Bank and the Inter-American Development Bank.

International Organization for Migration (2008). *World Migration 2008: Managing Labour Mobility in the Evolving Global Economy*. United Nations publication, Sales No. 07.III.S.8. Geneva.

Iqbal, Farrukh (2006). *Sustaining Gains in Poverty Reduction and Human Development in the Middle East and North Africa*. Washington, D.C.: World Bank.

Irudayam, Aloysius S. J., Jayshree P. Mangubhai and Joel G. Lee (2006). Dalit women speak out: violence against Dalit women in India, vol. I, Study report. New Delhi: National Campaign on Dalit Human Rights.

Islam, Rizwanul, and Graeme Buckley (2009). *Rising Food Prices and Their Implications for Employment, Decent Work and Poverty Reduction*. Employment Sector Employment Working Paper, No. 30. Geneva: International Labour Office, Economic and Labour Market Analysis Department.

Islam, Yan (2009). Notes on unemployment compensation programmes in developing and emerging economies. International Labour Organization Global Job Crisis Observatory (27 March). Available from http://www.ilo.org/public/english/support/lib/financialcrisis/featurestories/story7.htm.

Jackson, Cecile (1996). Rescuing gender from the poverty trap. *World Development*, vol. 24, No. 3, pp. 489-504.

_____ (2002). Disciplining gender? *World Development*, vol. 30, No. 3, pp. 497-509.

Johnson, Jessica K. M., and John B. Williamson (2006). Do universal non-contributory old-age pensions make sense for rural areas in low-income countries? *International Social Security Review*, vol. 59, No. 4, pp. 47-65.

Jomo K. S. and Jacques Baudot (2007). *Flat World, Big Gaps: Economic Liberalization, Globalization, Poverty & Inequality*. United Nations publication, Sales No. E.06.IV.5; and London: Zed Books.

Jones, Richard C. (1998). Remittances and inequality: a question of migration stage and geographical scale. *Economic Geography*, vol. 74, No. 1, pp. 8-25.

Jorgensen, Steen L., and Rodrigo Serrano-Berthet (2009). Comprehensive social policy for inclusive and sustainable globalization. In *Building Equality and Opportunity Through Social Guarantees: New Approaches to Public Policy and to Realization of Rights*, Estanislao Gacitúa-Marió, Andrew Norton and Sophia Georgieva, eds. Washington, D.C.: World Bank.

Kabeer, Naila (2006a). Poverty, social exclusion and the MDGs: the challenge of "durable inequalities" in the Asian context. *IDS Bulletin*, vol. 37, No. 3, pp. 64-78. Brighton, United Kingdom: Institute of Development Studies.

_____ (2006b). Social exclusion and the MDGs: the challenge of 'durable inequalities' in the Asian context. Paper prepared for the Asia 2015 Conference: Promoting Growth, Ending Poverty, organized by the United Kingdom Department for International Development, London, 6 and 7 March 2006. Available from http://www.eldis.org/vfile/upload/1/document/0708/DOC21178.pdf.

Kakwani, Nanak, Fabio V. Soares and Hyun H. Son (2005). Conditional cash transfers in African countries. International Poverty Centre Working Paper, No. 9 (November). Brasília, Brazil: United Nations Development Programme, International Poverty Centre.

Kakwani, Nanak, and Hyun H. Son (2006). New global poverty counts. International Poverty Centre Working Paper, No. 29 (September). Brasília: United Nations Development Programme, International Poverty Centre.

Kaminsky, Graciela L., and Carmen M. Reinhart (1999). The twin crises: the causes of banking and balance-of-payments problems. *American Economic Review*, vol. 89, No. 3, pp. 473-500.

Kannan, Narayanan (2008). *Rural Development and Social Change*. New Delhi: Abhijeet Publications.

Keynes, John M. (1936). *The General Theory of Employment, Interest and Money*. New York: Harcourt, Brace and Company.

Khan, Azizur Rahaman (2007). Growth, employment and poverty: an analysis of the vital nexus based on some recent UNDP and ILO/SIDA studies. DESA Working Paper No. 49. ST/ESA/2007/DWP/49. New York: Department of Economic and Social Affairs of the United Nations Secretariat, July.

Khan, Mushtaq H. (2009). Governance, growth and poverty reduction. DESA Working Paper No. 75 (June). ST/ESA/2009/DWP/75. New York: Department of Economic and Social Affairs of the United Nations Secretariat, June.

Khandker, Shahidur R. (2005). Microfinance and poverty: evidence using panel data from Bangladesh. *World Bank Economic Review*, vol. 19, No. 2, pp. 263-286.

King, Russell, and Julie Vullnetari (2003). Migration and development in Albania. Working Paper C5 (December). Brighton, United Kingdom: Development Research Centre on Migration, Globalisation and Poverty, University of Sussex.

Klugman, Jeni, ed. (2002). *A Sourcebook for Poverty Reduction Strategies, Volume I: Core Techniques and Cross-cutting Issues*. Washington, D.C.: World Bank, technical note A2 entitled "Estimating poverty lines: the example of Bangladesh".

Kochhar, Rakesh (2008). Latin labor report 2008: construction reverses job loss for Latinos. Washington, D.C.: Pew Hispanic Center, June.

Kose, M. Ayhan, Eswar S. Prasad and Marco E. Terrones (2003). Financial integration and macroeconomic volatility. IMF Working Paper, No. 03/50. Washington, D.C.: International Monetary Fund.

_____ (2006). How do trade and financial integration affect the relationship between growth and volatility? *Journal of International Economics*, vol. 69, No. 1, pp. 176-202.

Kroft, Kory, and Huw Lloyd-Ellis (2002). Further cross-country evidence on the link between growth, volatility and business cycles. Department of Economics Working Paper. Kingston, Ontario: Queens University.

Laird, Sam, and Santiago Fernández de Córdoba (2006). *Coping with Trade Reforms: A Developing Country Perspective on the WTO Industrial Tariff Negotiations*. New York: Palgrave Macmillan.

Laursen, Thomas, and Sandeep Mahajan (2005). Volatility, income distribution, and poverty. In *Managing Volatility and Crises: A Practitioner's Guide*, Joshua Aizenman and Brian Pinto, eds. Cambridge, United Kingdom: Cambridge University Press, pp. 101-136.

Lee, Eddy (1998). *The Asian Financial Crisis: The Challenge for Social Policy.* Geneva: International Labour Office.

Leibenstein, Harvey (1957). *Economic Backwardness and Economic Growth.* New York: Wiley.

Lerner, Abba (1943). Functional finance and the federal debt. *Social Research*, vol. 10, No. 1, pp. 38-57.

Levitas, Ruth (2000). What is social exclusion? In *Breadline Europe: The Measurement of Poverty*, David Gordon and Peter Townsend, eds. Bristol, United Kingdom: Policy Press, pp. 357-384.

Levy, Frank, and Peter Temin (2007). Inequality and institutions in 20th century America. *NBER Working Paper,* No. 13106. Cambridge, Massachusetts: National Bureau of Economic Research.

Lin, Justin Yifu (2008). The impact of the financial crisis on developing economies. Paper prepared for the Korea Development Institute, Seoul, 31 October.

Lobina, Emanuele (2000). Cochabamba: water war. *Focus* (PSI Journal), vol. 7, No. 2. London: Public Services International Research Unit, University of Greenwich.

Lora, Eduardo (2007). Public investment in infrastructure in Latin America: is debt the culprit? Inter-American Development Bank Research Department Working Paper, No. 595 (January). Washington, D.C.: Inter-American Development Bank. Available from http://www.iadb.org/res/publications/pubfiles/pubWP-595.pdf.

Lustig, Nora (2000). Crises and the poor: socially responsible macroeconomics. *Economia: Journal of the Latin American and Caribbean Economic Association*, vol. 1, No. 1 (fall), pp. 1-30.

_____ (2009). Coping with rising food prices: policy dilemmas in the developing world. Working Paper, No. 164 (March). Washington, D.C.: Center for Global Development.

Macarov, David (2003). *What the Market Does to People: Privatization, Globalization and Poverty.* London: Zed Books.

Magdahl, Jørgen, and others (2006). Privatisation of water public-private partnerships: do they deliver to the poor? Technical Report, No. 4 (1 April). Oslo: Norwegian Forum for Environment and Development. Available from http://www.forumfor.no/Artikler/4961.html.

Maluccio, John A., and Rafael Flores (2005). *Impact Evaluation of a Conditional Cash Transfer Program: The Nicaraguan Red de Protección Social.* Research Report Abstract No. 141. Washington, D.C.: International Food Policy Research Institute. Available from http://www.ifpri.org/sites/default/files/publications/pubs_pubs-abstract_141_rr141.pdf

Mamdani, Mahmood (1972). *The Myth of Population Control: Family, Class and Caste in an Indian Village.* New York: Monthly Review Press.

Martin, John P. (2000). What works among active labour market policies: evidence from OECD countries' experiences. *OECD Economic Studies*, No. 30 (2000/I). Paris: Organization for Economic Cooperation and Development.

Mayor, Susan (2001). Poorest women 20 times more likely to die in childbirth. *British Medical Journal*, vol. 323, No. 7325, pp. 1324-1324.

McGillivray, Mark, Indrani Dutta and Nora Markova (2009). Health inequality and deprivation. *Health Economics*, vol. 18, No. S1, pp. S1-S12.

McKenzie, David, and Hillel Rapoport (2007). Network effects and the dynamics of migration and inequality: theory and evidence from Mexico. *Journal of Development Economics*, vol. 84, No. 1 (September), pp. 1-24.

McKinley, Terry (2004). Economic policies and poverty reduction in Asia and the Pacific: alternatives to neoliberalism. New York: United Nations Development Programme, February.

_____ (2008). Economic policies for growth and poverty reduction: PRSPs, neoliberal conditionalities and 'post-consensus' alternatives. *IDS Studies Bulletin*, vol. 39, No. 2, pp. 93-103. Brighton, United Kingdom: Institute of Development Studies.

McKinnon, Ronald I. (1973). *Money and Capital in Economic Development*. Washington, D.C.: Brookings Institution.

McKinnon, Ronald, and Huw Pill (1999). Exchange-rate regimes for emerging markets: moral hazard and international overborrowing. *Oxford Review of Economic Policy* (London), vol. 15, No. 3, pp. 19-38.

Medina, Martin (2005). Waste picker cooperatives in developing countries. Paper prepared for the Conference on Membership-Based Organizations of the Poor, organized by Women in Informal Employment Globalizing and Organizing (WIEGO), Cornell University and Self-employed Women's Association (SEWA), Ahmedabad, India, 17-21 January 2005.

Meinzen-Dick, Ruth, Patricia Kameri-Mbote and Helen Markelova (2007). Property rights for poverty reduction. 2020 FOCUS BRIEF on the World's Poor and Hungry People (October). Washington, D.C.: International Food Policy Research Center.

Migration News (2005). Canada: brain waste. *Migration News*, vol. 12, No. 3 (July).

Migration Policy Institute (2008). Top 10 migration issues of 2008: issue #1—"buyer's remorse" on immigration policy. Migration Information Source (December). Migration Policy Institute. Available from http://www.migrationinformation.org/Feature/display.cfm?ID=710.

Minoiu, Camelia, and Sanjay Reddy (2007). Aid does matter after all: revisiting the relationship between aid and growth. *Challenge*, vol. 50, No. 2, pp. 39-58.

Minsky, Hyman P. (1965). The role of employment policy. In *Poverty in America*, M. S. Gordon, ed. San Francisco, California: Chandler Publishing Company.

_____ (1966). Tight full employment: let's heat up the economy. In *Poverty American Style*, H. P. Miller, ed. Belmont, California: Wadsworth Publishing Company.

_____ (1986). *Stabilizing an Unstable Economy. A Twentieth Century Fund Report*. New Haven, Connecticut: Yale University Press.

Mishel, Lawrence, Jared Bernstein and Heidi Shierholz (2009). *The State of Working America, 2008/2009*. Economic Policy Institute Book. Ithaca, New York: ILR Press (an imprint of Cornell University Press).

Mkandawire, Thandika (2005). Targeting versus universalism in poverty reduction. *Social Policy and Development Programme Paper*, No. 23. Geneva: United Nations Research Institute for Social Development (UNRISD).

_____ (2007). Targeting and universalism in poverty reduction. In *Policy Matters: Economic and Social Policies to Sustain Equitable Development*, José Antonio Ocampo, Jomo K. S. and Sarbuland Khan, eds. London: Zed Books, pp. 305-330.

Morduch, Jonathan (2008). *How Can the Poor Afford Microfinance?* Focus note (January). New York: Financial Access Initiative, NYU Wagner Graduate School.

Morris, David, and Michelle B. McAlpin (1982). Measuring the conditions of the world's poor: the Physical Quality of Life Index. New Delhi: Promilla and Company.

Mosse, David (2007). *Power and the Durability of Poverty: A Critical Exploration of the Links Between Culture, Marginality and Chronic Poverty*. CPRC Working Paper, No. 107. London: Chronic Poverty Research Centre.

Mushinski, David W., and Kathleen A. Pickering (2007). Heterogeneity in informal sector mitigation of micro-enterprise credit rationing. *Journal of International Development*, vol. 19, No. 5, pp. 567-581.

Narayan, Deepa, Lant Pritchett, and Soumya Kapoor (2009). *Moving Out of Poverty*, vol. 2, *Success from the Bottom Up*. Washington, D.C.: World Bank; London: Palgrave Macmillan.

Ndulu, Benno J. (2006). Infrastructure, regional integration and growth in sub-Saharan Africa: dealing with the disadvantages of geography and sovereign fragmentation. *Journal of African Economies*, vol. 15, Supplement 2, pp. 212-244.

New York Times (2009). As jobs die, European migrants head home, 25 April.

Nixson, Frederick, and Bernard Walters (2006). Privatization, income distribution, and poverty: the Mongolian experience. *World Development*, vol. 34, No. 9, pp. 1557-1579.

Nordhaus, William D., and Xi Chen (2009). Geography: graphics and economics. *The B.E. Journal of Economic Analysis & Policy*, vol. 9, No. 2, pp. 1-2.

Ocampo, José Antonio, Jomo K. S. and Sarbuland Khan, eds. (2006). *Policy Matters: Economic and Social Policies to Sustain Equitable Development*. London: Zed Books.

Ocampo, José Antonio, and María Ángela Parra (2003). The terms of trade for commodities in the twentieth century. *CEPAL Review* (Santiago), No. 79, pp. 7.

Organization for Economic Cooperation and Development (2003). *OECD Employment Outlook 2003: Towards More and Better Jobs*. Paris: OECD.

_____ (2007). *Gaining from Migration: Towards a New Mobility System*. Paris: OECD.

_____ (2008a). *Growing Unequal? Income Distribution and Poverty in OECD Countries*. Paris: OECD.

_____ (2008b). *OECD Factbook 2008: Economic, Environmental and Social Statistics*. Paris: OECD.

Osmani, Siddiqur (2005). Defining pro-poor growth. One pager, No. 9 (January). Brasília: United Nations Development Programme, International Poverty Centre.

Oxford Analytica (2008). Labour Migration Policy Index, phase II: a report produced for the Business Advisory Board, International Organization for Migration. Oxford, 1 October.

Oyen, Else (1997). The contradictory concepts of social exclusion and social inclusion. In *Social Exclusion and Anti-Poverty Policy: A Debate*, Charles Gore and Jose B. Figueiredo, eds. Geneva: International Institute for Labour Studies.

Panda, Pradeep, and Bina Agarwal (2005). Marital violence, human development, and women's property status in India. *World Development*, vol. 33, No. 5, pp. 823-850.

Papademetriou, Demetrios G., Madeleine Sumption and Will Somerville (2009). Migration and the economic downturn: what to expect in the European Union. Washington, D.C.: Migration Policy Institute, January.

Papademetriou, Demetrios G., and Aaron Terrazas (2009). Immigrants and the current economic crisis: research evidence, policy challenges, and implications. Washington, D.C.: Migration Policy Institute, January.

Pécoud, Antoine (2006). Circulations migratoires et contrôles aux frontières. *Migrations Société*, vol. 18, No. 107 (September-October), pp. 51-63.

Perry, Guillermo E., and others (2006). *Poverty Reduction and Growth: Virtuous and Vicious Circles*. Washington, D.C.: World Bank.

Pickering, Kathleen A., and Bethany Mizushima (2007). Lakota health care access and the perpetuation of poverty on Pine Ridge. In *The Economics of Health and Wellness: Anthropological Perspectives,* Donald C. Wood, ed. (vol. 26 of *Research in Economic Anthropology*); pp. 11-33.

Pogge, Thomas, and Sanjay Reddy (2006). Unknown: the extent, distribution and trend of global income poverty. *Economic and Political Weekly,* 3 June.

Pollin, Robert (1998). Can domestic expansionary policy succeed in a globally integrated environment? an examination of alternatives. In *Globalization and Progressive Economic Policy,* Dean Baker, Gerald A. Epstein and Robert Pollin, eds. New York: Cambridge University Press.

Prasad, Eswar S., Raghuram G. Rajan and Arvind Subramanian (2007). Foreign capital and economic growth. *Brookings Papers on Economic Activity,* vol. 38 (2007-1), pp. 153-230.

Psacharopoulos, George, and Harry A. Patrinos (2004). Returns to investment in education: a further update. *Education Economics,* vol. 12, No. 2, pp. 111-134.

Quinn, Lois M., and Robert S. Magill (1994). Politics versus research in social policy. *Social Service Review,* vol. 68, No. 4, pp. 503-520.

Rahman, Tauhidur, and Satheesh Aradhyula (2007). Cross-country evidence on the link between health and macroeconomic volatility. Paper presented at the Singapore Economic Review Conference 2007, Singapore, 2-4 August 2007. Tucson, Arizona: Department of Agricultural and Resource Economics, University of Arizona.

Ravallion, Martin (2008). Bailing out the world's poorest. Policy Research Working Paper, No. 4763 (December). Washington, D.C.: World Bank.

_____, and Shaohua Chen (2004). China's (uneven) progress against poverty. World Bank Policy Research Working Paper, No. 3408 (September). Washington, D.C.: World Bank.

Ravallion, Martin, and Jyotsna Jalan (1999). China's lagging poor areas. *American Economic Review (Papers and Proceedings),* vol. 89, No. 2 (May), pp. 301-305.

Ravi, Changanti, and S. Mahendra Dev (2008). Revising estimates of poverty. *Economic and Political Weekly,* vol. 43, No. 10, pp. 8-13.

Ray, Ranjan, and Geoffrey Lancaster (2005). On setting the poverty line based on estimated nutrient prices: condition of socially disadvantaged groups during the reform period. *Economic and Political Weekly,* vol. 40, No. 1 (January), pp. 46-56.

Reddy, Sanjay (2009). The emperor's new suit: global poverty estimates reappraised. Working paper prepared for the Division for Social Policy and Development, Department of Economic and Social Affairs of the United Nations Secretariat. Draft, March.

_____, and Thomas Pogge (forthcoming). How not to count the poor. In *Debates on the Measurement of Global Poverty*, Joseph Stiglitz, Sudhir Anand and Paul Segal, eds. Oxford: Oxford University Press.

Reinhart, Carmen, and Tokatlidis Ioannis (2008). Before and after financial liberalization. MPRA Paper, No. 6986. Munich, Germany: Munich Personal RePEc Archive, 4 February. Available from http://mpra.ub.uni-muenchen.de/6986/.

Reinhart, Carmen M., and Kenneth S. Rogoff (2009). The aftermath of financial crises. *NBER Working Paper*, No. 14656. Cambridge, Massachusetts: National Bureau of Economic Research. Available from http://www.nber.org/papers/w14656.

Robbins, Richard H. (1999). *Global Problems and the Culture of Capitalism*. Boston: Allyn and Bacon, chap. 5 ("The problem of population growth"), pp. 147-178.

Robeyns, Ingrid, ed. (2008). Debate: should feminists endorse basic income? *Basic Income Studies* (special issue: "Debate: should feminists endorse basic income?"), vol. 3, No. 3 (December).

Rodríguez, Francisco (2007). Openness and growth: what have we learned. DESA Working Paper, No. 51. ST/ESA/2007/DWP/51. New York: Department of Economic and Social Affairs of the United Nations Secretariat, August.

Rodrik, Dani (1998). Who needs capital-account convertibility? *Essays in International Finance*, No. 207, pp. 55-65.

_____ (2001). Globalization, growth and poverty: is the World Bank beginning to get it? 6 December. Available from http://ksghome.harvard.edu/~drodrik/WB%20oped.pdf (accessed 12 August 2009).

_____ (2004). Rethinking growth policies in the developing world. Draft of the Luca d'Agliano Lecture in Development Economics, delivered in Turin, Italy, on 8 October 2004. Available from http://ksghome.harvard.edu/~drodrik/Luca_d_Agliano_Lecture_Oct_2004.pdf.

_____, and Arvind Subramanian (2008). Why did financial globalisation disappoint? Available from http://www.iie.com/publications/papers/subramanian0308.pdf (accessed 10 May 2009).

Roig, Marta, and Joachim Singelmann (2009). The socioeconomic selectivity of migrants: a comparative analysis. Paper prepared for the XXVI IUSSP International Migration Conference, Marrakesh, Morocco, 27 September–2 October 2009.

Roodman, David, and Uzma Qureshi (2006). Microfinance as business. Washington, D.C.: Center for Global Development, November.

Roy, Rathin, and John Weeks (2004). Making fiscal policy work for the poor. United Nations Development Programme, Asia-Pacific Regional Programme on Macroeconomics of Poverty Reduction.

Sachs, Jeffrey (2008). *Common Wealth: Economics for a Crowded Planet*. New York: Penguin Press.

Saith, Ashwani (2005). Poverty lines versus the poor: method versus meaning. *Economic and Political Weekly*, vol. 40, No. 43 (October), pp. 4601-4610.

_____ (2007). Downsizing and distortion of poverty in India: the perverse power of official definitions. *Indian Journal of Human Development*, vol. 1, No. 2 (July-December), pp. 247-282.

_____ (2008). Towards universal socio-economic security: strategic elements of a policy framework. *Indian Journal of Human Development*, vol. 2, No. 1 (January-June), pp. 9-38.

Sala-i-Martin, Xavier (2006). The world distribution of income: falling poverty and ... convergence, period. *Quarterly Journal of Economics*, vol. 121, No. 2, pp. 351-398.

Salop, Steven C. (1979). A model of the natural rate of unemployment. *American Economic Review*, vol. 69, No. 1, pp. 117-125.

Samba, Ebrahim Malick (2004). African health care systems: what went wrong, editorial. The Medical News, 8 December. Available from http://www.news-medical.net/news/2004/12/08/6770.aspx.

Schiantarelli, Fabio, and Fidel Jaramillo (1996). Access to long-term debt and effects on firms' performance: lessons from Ecuador. World Bank Policy Research Working Paper, No. 1725 (November). Washington, D.C.: World Bank.

Schubert, Bernd, and Rachel Slater (2006). Social cash transfers in low-income African countries: conditional or unconditional? *Development Policy Review*, vol. 24, No. 5, pp. 571-578.

Schultz, T. Paul (1993). Returns to women's education. In *Women's Education in Developing Countries: Barriers, Benefits, and Policies*. Elizabeth M. King and M. Ann Hill, eds. Washington, D.C.: World Bank; and Baltimore, Maryland: The Johns Hopkins University Press. pp. 51-59.

Sen, Amartya K. (1979). Personal utilities and public judgements: or what's wrong with welfare economics. *The Economic Journal*, vol. 89, pp. 537-558.

_____ (1985). *Commodities and Capabilities*. Amsterdam: North-Holland.

_____ (1987). The standard of living: lecture II, lives and capabilities. In *The Standard of Living*, Amartya K. Sen, Geoffrey Hawthorn and John Muellbauer, eds. Cambridge, United Kingdom: Cambridge University Press, pp. 20-38.

_____ (1999). *Development as Freedom*. New York: Knopf.

_____ (2000). *Social Exclusion: Concept, Application, and Scrutiny*. Social Development Paper, No. 1. Manila: Office of Environment and Social Development, Asian Development Bank, June.

Sen, Binayak (2003). Drivers of escape and descent: changing household fortunes in rural Bangladesh. *World Development*, vol. 31, No. 3, pp. 513-534.

Sengupta, Arjun, K. P. Kannan and G. Raveendran (2008). India's common people: who are they, how are they and where do they live? *Economic and Political Weekly*, vol. 43, No. 11, March, pp. 49-63.

Shapiro, Carl, and Joseph E. Stiglitz (1984). Equilibrium unemployment as a worker discipline device. *American Economic Review*, vol. 74, No. 3, pp. 433-444.

Sharma, Savita (2004). Poverty estimates in India: some key issues. *ERD Working Paper*, No. 51. Manila: Asian Development Bank, Economics and Research Department, May.

Shaw, Edward S. (1973). *Financial Deepening in Economic Development*. New York: Oxford University Press.

Singer, Peter (2009). *The Life You Can Save: Acting Now to End World Poverty*. New York: Random House.

Singh, Gopal K., and Mohammed Siahpush (2006). Widening socioeconomic inequalities in US life expectancy, 1980-2000. *International Journal of Epidemiology*, vol. 35, pp. 969-979.

Skoufias, Emmanuel (2001). PROGRESA and its impacts on the human capital and welfare of households in rural Mexico: a synthesis of the results of an evaluation by IFPRI. Washington, D.C.: International Food Policy Research Institute, Food Consumption and Nutrition Division, December.

Social Watch (2007). *Social Watch Report 2007: In Dignity and Rights—Making the Universal Right to Social Security a Reality*. Montevideo: Instituto del Tercer Mundo.

Soubbotina, Tatyana P. (2004). *Beyond Economic Growth: An Introduction to Sustainable Development*, 2nd ed. World Bank Institute Learning Resources Series. Washington, D.C.: World Bank.

South Dakota Vital Statistics (2007). State and county comparison of leading health indicators—2007 report. South Dakota vital statistics. Available from http://doh.sd.gov/statistics/2007Vital/default.aspx (accessed 19 May 2009).

Srinivasan, T. N. (2007). Poverty lines in India: reflections after the Patna Conference. *Economic and Political Weekly*, vol. 42, No. 41 (October), pp. 4155-4165.

Stalker, Peter (2000). *Workers Without Frontiers: The Impact of Globalization on International Migration*. Boulder, Colorado: Lynne Rienner Publishers.

Standing, Guy (2007). How cash transfers boost work and economic security. DESA Working Paper, No. 58. ST/ESA/2007/DWP/58. New York: Department of Economic and Social Affairs of the United Nations Secretariat, October.

_____ (2008). Economic insecurity and global casualisation: threat or promise? *Social Indicators Research*, vol. 88, No. 1, pp. 15-30.

Stern, Nicholas, and Joseph Stiglitz (1996). A framework for a development strategy in a market economy: objectives, scope, institutions and instruments. *EBRD Working Paper*, No. 20. London: European Bank for Reconstruction and Development.

Stewart, Frances (2002). Horizontal inequalities: a neglected dimension of development. QEH Working Paper, No. 81. Oxford: Queen Elizabeth House, University of Oxford.

Subbarao, Kalanidhi (2003). Systemic shocks and social protection: role and effectiveness of public works programs. Social Protection Discussion Paper, No. 0302 (January). Washington, D.C.: World Bank.

Sukhatme, P. V. (1988). Energy intake and nutrition: on the auto-regulatory homeostatic nature of the energy requirement. In *Rural Poverty in South Asia*, T. N. Srinivasan and Pranab K. Bardhan, eds. New Delhi: Oxford University Press.

Svedberg, Peter (2000). *Poverty and Undernutrition: Theory, Measurement, and Policy*. New York: Oxford University Press.

Taran, Patrick, and others (2009). *Economic Migration, Social Cohesion and Development: Towards and Integrated Approach*. Luxembourg: Council of Europe.

Taylor, Edward J. (1999). The new economics of labour migration and the role of remittances in the migration process. *International Migration*, vol. 37, No. 1, pp. 63-88.

_____, Jorge Mora and Richard Adams (2005). Remittances, inequality and poverty: evidence from rural Mexico. Paper presented at the American Agricultural Economics Association Annual Meeting, Providence, Rhode Island, 24-27 July 2005.

Teixeira, Clarissa Gondim (2008). Análise do impacto do Programa Bolsa Família na oferta de trabalho dos homens e mulheres. Available from: http://www.ipc-undp.org/publications/mds/27P.pdf (accessed 4 August 2009).

Thomas, Duncan, and others (2004). Education in a crisis. *Journal of Development Economics*, vol. 74, No. 1, pp. 53-85.

Townsend, Peter (2002). Poverty, social exclusion and social polarisation: the need to construct an international welfare state. In *World Poverty: New Policies to Defeat an Old Enemy*, Peter Townsend and David Gordon, eds. Bristol, United Kingdom: Policy Press, pp. 3-24.

United Nations (1996). *Report of the World Summit for Social Development, Copenhagen, 6-12 March 1995*. Sales No. E.96.IV.8.

_____ (2002a). *Report of the Second World Assembly on Ageing, Madrid, 8-12 April 2002*. Sales No. E.02.IV.4.

_____ (2002b). *Report of the World Summit on Sustainable Development, Johannesburg, South Africa, 26 August–4 September 2002*. Sales No. E.03. II.A.1 and corrigendum.

_____ (2005a). *The Inequality Predicament: Report on the World Social Situation 2005*. Sales No. E.05.IV.5.

_____ (2005b). Report of the Secretary-General on the monitoring of population programmes, focusing on international migration and development. 27 December. E/CN.9/2006/4.

_____ (2006). *Building Inclusive Financial Sectors for Development*. Sales No. E.06.II.A.3.

_____ (2007a). *The Employment Imperative: Report on the World Social Situation*. Sales No. E.07.IV.9.

_____ (2007b). *The Millennium Development Goals Report 2007*. Sales No. E.07.I.15.

_____ (2008). *World Economic and Social Survey 2008: Overcoming Economic Insecurity*. Sales No. 08.II.C.1.

_____ (2009a). *The Millennium Development Goals Report 2009*. Sales No. E.09.I.12.

_____ (2009b). *World Economic Situation and Prospects 2009*. Sales No. E.09.II.C.2.

_____, Conference on the World Financial and Economic Crisis and Its Impact on Development (2009). Report of the Secretary-General on the world financial and economic crisis and its impact on development, A.CONF.214/4.

United Nations, Department of Economic and Social Affairs, Population Division (2009). World Population Prospects: the 2008 Revision Population Database. Available from http://esa.un.org/unpp/ (accessed 16 July 2009).

United Nations, Department of Economic and Social Affairs, Statistics Division (2009). Key Global Indicators database. Available from http://data.un.org.

United Nations, Economic and Social Commission for Asia and the Pacific (2007). Persistent and emerging issues in rural poverty reduction. ST/ESCAP/2433. Bangkok.

_____ (2008a). *Economic and Social Survey of Asia and the Pacific 2008: Sustaining Growth and Sharing Prosperity*. Sales No. E.08.II.F.7.

_____ (2008b). *A Future within Reach 2008: Regional Partnerships for the Millennium Development Goals in Asia and the Pacific*. Sales No. E.08.II.F.15.

United Nations, Economic Commission for Africa (2008). *Economic Report on Africa 2008: Africa and the Monterrey Consensus—Tracking Performance and Progress.* Sales No. E.08.II.K.3.

United Nations, Economic Commission for Latin America and the Caribbean (2008). *Social Panorama of Latin America 2007.* Sales No. S.07.II.G.124.

_____ (2009). *Social Panorama of Latin America 2008.* Sales No. S.08.II.G.89.

United Nations Children's Fund (1987). *Adjustment with a Human Face.* New York: Oxford University Press.

_____ (1999). *The State of the World's Children 1999: Education.* New York.

_____ (2000). *The Progress of Nations 2000.* New York.

United Nations Conference on Trade and Development (2006). *Trade and Development Report 2006: Global Partnership and National Policies for Development.* Sales No. E.06.II.D.6.

_____ (2008). *Economic Development in Africa 2008: Export Performance Following Trade Liberalization: Some Patterns and Policy Perspectives.* Sales No. E.08.II.D.22.

United Nations Development Programme (2006). *Human Development Report 2006: Beyond Scarcity—Power, Poverty and the Global Water Crisis.* Basingstoke, United Kingdom: Palgrave Macmillan.

_____ (2007). *Human Development Report 2007/2008: Fighting Climate Change—Human Solidarity in a Divided World.* Basingstoke, United Kingdom: Palgrave Macmillan.

United States Census Bureau (2000). Census 2000 summary file 3 (SF 3). United States Census Bureau. Available from http://factfinder.census.gov (accessed 21 May 2009).

United States Department of Health and Human Services, Centers for Disease Control and Prevention, National Center for Health Statistics (2009). Health, United States, 2008, with Chartbook. Hyattsville, Maryland. Available from http://www.cdc.gov/nchs/ hus.htm (accessed 11 May 2009).

Van Arkadie, Brian (2005). Good governance, markets and donors. In *Globalization, Neo-Conservative Policies and Democratic Alternatives: Essays in Honour of John Loxley*, A. Haroon Akram-Lodhi, Robert Chernomas and Ardeshir Sepehri, eds. Winnipeg, Manitoba: Arbeiter Ring Publishing, chap. 11, pp. 201-222.

Van der Hoeven, Rolph, and György Sziráczki, eds. (1998). *Lessons from Privatization: Labour Issues in Developing and Transitional Countries.* Geneva: International Labour Organization.

Vera Soares, Fabio, Rafael Perez Ribas and Guilherme Issamu Hirata (2008). Achievements and shortfalls of conditional cash transfers: impact evaluation of Paraguay's *Tekoporã* programme. IPC evaluation note, No. 3 (March). Brasília: United Nations International Poverty Centre.

Vroman, Wayne (1999). Unemployment and unemployment insurance in three groups of countries. World Bank Social Protection Discussion Paper, No. 1911 (May). Washington, D.C.: World Bank, Human Development Network, Social Protection Unit.

_____, and Vera Brusentev (2005). *Unemployment Compensation Throughout the World: A Comparative Analysis*. Kalamazoo, Michigan: W. E. Upjohn Institute for Employment Research.

Walsh, Carl E. (2000). Should central banks stabilize prices? FRBSF Economic Letter (Federal Reserve Bank of San Francisco), No. 2000-24 (August 11), p. 1.

Williamson, John (1990). What Washington means by policy reform. In *Latin American Adjustment: How Much Has Happened?*, John Williamson, ed. Washington, D.C.: Institute for International Economics.

Wily, Liz Alden (2006). Land rights reform and governance in Africa: how to make it work in the 21st century. UNDP Discussion Paper (March). New York: United Nations Development Programme.

Woodward, David (1992). *Debt, Adjustment, and Poverty in Developing Countries*. London: Pinter Publishers.

World Bank (1978). *World Development Report 1978* (August). New York: Oxford University Press.

_____ (1990). *World Development Report 1990*. Washington, D.C.: World Bank.

_____ (1993). *The East Asian Miracle: Economic Growth and Public Policy*. World Bank Policy Research Report. New York: Oxford University Press.

_____ (2002). *Globalization, Growth and Poverty: Building an Inclusive World Economy*. World Bank Policy Research Report. Washington, D.C.: World Bank; New York: Oxford University Press.

_____ (2003). *World Development Report 2004: Making Services Work for Poor People*. Washington, D.C.: World Bank; New York: Oxford University Press.

_____ (2004). Poverty in MENA. Sector brief.

_____ (2005). *Economic Growth in the 1990s: Learning from a Decade of Reform*. Washington, D.C.: World Bank.

_____ (2008a). Edstats: Educations statistics version 5.3. World Bank. Available from www.worldbank.org/education/edstats (accessed 20 May 2009).

_____ (2008b). Trade is key to overcome crisis. Press release, 1 December.

_____ (2008c). *World Development Indicators 2008*. Washington, D.C.

_____ (2009a). *Conditional Cash Transfers: Reducing Present and Future Poverty*, Ariel Fiszbein and others. Washington, D.C.: World Bank.

_____ (2009b). Crisis hitting poor hard in developing countries. Press release No. 2009/220/EXC, 12 February.

_____ (2009c). *Global Economic Prospects 2009: Commodities at the Crossroads*. Washington, D.C.: World Bank.

_____ (2009d). *Global Monitoring Report 2009: A Development Emergency*. Washington, D.C.: World Bank.

_____ (2009e). In Africa, "Poverty has a female face". Feature story, 15 May.

_____ (2009f). People Move: a blog about migration, remittances, and development. Remittances expected to fall by 5 to 8 per cent in 2009. Submitted by Dilip Ratha. Available from http://peoplemove.worldbank.org (accessed 15 May 2009).

_____ (2009g). Swimming against the tide: how developing countries are coping with the global crisis. Background paper prepared by World Bank staff for the Group of 20 Finance Ministers and Central Bank Governors Meeting, Horsham, United Kingdom, 13 and 14 March 2009.

World Bank, Development Economics Research Group. Living Standards Measurement Study. Available from http://go.worldbank.org/IFS9WG7EO0.

World Bank, Development Research Group (2009). PovcalNet Online Poverty Analysis Tool. Available from http://go.worldbank.org/NT2A1XUWP0 (accessed April 2009).

World Health Organization, Regional Office for the Western Pacific (2002). Pro-poor health policies: a framework for analysis and action. November. Available from http://www.wpro.who.int/health_topics/equity/.

Wray, L. Randall (2007). *The Employer of Last Resort Programme: Could It Work for Developing Countries? Economic and Labour Market Paper*, No. 2007/5. Geneva: International Labour Office, August.

Yates, Rob (2009). Universal health care and the removal of user fees. *The Lancet*, vol. 373, No. 9680, pp. 2078-2081.

Yunus, Muhammad (2003). *Banker to the Poor: Micro-lending and the Battle Against World Poverty*. New York: Public Affairs.

Zepeda, Eduardo (2007). Addressing the employment-poverty nexus in Kenya: comparing cash-transfer and job-creation programmes. International Poverty Centre Working Paper, No. 40. Brasília: United Nations Development Programme, International Poverty Centre, October.

Zoellick, Robert (2009). A stimulus package for the world. *New York Times*, 23 January, Op-Ed, p. A27.